Analysing Conversation

An Introduction to Prosody

Beatrice Szczepek Reed

palgrave
macmillan

First published 2011 by
PALGRAVE MACMILLAN

Palgrave Macmillan in the UK is an imprint of Macmillan Publishers Limited, registered in England, company number 785998, of Houndmills, Basingstoke, Hampshire RG21 6XS.

Palgrave Macmillan in the US is a division of St Martin's Press LLC, 175 Fifth Avenue, New York, NY 10010.

Palgrave Macmillan is the global academic imprint of the above companies and has companies and representatives throughout the world.

Palgrave® and Macmillan® are registered trademarks in the United States, the United Kingdom, Europe and other countries.

ISBN 978–0–230–22344–8 hardback
ISBN 978–0–230–22345–5 paperback

This book is printed on paper suitable for recycling and made from fully managed and sustained forest sources. Logging, pulping and manufacturing processes are expected to conform to the environmental regulations of the country of origin.

A catalogue record for this book is available from the British Library.

A catalog record for this book is available from the Library of Congress.

10   9   8   7   6   5   4   3   2   1
20 19 18 17 16 15 14 13 12 11

Printed and bound in Great Britain by
CPI Antony Rowe, Chippenham and Eastbourne

This book is dedicated to
Elizabeth Couper-Kuhlen

Brief Contents

Contents

List of Figures

Acknowledgements

In the writing of this book I am greatly indebted to Elizabeth Couper-Kuhlen, whose passionate and meticulous study of prosody first inspired me to take up the subject, and whose work I have admired ever since. Furthermore, I would like to express my sincerest thanks to Rebecca Hughes for numerous inspiring conversations about spoken language, and for very helpful comments on earlier drafts of this book.

Very special thanks also to my students, particularly those whose first language is not English, as their insightful comments and questions have inspired me greatly in thinking through many issues concerning the prosody of English conversation.

For their kind support and efficient handling of the entire publishing process I warmly thank Kitty van Boxel and Felicity Noble at Palgrave Macmillan.

For his continuous patience and encouragement in the writing of this book I am deeply grateful to my husband Darren Reed.

BEATRICE SZCZEPEK REED

The author and publishers wish to thank the following for kind permission to use copyright material:

Black and white headphone © istock International Inc.

TalkBank, for kind permission to use the Santa Barbara Corpus of Spoken American English.

Preliminaries

This book is concerned with the prosody of naturally occurring conversation. It explores the ways in which participants in everyday talk use and interpret the 'musical' aspects of speech, that is, pitch, timing, loudness and voice quality, as part of social interaction. This book is not an introduction to phonetics or phonology, although it does make use of some phonetic concepts to describe prosodic phenomena. My central aim is to introduce the non-expert reader to the analysis of the prosody of spontaneous talk. All descriptions, definitions and analyses are presented in combination with examples from everyday conversations. In following this approach I treat prosody as an integral part of human interaction, and interaction as a collaborative achievement by interactants themselves. This perspective on language has been developed by researchers in the fields known as conversation analysis (CA) and interactional linguistics, and the approach to language study adopted here is a conversation analytic/interactional linguistic one.

During the second half of the 20th century, a way of investigating language emerged that took an entirely new perspective on language itself and its role for human communication. From the mid-1960s, the sociologists Harvey Sacks and Emanuel A. Schegloff were among the first to suggest that the primary habitat of language is natural conversation. This position was, and still is, in stark contrast to traditional enquiry into language in the field of linguistics, whose typical object of study is language as a primarily cognitive and mono-logical activity. Sacks and Schegloff postulated that all aspects of interaction, including all features of language, must be studied in the context of their occurrence and from the perspective of the conversational participants themselves. Analytical claims and interpretations regarding any part of human interaction must be based entirely on evidence that shows their reality for those interacting with one another. Again, this marked a significant change from conventional linguistic investigation, where language is typically either studied in isolation from its speakers and from natural contexts, or where language production is experimentally elicited and controlled.

This new approach soon found its way from sociology into linguistics and established itself as 'interactional linguistics'. Students of language in this area adopted the view that language must be analysed as a human activity, rather than a theoretical system of rules, and interactional linguists began exploring many different aspects of language in this new light. Previously unquestioned linguistic categories were investigated for their relevance for conversational participants themselves; some survived this 'reality check', others did not. Alongside the field of syntax, the fields of phonetics and phonology became a particularly fruitful area of interactional linguistic investigation. From the mid-1980s onwards, groundbreaking research by phonologists such as Elizabeth Couper-Kuhlen, Margret Selting and John Local brought to light the crucial role played by prosody for natural conversation. While it could be shown that participants orient to prosodic patterns as relevant for a variety of conversational activities, prosody as such emerged as integral to all aspects of spontaneous spoken interaction.

This book introduces the most relevant analytical tools and concepts for a prosodic analysis of naturally occurring talk. For this purpose, the present chapter gives an overview of the most relevant terminology and analytical practice regarding both the analysis of conversation and of prosody. Subsequently, some of the most central findings in recent research on prosody are presented and the transcription system used in this book is introduced. The final section contains an outline of the chapters in the rest of the book.

All examples used in this book can be found on the accompanying website (**www.palgrave.com/language/analysingconversation**). Each time the headphone icon ∩ appears next to a transcript, the sound file can be listened to on the website. I cannot recommend strongly enough that readers should make use of the opportunity to listen to the extracts, rather than simply read the transcripts, as the prosodic features described here only really come to life when they are heard. As this book takes seriously the importance of working with naturally occurring discourse, the data extracts take centre stage in almost every part of the book.

1.1   Analysing natural conversation

In many areas of linguistics the study of language typically involves isolating areas such as sounds, meaning or grammar and developing theories that are based on internal rules within these areas. Those rules are established through linguists' theoretical considerations and based on constructed examples. Language in this tradition is treated as a formal system with laws of its own and is often investigated independently of its use in natural contexts. In contrast, for conversation analysis and interactional linguistics it is precisely the real life uses of language that are of interest: language is considered a repertoire of resources for human interaction, and conversation analytic research shows that the employment of those resources is highly ordered. In contrast to the formal analysis typical of theoretical linguistics, practitioners of conversation analysis use a normative approach. They generally do not speak of 'rules', but of the normative orderliness of social interaction. For example, one action, such as a first greeting, may make a next action, such as a return greeting, relevant or expectable. However, those expectations are not rules in any strict sense: we may find them broken by participants themselves, leading to inferences and interactional strategies dealing with the noticeable deviation from an expectable pattern. A next participant may not offer a return greeting, but ask a question instead. In conversation analysis, this would not be considered a 'mistake', but an insight into how this participant interprets the interaction at hand; in this case, his or her next action may show that he or she did not interpret the prior utterance as a greeting. We should therefore not think of the organisation of conversation as rule governed, but as normatively ordered – with conversationalists themselves acting out this order at any given moment in time.

Participants employ a shared repertoire of routine conversational practices, some of which seem to be universal, while others depend on the individual ethnic, cultural and/or social group a speaker belongs to. Typically, these practices are accomplished in the form of 'turns', that is participants' contributions to conversations; 'turn constructional units' (TCUs), that is utterances which could potentially be complete turns; or their building blocks ('intonation phrases', see Chapter 3; or 'turn constructional phrases' (TCPs), see Szczepek Reed (2010a, 2010c)). Discovering this repertoire of conversational practices is one of the main aims in interactional linguistics and conversation analysis. And while we can observe participants using many well-known linguistic units, such as sounds, noun phrases or sentences, in their talk, thinking of these as fixed linguistic categories is not necessarily the best way forward in exploring language in interaction. Instead, thinking of them initially simply as conversational practices will allow us as analysts to free our mind from any preconceptions and investigate what is treated as interactionally relevant by participants themselves. See, for example, the utterance *can I say something* at line 12 in Extract 1.1.

Extract 1.1 SBC033 Guilt 🎧

```
 1 Leann:   Apropos something [JENnifer said in MAY;
 2 Laura:                     [well WAIT -
 3            you know [liz-
 4 Don:               [MA,
 5            [you HAVE to hear this;
 6 Leann:   [<< falsetto+f> WAIT WAIT - >
 7 Jenn:    WHAT -
 8 Bill:    [<<f> will you let leann FINish;>
 9 Jenn:    [did i -
10 Leann:   [<< falsetto+f> WAIT -
11           ↑TIME; >
12           <<falsetto> can i SAY sOmething - >
13 (0.42)
14           JENnifer and I and dana;
15           had a HU::GE Argument in mAY;
16           which creAted a RIFT;
17           for about a DAY. 💬
```

Line 12 shows Leann's utterance *can I say something*, a phrase that can be grammatically defined as a yes/no interrogative. However, in many social contexts, phrases such as this one (*Do you know what time it is? Can you pass me the gravy?*) are typically not interpreted by their recipients as yes/no questions, a fact that can easily be proven by the limited number of instances in everyday life in which such phrases are responded to by either *yes* or *no*. Instead, they are typically treated as requests, as next participants either grant or refuse the expressed wish of the first speaker.

However, a classification of the turn above, either as a question or as a request, does not provide a satisfactory interpretation of this particular interactional sequence. At the time of her utterance, Leann has been trying to enter into the conversation for quite some time. She has tried different strategies for taking the floor, such as speaking with increased loudness and pitch, and shouting *wait wait wait* and *time* (lines 6, 10–11). Eventually, she explicitly demands to be allowed to speak: *can I say something* in this instance is neither a question nor a request; it is an announcement that this speaker is determined to come in to speak, and will do so at any moment. The co-participants' behaviour reveals their interpretation of Leann's utterance in this way. If they treated it as a question, they could be expected to either provide an answer or to offer some sort of reply that shows that they are aware of the necessity to provide an answer. Similarly, a request would most probably be followed by some kind of acknowledgement that a request has been made, such as a granting or refusal of the request. However, following Leann's turn no one comes in to speak. Instead, the overlapping talk by several speakers that has been going on for a while comes to an immediate halt, leading to silence (line 13). The silence shows that the other participants are treating Leann's turn *can I say something* as an announcement which foreshadows an upcoming turn, rather than as a question or request, which a context-free interpretation of syntactic structure or social norms would infer.

From our considerations so far, the following main points concerning the analysis of naturally occurring conversation arise:

- Language is a human activity.
- The natural environment for language is human interaction.
- Language is always embedded in a context and must therefore be studied as part of that specific context.
- Interpretations of conversational language are most convincing when they can show that they match the interpretations of conversational participants themselves.
- Interactional order is achieved by conversationalists as they interact with each other.
- Language categories should be based on the repertoire of conversational practices shared by speakers from the same cultural and ethnic background.
- The meaning attributed to an utterance cannot be defined in isolation, based simply on the choice of words and grammatical structure. It is also based on its location as situated within an emerging interaction and its treatment by other participants as demonstrated in their subsequent utterances.

From these very general introductory notes on the analysis of conversation we now move on to some of the basic terms and concepts which have been established by previous research and which will be relevant throughout this book.

1.1.1   Naturally occurring talk-in-interaction

In conversation analysis and interactional linguistics, the data under analysis are often referred to as 'naturally occurring talk-in-interaction'. Both the terms 'naturally occurring' and 'talk-in-interaction' require some defining comments.

In order to investigate the organisation and, as in this book, the prosody of spontaneous talk, we use recordings and transcripts of real-life conversations. Rather than gathering data through experiments, questionnaires, interviews, focus groups or large written corpora, an interactional linguistic approach insists on data that have occurred *naturally* at the time the audio or video recording was made. Given the necessity for previous consent from participants, the interactions typically take place with participants' awareness of the recording device, and thus can never be claimed to be entirely 'natural'. Nevertheless, the overall patterns of interaction can be assumed to be roughly the same as they would be outside the context of their observation, or at least more so than in most of the other kinds of data mentioned above. However, while the data themselves may have occurred naturally, we must always bear in mind that the recording is already one step removed from the original interaction *in situ*. Furthermore, once a conversation has been recorded, analysts are able to listen to the same interactional sequence over and over again, thus knowing beforehand what will be said next – a privilege never shared by participants themselves. Therefore interpretations of the data must reflect analysts' awareness of the participants' reality of interactions as emerging, rather than their own experiences of the data as pre-existing.

Related to this issue is the necessity that analysts retain an understanding of the recording as a *version* of the original, rather than the original itself. This is particularly relevant for the analysis of face-to-face interactions, as opposed to those conducted via the telephone. During telephone conversations speakers have only their co-participant's voice to go by, and thus analysts have a chance of getting very close to participants' experiences of interactional reality. During face-to-face interactions, however, neither audio nor video recordings are able to catch every single detail in the environment of the speakers, and an analysis of those conversations is therefore always potentially incomplete.

A further step away from the original natural occurrence of an interaction is its transcription from the recording. Again, analysts must beware of the temptation to treat the transcript as the primary datum. As Ashmore and Reed (2000) argue convincingly, the transcript is always a rendition of a recorded interaction and, as such, two steps removed from the original itself.

The term 'talk-in-interaction' was coined by Emanuel Schegloff (1987, p. 207) and replaced the earlier term 'conversation' in most conversation analytic studies. In an early paper on 'opening up closings', Schegloff and Sacks (1973) define conversation as having two basic features: '(1) at least, and no more than, one party speaks at a time in a single conversation; and (2) speaker change recurs' (ibid., p. 293). Both features have been criticised, amongst other things, for being culturally biased towards American English; however, as a description of a systematic overall pattern, this broad definition is still valid. While the term 'conversation' in its vernacular use mainly covers casual talk without any externally imposed purpose, the term 'talk-in-interaction' covers all forms of spontaneous talk, including institutional and broadcast interaction.

1.1.2 Turn-taking

The term 'turn-taking' refers to participants' active management of changes of speakership during an ongoing interaction. The most important aspect of turn-taking in spontaneous conversation is that it is interactionally achieved, rather than given a priori. Aspects of talk, such as who speaks when, and for how long, and who comes in next, are constantly negotiated by conversationalists. This means that potential next speakers are listening not only to the 'information content' of what a current speaker is saying, but they are also engaged in an ongoing interpretation of where in the turn, sequence and overall conversation a current speaker is positioning him or herself as he or she speaks. Only by this continuous interpreting process is it possible for potential next speakers to start up at exactly the point at which a previous speaker has finished. For a currently speaking participant this means that he or she, too, is continuously involved in designing his or her talk in accordance to its position within the turn, sequence and conversation. For example, during an emerging turn, speakers design their talk differently depending on whether it is located at the beginning, middle or end of their turn, and whether it is initiating a new sequence or replying to a previous turn by someone else. Signs of such positioning are produced and interpreted by participants as part of a continuously emerging interaction.

Regarding turn-taking, some of the most crucial signals for participants concern 'turn initiation', that is, designing one's talk as the beginning of a new turn; 'turn continuation', that is, designing one's talk as not yet finished; 'turn completion', that is, designing one's talk as finished for the present moment; 'interruption', that is, initiating a turn illegitimately at a point at which another participant has not displayed signs of turn completion; and 'recipiency', that is, designing one's interactional behaviour as that of a non-turn holder. Extract 1.2 shows some of the above activities, and the brief analysis following it shows how they can be interpreted from the participants' perspective.

Extract 1.2   SBC006 Cuz 🎧

```
1 Alina:    <<h> remember TYKE?
2           lives next door to MOM?>
3 (1.54)
4 Lenore:   ↑YEAH:.
```

```
 5  Alina:     OkAY,
 6             .hh
 7  (0.29)
 8             twO wEEks ago i'm watching TV:,
 9             and dAvid HORowitz is going to ha:ve this former cAr: (0.31) rAdio
10             THIEF O:n,
11  (0.76)
12  Lenore:    <<p> it's her BOYfriend,>
13  Alina:     .hh
14  (0.32)
15             ↑yEAh her exBOYfriend.
16  (0.27)
17             MIKE. 🔊
```

In Extract 1.2, Lenore initiates a new sequence concerning her mother's neighbour's ex-boyfriend. She does so by starting an initial question/answer sequence at lines 1–2. Her sentences *remember Tyke? lives next door to mom?* are both not grammatically 'correct' in the strictest sense. The first one is missing the initial auxiliary verb and pronoun, 'do you'; the second is missing at least a relative or personal pronoun, 'who' or 'she'. However, neither of the conversational participants treats this as a problem: Alina does not correct herself, and Lenore does not come in to correct her. The two questions are used to introduce a new topic, or sequence, and as such are instances of 'preliminaries' (Schegloff, 1980) to a projected next action. The high pitch with which they are delivered is typical of new beginnings such as this one (Couper-Kuhlen, 2004).

The pause at line 3 allows us to interpret Alina's turn as complete. The very fact that she does not continue speaking is clear evidence for the fact that Alina has completed her turn for the moment. However, the pause is *noticeably* long, representing a delay in Lenore's response. Her reply *yeah* (line 4) shows us, among other things, that the turn had made a reply relevant. We can now safely say that Alina's first turn and Lenore's second turn together form an 'adjacency pair'. Adjacency pairs are the most basic sequences in interaction, and we will look at them in more detail below. They are often followed by a third turn from the original speaker, acknowledging the completion of the pair. This is provided here by Alina in the form of the token *okay* (line 5). Alina's *okay* closes the preliminary adjacency pair which foreshadows more talk to come from Alina, most probably on the topic of *Tyke*. *Okay* is also delivered with slightly rising intonation, a common signal that a current activity is not yet finished. Line 7 shows that Lenore shares this interpretation: the pause shows that she forgoes any attempt to take over the floor.

Alina's turn continuation contains the initial part of her telling (lines 8–10). At the end of this utterance, Alina once again uses slightly rising intonation. This is once more followed by a pause (line 11), showing that initially Lenore treats Alina's turn as projecting more talk. However, following the non-occurrence of such talk Lenore comes in to speak; she *self-selects* as next speaker (line 12). She does so, however, very quietly, and also with slightly rising intonation. The content of her turn is a candidate continuation of Alina's turn. Both the prosodic design and the verbal content show that this turn is not designed as an interruption, but as a non-competitive recipient activity that does not claim the floor. By producing such a turn Lenore designs her talk as that of a recipient, rather than that of a current floor-holder. Alina indeed treats it as such and confirms it is the correct candidate in her next turn (lines 13–17).

1.1.3   Sequences and sequence organisation

As conversations evolve, it is sometimes tempting to interpret them in terms of the topics participants are talking about. However, this presents problems for analysts, as defining the topic is not always a straightforward issue. It has therefore proven helpful to think of the building blocks of conversations as 'sequences', rather than topics. The most basic conversational sequence consists of two adjacent parts, with the first part making the second part expectable or *conditionally relevant*. For example, if one speaker greets another, the second speaker is generally expected to offer a return greeting. Thus, we would say that a first greeting makes a second greeting conditionally relevant; and a pair such as greeting–return greeting is an adjacency pair. Other typical kinds of adjacency pairs are question–answer; invitation–acceptance/rejection of the invitation; and *thank you–you're welcome* (see Schegloff, 2007, for a detailed exploration of sequences).

Many conversational sequences are longer than just two adjacent turns, and the talk within them can therefore be analysed as to *where in the sequence* it occurs. Such an analysis is called 'sequential analysis'. It results in talk not being interpreted initially in terms of its 'meaning' – such an interpretation would typically be made in connection with a perceived conversational topic – but in terms of its *sequential location*, that is its relation to what has been said previously and what is said subsequently, either by the same speaker or other participants. For example, in Extract 1.2 above, one way of interpreting Lenore's hesitation in coming in with a turn in spite of a lengthy silence (line 11) would be to see it as located mid-sequence: Alina is in the middle of a telling, which is not typically a position for speaker change.

1.1.4   Recipient design and participant orientation: interactional negotiation

The above paragraphs have already shown the general perspective of conversation analysis on language-in-interaction as emerging turn by turn. Talk is not analysed as having a predefined meaning or structure; rather its structure and meaning evolve step by step, as conversational participants work their way through any given interaction. This turn-by-turn development is a result of the continuous negotiation between participants concerning the next relevant action. Conversation analytic research has shown on numerous occasions that in interpreting conversational data not even the most basic social or linguistic categories should be taken for granted, but that almost every aspect of talk-in-interaction is collaboratively accomplished through participants' ongoing negotiations *in situ*. This kind of negotiation involves two main acting parties: the current turn-holding participant and the current non-turn holders or recipients. The current turn holder's part in interactional negotiation is to design his or her talk as appropriate for its current sequential location and recipient(s); this is referred to as 'recipient design'. A current recipient's part is to orient to the current turn at an appropriate next location – and by orienting to it in a certain way to show his or her interpretation of the previous speaker's talk. This is referred to as 'participant orientation'.

For example, Extract 1.1 showed that an instance of the phrase *can I say something* could not be analysed as a question or even as a request. It was designed by the speaker, and treated by the other participants, as an announcement. Another instance of interactional negotiation can be shown in Extracts 1.3 and 1.4, first analysed in Szczepek Reed (2009). The data come from a corpus of radio phone-in programmes called 'Brainteaser', broadcast on BBC radio in the 1980s. In both instances, the host Dave initiates interaction with his callers by offering what could easily be understood to be a first greeting: *hi Nige* in Extract 1.3 and *Ann hi* in Extract 1.4. Both turns contain greeting tokens and the caller's name. We know that this is how greetings are done by native speakers of this variety of English, and we could therefore be forgiven for analysing both as first greetings. However, a close analysis of the interactional negotiation between the participants reveals that the host's turn is only treated as a first greeting in one of the two cases.

Extract 1.3   Brainteaser: Nigel 🎧

```
1  Dave:   next is NIgel HIBbits;
2          who lives in PRESTwich.
3          <<h> ↑HI `NI:GE,>
4  Nigel:  <<h> ↑HI `DA:VE,>
5  Dave:   <<all> how ARE ya.>
6  (0.25)
7  Nigel:  .hh
8          nOt too BAD,
9  Dave:   GOOD to speak to you agAIn, 💬
```

Extract 1.4   Brainteaser: Ann 🎧

```
1  Dave:   a:nd we have ANN,
2          who lives in GORton.
3  (0.23)
4          who's FIRST.=
5          and then of COURSE,
6          .h
7          After our two callers we do have RAchel back again.
8          .h
```

```
 9           ANN.
10           HI.
11  (0.26)
12  Ann:    <<breathy> HELL:^O:.>
13  Dave:   <<breathy> HELL:^O:.>
14           <<h> how ARE you Ann,>
15  (0.25)
16  Ann:    I'm FINE,
17           THANKS,
18  Dave:   GOOD.
19           WELcome to piccadilly rAdio. 99
```

In Extract 1.3, the turn *hi Nige* (line 3) is designed by Dave and treated by Nigel as a first greeting. Dave uses the high pitch onset and register that is often associated with new sequences, and a rising-falling-rising intonation contour. This final rise is typical of first greetings. Nigel shows his interpretation of Dave's turn as a first greeting by offering a return greeting. This return greeting is delivered with exactly the same prosodic pattern: high pitch onset and register, rising-falling-rising intonation and lengthening on the name. By producing a second pair part, Nigel shows that he is orienting to Dave's turn as a first pair part. Thus, this sequence can safely be interpreted as a greeting pair.

In contrast, Extract 1.4 develops slightly differently. Once again, host Dave produces a greeting token and his caller's name, Ann (lines 9–10). In her next turn, Ann produces the potential greeting token *hello* (line 12). Thus, the two successive turns could be interpreted as a greeting pair. However, in a third turn, Dave produces another *hello* (line 13). Looking at the prosodic features of these three turns, we can see that the last two are strikingly similar: not only do the participants use the same word, they both employ breathy voice quality, lengthening on the final part of the word *hello*, and a rising-falling intonation contour on the final syllable. In contrast, Dave's *Ann hi* has little in common with Ann's following turn, except for the fact that both are commonly used as greeting tokens. Ann's non-matching prosody on her greeting token *hello* is a first indication that she is not designing this turn as a second greeting. Dave's production of a prosodically matching return greeting is evidence that he, too, treats Ann's turn not as a reply to his previous turn, but as a new first pair part. A closer analysis reveals that Dave's initial turn *Ann hi* is designed and treated as the summons of a new caller, rather than a first greeting.

The differences between these two extracts show that when interpreting talk-in-interaction analysts must be careful not to take anything for granted: the fact that a participant has used a word that is commonly used for greetings does not necessarily mean he or she is *doing* a greeting at that particular sequential location. Close observation of the turns that precede and follow, including their prosodic design in relation to prior prosody, reveal how conversationalists interactionally negotiate the sequential status and 'meaning' of any given turn.

1.1.5 Repair

A last crucial conversational phenomenon to be introduced here is the way in which participants deal with potential problems in interaction. This area is referred to as 'repair' and covers the wide-ranging number of practices of correcting, reformulating or redoing previous talk. Repair can be initiated by participants themselves, in which case we speak of 'self-initiated' repair. If repair is initiated by co-participants, this is called 'other-initiated' repair. Furthermore, the redoing of speech material by the participant who produced it is called 'self-repair'; participants' redoing of other speakers' talk is referred to as 'other-repair'. Talk that is being repaired is called the 'repairable' or 'trouble source'.

Conversation analytic research has shown that there is a general preference amongst conversationalists for self-repair over other-repair; that is, participants go to great lengths to avoid having to redo the talk produced by others (Schegloff et al., 1977). This means that even if participants have noticed a potential trouble source in a currently speaking participant's turn, they tend to give that participant time to execute the repair him or herself. Extract 1.5 below contains two instances of other-initiations of repair and one instance of self-initiated self-repair. Steven is looking up a potential birthday present for his friend in a catalogue and initially tells his mother Sheri the price is *nine ninety-nine* (lines 1–3). Sheri can be assumed to be at a spatial distance from Steven, as he later asks her to *come over here and look* (line 17).

Extract 1.5   SBC058 Swingin' Kid 🎧

```
 1 Steven:   Okay it cO:sts -
 2 (1.36)
 3           NI:NE NINEty-NI:NE.
 4 (1.15)
 5 Sheri:    are you SURE?
 6 (0.32)
 7 Steven:   YEAH.
 8 (0.3)
 9           [thAt's it;
10 Sheri:    [well wE could prObably afford THA:T huh?
11 (2.98)
12 Steven:   Oh WAIT a minute;
13 (0.64)
14           i think it says TWELVE ninety-nine.
15           [thirteen;
16 Sheri:    [TWELVE ninety-nine?
17 Steven:   cOme over here and LOOK.
```

Steven's initial claim is followed by a noticeably lengthy pause (line 4), after which Sheri initiates repair in her next turn by asking *are you sure?* (line 5). This is an instance of other-initiation. The preceding pause shows her to be giving

Steven an opportunity for self-repair, rather than repairing herself. Initially, Steven does not repair his claim (lines 7–9); however, after another long pause (line 11), in which we can assume he is re-reading the information in the catalogue, he self-initiates repair in his turn *oh wait a minute* (line 12). *Oh* has been shown to be a marker of news-receipt (Heritage, 1984b), the 'news' element here being the sudden realisation of the different price. The phrase *wait a minute* is frequently used by participants to other-initiate repair. Steven's actual self-repair can be seen at line 14, *i think it says twelve ninety-nine*. In the immediately following turn, Sheri other-initiates another repair with her turn *twelve ninety-nine?* (line 16). At this point Steven treats the situation as no longer repairable through spoken interaction alone and requests his mother to *come over here and look* (line 17) instead.

As can be seen in this short extract, repair takes a wide variety of forms. However, in spite of its dealing with *trouble* in interaction, it is not necessarily a sign of discord amongst participants. Instead, repair can be seen as an integral aspect of the ongoing negotiating process that is talk-in-interaction.

1.2 Prosody in natural conversation

Prosody is an essential part of speech: human beings do not speak without articulating, and usually not without using their voice. We may whisper, and thus not vocalise; however, even when we whisper we articulate sounds, lengthen and shorten syllables, and emphasise certain words over others. We can therefore say that speech without prosody does not exist. Likewise, prosody without speech does not exist, if we assume, as we do in this book, that vocalisations such as *m* or *uh* are always conversationally meaningful, and therefore a part of speech. Even the sounds we make outside speech, such as yawning, sobbing, coughing or singing, are always socially relevant, although they are not included in this book.

In spite of the integral part that prosody plays for speech, prosodic events have no meaning of their own. Unlike the various kinds of meanings and functions associated with words – such as the concept of 'faith' underlying the word *faith*; or the connecting function associated with the word *and* – there are no such concepts or functions inherent in prosodic events. Although native speakers of any language may have intuitions concerning the 'meaning' conveyed by, say, a certain intonation contour, these meanings can only be described in the vaguest of terms. Falling pitch or sound lengthening, for example, have no meaning independent of the specific social and interactional environment in which they are being used. Therefore, we can only describe and interpret prosodic patterns in relation to the linguistic and other interactional events co-occurring with them at a given moment in time. To name some of the most important considerations for such an interpretation, we have to ask

- What words, grammatical constructions and, in the case of face-to-face interaction, what gestures, gazes and other physical movements do prosodic events co-occur with?

- Where in the conversational sequence do prosodic events occur?
- What activities is their speaker currently involved in?
- Where in a participant's utterance are they located?
- What social and regional variety does the participant speak?

With all this in mind it becomes clear that prosody must always be treated as a part of a broader speaking event, rather than as an isolated event in itself.

While prosodic patterns have no independent meaning or interpretation outside the context in which they occur, they do *contribute* to conversational meaning, or, more accurately, to conversational *actions*. As much as conversational meanings or actions are not accomplished by prosody alone, they are also rarely accomplished without prosody.

With this in mind, we can define prosody as covering *all interactionally relevant, suprasegmental aspects of talk, comprising the features of pitch, loudness, time and voice quality*. We exclude from our definition the articulation of individual sounds (segments), which is traditionally studied in the field of phonetics. We focus instead on the *suprasegmental* aspects of talk, that is on those aspects that are relevant beyond the domain of single sounds.

The wording *interactionally relevant* is particularly significant for our inclusion of voice quality into a definition of prosody. In the past, voice quality has been classified as a 'paralinguistic' or 'extralinguistic' aspect of speech, that is one that does not carry, or contribute to, linguistic contrasts. This has been the case because phonologists have assumed that a speaker's voice quality is determined by non-linguistic factors, such as an individual person's vocal setting, speaking habit, age and health condition. For example, a speaker may have a bad cold and therefore only be able to whisper; whispering in this instance does not add to the linguistic message itself, but is a result of a physiological condition.

Voice quality has been included into a definition of prosody here because it can at times be shown to be interactionally relevant. For example, a speaker may whisper because he or she has a cold; he or she may, however, also whisper for interactional reasons, such as indicating intimate information or ending a long sequence of talk. In those latter instances, voice quality, like other prosodic parameters, contributes to the accomplishment of conversational actions and must be included in the analysis of an interactional event.

Research on prosody in interaction has brought to light fundamental connections between prosody and some of the interactional practices described above. In the following sections we briefly consider the role prosody plays for turn-taking, sequence organisation and interactional negotiation.

1.2.1 Prosody and turn-taking

For many varieties of English, prosody, along with other interactional resources, has been shown to be used by participants to signal turn-related activities. For example, currently speaking participants employ different clusters of prosodic features to show that their turn is approaching completion or is being continued (Local et al., 1985, 1986; Wells and Peppé, 1996); whereas incoming participants use different prosodic practices for legitimate turn initiations on the one hand, and illegitimate interruptions on the other (French and Local, 1983, 1986). The prosodic features that have been shown to be primarily involved in turn-taking are pitch, voice quality, speech rate, rhythm and loudness.

While it is tempting to generalise that certain prosodic patterns always 'mean' turn completion or continuation, in reality participants may employ a variety of patterns depending on the sequential location of a specific turn-related activity. One aspect of turn-taking that can be attributed almost entirely to prosody is what is frequently referred to as participants' 'split-second precision' in timing their next turn onset at precisely the moment at which a previous participant has finished speaking (Jefferson, 1973). The main explanation for this ability lies with participants' collaborative orientation to speech rhythm. In her seminal book on rhythm, Couper-Kuhlen (1993) demonstrates that rhythmic patterns established by first speakers are frequently continued by next speakers: as a currently speaking participant approaches the end of his or her turn, the rhythmic pattern created by the stressed syllables is monitored by potentially next speakers. They begin their next turn by placing their first stressed syllable on the next rhythmic beat, according to the rhythmic pattern established by the previous speaker.

Extract 1.6 is an example of an orientation to prosody by an incoming speaker. The participants are two retired women. Angela, who is 90 years old, has just explained that she is looking for a service that would allow her to phone in every morning to confirm that she is up and well, so that in the case of her not phoning in relevant action would be taken. Her friend Doris offers – partly in jest – to provide this service for her, to which Angela replies that she would like to have it on a *business basis* (line 2).

Extract 1.6   SBC011 This retirement bit   🎧

```
66 1  Angela:   WELL,
   2            I would like to hAve it on a BUSIness BAsis with [sOmebody.
   3  Doris:                                                     [Oh well ALRIGHT;
   4            WE'LL put it on a bUsiness bAsis?
   5  (0.25)
   6  Angela:   you WILL?
   7  Doris:    ↑YEAH. 99
```

Angela's turn *well I would like to have it on a business bass with somebody* contains two heavily accented syllables on *BUSIness* and *BAsis*. The pitch pattern on both is a fall-to-low. This combination of rhythmically delivered final stressed syllables and low falling intonation is treated by Doris as a place to come in to speak: line 3 shows her to be starting up following these cues. While we can find many instances of participants starting up after a combination of rhythmic patterns and low falling pitch, this instance of overlap shows us that an incoming speaker is not orienting to an actual completion, but only a potential one. Angela continues her turn: as it turns out she had not quite finished. Doris takes the prosodic pattern, in combination with the potential syntactic completion, and possibly gestures and/or gaze, and interprets their combination as signalling a point of potential turn transition.

The following chapters will deal with individual prosodic parameters and their role for talk-in-interaction in much greater detail. While this book presents prosodic features in separate chapters, we must not forget that in real life interaction they are produced and interpreted by participants as clusters of prosodic events, which in addition continuously co-occur with other interactional activities.

1.2.2   Prosody and sequence organisation

Interactional linguistic research has also explored the relevance of prosody for sequence organisation beyond its role for the finality or continuity of individual turns. Interactional linguists generally seem to agree that the beginning of a new conversational activity or sequence is typically accompanied by a change to higher pitch and possibly by a break in the rhythmic pattern. For example, Couper-Kuhlen (2004) shows that new sequential beginnings frequently coincide with an extreme upwards shift in pitch in environments in which prior talk has reached a point of possible closure; while sequence continuations co-occur with a continuation of the previous pitch register. However, Extract 1.3, above, shows that, in environments where previous talk does not have the potential for closure, sequential continuations may also involve high pitch; while Extract 1.4, on the other hand, is an example of a new beginning without a pitch step-up.

In Extract 1.3, line 4, caller Nigel shows that he is continuing the greeting sequence started by Dave by repeating Dave's high pitch step-up and overall high pitch register; thus, in this context sequential continuation co-occurs with a high pitch onset. It is part of Nigel's *prosodic orientation* (see section 1.2.3 below) to Dave's turn which designs Nigel's utterance as a direct response to Dave's. In contrast, Ann's pitch onset in Extract 1.4, line 12, is no higher than normal, but clearly accompanies a new sequential beginning. This new beginning is achieved simply by not repeating Dave's prosody in his previous turn (lines 9–10).

The above extracts show that prosody plays a locally negotiated part in sequential organisation that can only be investigated through detailed and context-sensitive analysis. They also show that it is impossible to attribute general meanings or functions to individual prosodic patterns. Later chapters will focus in more detail on some of the sequence-related practices in which prosody plays a role.

1.2.3   Prosody and interactional negotiation

As we have seen in the above sections on prosody and turn and sequence organisation, prosodic patterns play a significant role in participants' collaborative accomplishment of conversational activities. A large body of interactional linguistic research has covered the contributions of prosody to specific actions. For example, Freese and Maynard (1998) investigate the prosodic features associated with the delivery and receipt of good and bad news; Couper-Kuhlen (1996a) shows that participants distinguish between prosodically quoting and mimicking another speaker; and Uhmann (1996) explores prosodic aspects of assessment sequences in German talk-in-interaction.

However, prosody has also been shown to be more universally involved in interactional negotiation amongst conversational participants. Turning once again to Extracts 1.3 and 1.4, the participants in those sequences display what I have called 'prosodic orientation' (2006). In extreme cases such as the greeting pairs *hi nige–hi dave* in Extract 1.3 and *hello–hello* in Extract 1.4, we see participants matching each others' prosodic design in several respects, such as intonation, pitch register, voice quality, stress pattern and lengthening. Other instances of prosodic orientation are not so clearly marked, and may in fact not involve matching of prosodic designs at all, but, for example, noticeable non-matching of a previous turn. However, most second-position turns show some form of orientation to prior turns in the realm of prosody, particularly if those next turns also contain strong interactional backwards orientation, as is the case for adjacency pairs.

Consider for example Extract 1.7. Miles has just told his friends a story about a young woman who has been dancing in a sexually explicit manner with a stranger in his fifties. Harold and Pete agree in their assessment of the reaction of the man, and their agreement sequence contains the repeated use of the same prosodic pattern.

Extract 1.7   SBC002 Lambada 🎧

```
1  Miles:    I mean y- y- you're FIFty year old GUY: and;
2            some TWENty year old wOman comes up dOing that to you u-
3            <<h> what do you ↑THINK;>
4  (2.05)
5  Harold:   I think you THINK you better go bAck to your tAble ↑FA:ST.
6  Pete:     ↑RI:GHT.
7  Harold:   ap↑PARently,
```

At line 5, Harold uses a high pitch step-up and a subsequent fall-to-low, and syllable lengthening on his final word *fast*. Pete comes in to agree (*right*, line 6), also using lengthening and a pitch step-up followed by a fall-to-low. As Harold closes the assessment sequence with *apparently* (line 7), he employs the same pitch movement once again. This practice of prosodic matching shows that participants are continuously aware of their co-participants' prosodic behaviour. At certain times during interaction it becomes necessary to show such awareness, either by repeating the prosodic pattern of a previous speaker or by complementing it in some other way. For example, participants may also produce a noticeably opposite prosodic design, such as a soft reply to a very loud prior turn. They may also continue a previous intonation contour, as is the case in Extract 1.8, taken from Szczepek Reed (2006, pp. 159–60). Patrick is in the process of making his point that the meat that is used for sausages is not of very high quality. As he approaches the main claim of his argument, Beverly offers a candidate completion for his utterance-in-progress. She does so with an intonation contour that continues the one Patrick has begun.

Extract 1.8   Rubbish   🎧

```
66    1  Patrick:   but you CA:N use quality meat [for SAUsages.
      2  Beverly:                                 [VEAL actually,
      3  Robert:    ↑Oh you nO you you CA:N,
      4             and and they DO:,
      5             [in in GERmany ↑And swItzerland,
      6  Patrick:   [but the but the ma↑JORity of sAUsage:s,
      7             A::RE,
      8  (0.26)
      9                  [(     ) what-
     10  Beverly:   [↑RUBbish.
     11  (1.27)
     12  Patrick:   what they CAN'T sEll as ROASTing BOILing,
     13  (0.4)
     14  Beverly:   that's ↑RIGHT;
     15  Patrick:   ↑FRYing joints. 99
```

Patrick's turn *but the majority of sausages are* (lines 6–7) is split up into two intonation phrases, both of which end in lengthening and rising pitch (*sausages* and *are*). This list of rises is completed by Beverly when she produces a candidate completion of Patrick's turn. *Rubbish* (line 10) starts with a high pitch step-up and ends on a fall-to-low. Thus, she continues and completes Patrick's turn prosodically, as well as syntactically and interactionally. Once again, this extract shows how a participant displays her awareness of a previous prosodic pattern by producing a prosodically orienting one in her immediately following turn.

Prosodic orientation is not a feature limited to certain conversational activities, but it permeates spoken interaction as a whole. Wherever participants display next turns as at least partially rooted in prior turns, we find aspects of prosodic backward orientation. This phenomenon shows how prosody is employed by participants not only in conjunction with, and for the purpose of, other conversational accomplishments, but as an interactional domain in its own right.

1.3   The data

The data for this book come from the Santa Barbara Corpus of Spoken American English (SBCSAE), a collection of naturally occurring spoken language data from across the USA. Recordings have been obtained from www.talkbank.org (MacWhinney, 2007); they can also be obtained from the Linguistic Data Consortium (Du Bois and Englebretson, 2004; 2005; Du Bois et al., 2000; 2003). For the purposes of this book we have primarily used dialogic data, with the exception of a theology lecture (Extracts 3.5 and 3.9). A small number of other extracts, such as 1.3, 1.4 and 1.8, are taken from cited publications.

1.4 Transcription conventions

This book follows a slightly modified version of the Gesprächsanalytisches Transkriptionssystem (GAT), a set of transcription conventions outlined by Selting et al. (1998). The conventions were specifically developed for the transcription of naturally occurring talk, with easily adaptable features for the notation of a large variety of prosodic events. In the following, the most basic conventions are described; the entire list of conventions used in this book can be found in the Appendix. We start with a highly simplified transcript of an extract from a conversation about Mexico as a holiday destination.

Extract 1.9(a)   SBC015 Deadly diseases 🎧

```
  1 Joanne:   i think mexico's like the place
  2           to go
  3           because it's got everything
  4           .hh
  5           it's got history
  6           it's [got big cities
  7 Ken:           [yeah it's got-
  8           [it's got disea[ses that i keep [ca[tching
  9 Joanne:   [it's got ruins
 10                          [and it's got-
 11                                         [.hh
 12                                            [and it's got resorts
 13           you know i oh
 14 Lenore:   god listen [to you
 15 Joanne:              [god
 16           [the the [caribbean is incredible
 17 Lenore:   [.hh
 18                    [resorts
 19 Joanne:   .hh
 20           it's this bl-
 21           beautiful
 22 (0.11)
 23           beautiful
 24           blue water
 25 (1.35)
 26           what
```

Each line containing words represents a single intonation phrase (see Chapter 3.1.2); or an aborted intonation phrase, indicated by a dash immediately following the last letter: see lines 7, 10 and 20 (this practice deviates from the GAT conventions, in which aborted speech is only marked if it ends in a glottal stop). Furthermore, individual lines may contain in-breaths (.hh) or out-breaths (hh.), as in lines 4, 11, 17 and 19; and measurements of pauses in parentheses, as in lines 22 and 25 (see Chapter 8). When participants speak simultaneously, the beginning of the overlap is indicated by square brackets: see lines 6–7, 8–12 and 14–18.

In addition to these features, the transcript contains information concerning the degree of syllable stress; a distinction is made between *primary* and *secondary* stress, transcribed as capitalized syllables, or vowels, respectively. In order to be heard as having primary stress, a syllable will typically contain a noticeable pitch movement, such as a rise or a fall (see Chapter 3.1.1), as well as increased loudness and duration. Syllables with secondary stress only have a certain degree of increased loudness and/or duration. With this information included, the above transcript looks as follows:

Extract 1.9(b) SBC015 Deadly diseases 🎧

```
 1 Joanne:   i thInk MEXico's like the PLACE
 2             to GO
 3             becAUse it's got EVErything
 4             .hh
 5             it's got HIStory
 6             it's [got big CITies
 7 Ken:            [YEAH it's got-
 8             [it's got disEA[Ses that i keep [CA[TCHing
 9 Joanne:    [it's got RUins -
10                          [and it's got-
11                                      [.hh
12                                          [and it's got reSORTS
13             you know i- Oh
14 Lenore:   GOD LISten [to you
15 Joanne:                [GOD
16             [the the [caribBEan is inCREDible
17 Lenore:   [.hh
18                     [reSORTS
19 Joanne:   .hh
20            it's this bl-
21            BEAUtiful
22 (0.11)
23            BEAUtiful
24            BLUE WAter
25 (1.35)
26            WHAT
```

In addition to the degree of stress, the transcript indicates the type of intonation movement at the end of each intonation phrase, as this can be of great interactional relevance (see Chapter 3.1.2). This description includes the intonation movement from the last stressed syllable onwards. The possibilities are

- rise-to-high, indicated by ?
- rise-to-mid, indicated by ,
- level pitch, indicated by -
- fall-to-mid, indicated by ;
- fall-to-low, indicated by .

Furthermore, some pitch movements on individual syllables are so noticeable that they are transcribed separately. ↑ represents a single high pitch step-up; ↓ represents a single low step-down. In this transcript a pitch step-up occurs on the final word *what* (Extract 1.9(c), line 26).

Lengthening of individual sounds or syllables is indicated by one or more colons, depending on the duration of the lengthening (Chapter 5); see Extract 1.9(c), lines 1, 2, 5, 12, 13, 15, 16, 18, 21, 23–24 and 26. With this information, our transcript looks like this:

Extract 1.9(c) SBC015 Deadly diseases 🎧

```
 1 Joanne:   i thInk [MEXico's like the PLA:CE: -
 2           to GO: -
 3           becAUse it's got EVErything.
 4           .hh
 5           it's got HIStory: -
 6           it's [got big CITies -
 7 Ken:           [YEAH it's got-
 8           [it's got disEA[Ses that i keep [CA[TCHing,
 9 Joanne:   [it's got RUins -
10                          [and it's got-
11                                           [.hh
12                                              [and it's got reSO:RTS;
13           you know i- Oh:;
14 Lenore:   GOD LISten [to you;
15 Joanne:              [GO:::D;
16           [the the [caribBEan is inCR:E:Dible.
17 Lenore:   [.hh
18                  [re:SO:RTS,
19 Joanne:   .hh
20           it's this bl-
21           BEAU:tiful;
22 (0.11)
23           BEAU:tiful;
24           BLUE: WAter,
25 (1.35)
26           ↑WHA:T.
```

Finally, prosodic information that spans more than a single syllable is indicated by <<prosodic information>, with the end of the prosodic change marked by >. This may include information regarding the overall loudness, where 'f' stands for forte and 'p' for piano (Chapter 9); see Extract 1.9(d), lines 7–8, 12–13; 19 and 27; overall voice quality, such as creaky, falsetto, breathy or smiley (Chapter 10), as in lines 7–8, 15, 16, 19, 21–24, 27; overall pitch register, marked as 'h' for high or 'l' for low (Chapter 4), as in line 19; overall fast or slow speech rate, marked as 'len' for lento or 'all' for allegro (Chapter 6), as in lines 1–2, 16–17, 21–25; or other information, such as whether a participant is laughing, see lines 8 and 15.

Individual articulation can also be marked. See, for example, Joanne's aspirated pronunciation of the sound [b] in the word *beautiful* at line 22. Finally, if two intonation phrases are latched, that is if they are produced with no gap between them, this is indicated by = (see line 13). The final version of our transcript contains all of the above information.

Extract 1.9(d)   SBC015 Deadly diseases 🎧

66

```
 1  Joanne:  i thInk [MEXico's like the <<len> PLA:CE: -
 2           to GO: - >
 3           becAUse it's got EVErything.
 4           .hh
 5           it's got HIStory: -
 6           it's [got big CITies -
 7  Ken:         [<<creaky+p> YEAH it's got-
 8           [it's got disEA[Ses that i keep <<laughing> [CA[TCHing,>
 9  Joanne:  [it's got RUins -
10                          [and it's got-
11                                                    [.hh
12                                                       [<<f> and it's got
13           reSO:RTS;=>
14           you know i- Oh:;
15  Lenore:  <<falsetto+laughing> GOD LISten [to you;>
16  Joanne:                                  [<<breathy+len> GO:::D;
17           [the the [caribBEan is inCR:E:Dible.>
18  Lenore:  [.hh
19                   [<<smiley+h+p> re:SO:RTS,>
20  Joanne:  .hh
21           <<breathy+len> it's this bl-
22           BʰEAU:tiful;
23  (0.11)
24           BEAU:tiful;>
25           <<len> BLUE: WAter,>
26  (1.35)
27           <<breathy+p> ↑ WHA:T.> 99
```

1.5 Chapter overview

The following chapters present the prosodic parameters of pitch, time, loudness and voice quality. In the case of pitch, Chapter 2 introduces some basic definitions and raises fundamental issues for an analysis of pitch by speech analysis software. Chapter 3 is concerned with pitch from the perspective of intonation; while Chapter 4 introduces pitch range and pitch register. Chapters 5–8 are concerned with different prosodic manifestations of timing in interaction: Chapter 5 considers lengthening and shortening of sounds and syllables; Chapter 6 describes speech rate; Chapter 7 explores speech rhythm; and Chapter 8 is concerned with pauses. Chapter 9 turns to loudness and Chapter 10 introduces voice quality. Chapter 11 provides a brief final outlook for research on prosody in conversation.

Chapters 3–10 all follow a similar outline: a first section introduces the contrasts that are made relevant by the prosodic feature in question. A second section presents a single longer data extract and a sample analysis of the prosodic patterns and their role in the interaction. This section is followed by short data extracts in which readers can practice their analytical skills. A third section demonstrates how previous research has analysed the prosodic parameter. A further reading section completes each chapter.

FURTHER READING

On conversation analysis

There are a number of introductory textbooks on conversation analysis, notably Ian Hutchby and Robin Wooffitt's *Conversation Analysis* (2008, 2nd edition); Paul ten Have's *Doing Conversation Analysis: A Practical Guide* (2007, 2nd edition); Anthony J. Liddicoat's *An Introduction to Conversation Analysis* (2007); and George Psathas's *Conversation Analysis: The Study of Talk-in-interaction* (1995).

For more advanced reading, Harvey Sacks's original lectures, collected by his student Gail Jefferson, and introduced by his colleague Emanuel A. Schegloff, are published as *Lectures on Conversation* (1992). Emanuel A. Schegloff has recently published *Sequence Organization in Interaction: A Primer in Conversation Analysis* (2007).

Among the most influential edited volumes, containing some of the seminal research on conversation analysis and interactional linguistics, are Peter Auer and Aldo di Luzio's *The Contextualization of Language* (1992); Maxwell Atkinson and John Heritage's *Structures of Social Action: Studies in Conversation Analysis* (1984); Deirdre Boden and Don H. Zimmerman's *Talk and Social Structure: Studies in Ethnomethodology and Conversation Analysis* (1991); Alessandro Duranti and Charles Goodwin's *Rethinking Context: Language as an Interactive Phenomenon* (1992); Cecilia Ford, Barbara Fox and Sandra Thompson's *The Language of Turn and Sequence* (2002); Paul ten Have and George Psathas's *Situated Order: Studies in the Social Organization of Talk and Embodied Activities* (1995); Gene Lerner's *Conversation Analysis: Studies from the First Generation* (2004); Elinor Ochs, Emanuel A. Schegloff and Sandra A. Thompson's *Interaction and Grammar* (1996); George Psathas's *Everyday Language: Studies in Ethnomethodology* (1979); James Schenkein's *Studies in the Organization of Conversational Interaction* (1978); Margret Selting and Elizabeth Couper-Kuhlen's *Studies in Interactional Linguistics* (2001); and Deborah Tannen's *Analyzing Discourse: Text and Talk* (1982).

Further reading on conversation analysis, its predecessor ethnomethodology, and other related approaches to language in interaction can be found in Auer (1999); Berger and Luckmann (1966); Bergmann (1994); Billig (1999a, 1999b); Boden (1990); Button (1991); Clayman and Gill (2004); Drew (2003, 2005); Garfinkel (1967, 1996); Goodwin (1981); Goodwin and Heritage (1990); Gumperz (1982); ten Have (2004a, 2004b); Heritage (1984a, 1995); Kallmeyer and Schütze (1976); Leiter (1980); Levinson (1983); Lynch (2000); Nofsinger (1991); Peräkylä (2004); Pomerantz and Fehr (1997); Sacks et al. (1974); Silverman (1998, 2006); Streeck (1983); Taylor and Cameron (1987); Wooffitt (2005); and Zimmerman (1988).

On prosody in conversation

The largest contribution to the field of prosody in natural conversation has been made by Elizabeth Couper-Kuhlen. Her *An Introduction to English Prosody* (1986), and her introductory articles (2001b, 2002, 2007a), provide in-depth overviews of many aspects, complexities and implications of the field. She has also co-edited the two influential volumes *Prosody in Conversation* (1996a, with Margret Selting) and *Sound Patterns in Interaction* (2004, with Cecilia Ford). Margret Selting's book *Prosodie im Gespräch. Aspekte einer interaktionalen Phonologie der Konversation* (1995) sets out an interactional linguistic approach to prosody in conversation in German; while John Kelly and John Local's *Doing Phonology: Observing, Recording, Interpreting* (1989) introduces their detailed phonetic analysis beyond traditional phonetic categories. Two recent volumes containing research on prosody in interaction are Barth-Weingarten et al. (2009, 2010).

Among the seminal articles on prosody and turn and sequence organisation are three famous pieces of research on turn-taking in three English varieties: Local et al. (1985) on London Jamaican; Local et al. (1986) on Tyneside English; and Wells and Peppè (1996) on Ulster English.

Among the many other works on prosody in interaction are Altenberg (1987); Auer et al. (1999); Couper-Kuhlen (1991, 1992, 1993, 1999, 2001a, 2003, 2007b, forthcoming); Erickson (1992); Flowe (2002); Fox (2001); Freese and Maynard (1998); French and Local (1983, 1986); Goldberg (1978); Günthner (1999); Klewitz and Couper-Kuhlen (1999); Local (1992); Local and Kelly (1986); Local and Walker (2004); Ogden (2001); Schegloff (1998); Selting (1992a, 1992b, 1994c, 1996a); Szczepek Reed (2006, 2009, 2010a, 2010); Uhmann (1989, 1992); and Wells and Macfarlane (1998).

On phonetics and phonology

For introductory reading on phonetics and phonology see Abercrombie (1967); Carr (1999); Catford (2002); Clark and Yallop (1995); Collins and Mees (2008); Fry (1979); Giegerich (1992); International Phonetic Association (1999); Johnson (2003); Ladefoged (2001, 2005); Lass (1984, 2009); Laver (1994); Local et al. (2003); Ogden (2009); Roach (2001, 2003); and Rogers (2000).

On transcription of conversational data

For discussions of the transcription of conversational speech data, see Du Bois (1991); Du Bois et al. (1993); Edwards and Lampert (1993); Gumperz (1993); ten Have (2002); O'Connel and Kowal (1994); Ochs (1979); Psathas and Anderson (1990); and Selting et al. (1998).

Pitch: Introduction

Out of all prosodic features, pitch is the one that is most frequently referred to in research on conversation, both by linguists and non-linguists. We shall therefore begin our exploration of conversational prosody with the two prosodic parameters in which pitch is made meaningful by participants in interaction: *intonation*, that is changes in pitch through time (Chapter 3); and *pitch range* and *pitch register*, that is the overall positioning of a participant's voice in a higher or lower speaking range (Chapter 4).

Physiologically, what we perceive as pitch is produced by the vibration of the vocal folds in the larynx. The auditory impression of high or low pitch is the result of the frequency with which a speaker's vocal folds are opening and closing: the higher the frequency of vibration, the higher we perceive the pitch. The term 'fundamental frequency', or 'F0', is used to describe the number of complete opening and closing cycles of the vocal folds per second. Frequency is measured in Hertz (Hz); therefore, a pitch value of 250 Hz is created by 250 complete cycles of vocal fold openings and closings in one second.

When it comes to analysing pitch in natural conversation, individual Hz values are not very meaningful in themselves; they only tell us what pitch a given speaker is producing at a given moment in time. Individual pitch values have to be interpreted in the context of the other pitch events that surround them. Firstly, they have to be considered in the light of those pitch values that immediately precede them. An individual 'high' pitch is only meaningfully so when surrounded by other, lower pitch events. Pitch changes like this will be discussed in Chapter 3 under intonation. Secondly, pitch values have to be interpreted in the light of a speaker's overall pitch range. A certain pitch value may be high for one speaker but not for another, depending on his or her overall speaking range. Thirdly, pitch values only become meaningful in the context of the local pitch register a conversational participant is using at the time of speaking. A pitch value may be low for a particular speaker at one point in the conversation, but not at another. The last two issues will be discussed in Chapter 4 under pitch range and register. However, before we take a closer look at the manifestations of pitch in natural talk, I will present in this chapter some of the issues surrounding the use of speech analysis software.

2.1   Pitch analysis using speech analysis software

Analysis of conversational speech data is typically conducted from audio or video recordings, and the pitch can therefore be extracted and analysed by specialist software, such as PRAAT[1] or Adobe Audition.[2] However, in producing pitch analyses it is of vital importance that the analyst is also able to make reliable judgements via his or her auditory impression. In fact, computer-generated pitch analyses should never be treated as the primary data source; instead, they should be used as a way to measure, compare and represent pitch events as situated in a given conversational context. In general, the following points should be borne in mind when analysing pitch by speech analysis software.

First, the audio file under analysis is best kept as short as possible, should not contain excessive overlapping background noise and ideally no overlapping talk by other participants. The longer the stretch of speech, the less clear the representation of detail in the analysis window will be. This means that any speech material before and after the immediate extract of interest should be cut from the audio file under analysis. In addition, any pauses preceding and/or following the extract should be cut. Decisions over what can be left out of the analysis should be made with the pitch event of interest in mind; the pitch analysis must contain just enough speech material to reveal the relevant pitch contrasts. The final drawing should show how the pitch movement under analysis is meaningful in relation to the pitch events immediately surrounding it.

Second, a pitch floor and ceiling should be determined, that is a decision should be made concerning the bottom and top Hz values in the window of analysis. The window needs to be wide enough to accommodate the speech material in question, but not too wide, in case details are not represented clearly. If a pitch analysis for one speaker is to be presented or compared with pitch analyses for other speakers it is best to use the same top and bottom values for all analyses. This allows analysts and readers to compare speech material and speakers. If drawings do not use the same analysis window, for example in order to be able to bring out certain details more precisely, or in order to accommodate a particularly low or high pitch, the reader's attention should be drawn to this fact. In this book, a default analysis window of 50–500 Hz has been chosen, as the speech presented here originates from many different speakers of varying age and gender, and a large number of conversational contexts. However, Figure 3.9 in section 3.1.1 is an exception, as the participant in this particular instance reaches values of around 700 Hz. The window in this instance has therefore been widened to 50–700 Hz.

Third, it is always possible that the software produces 'stray values', that is pitch paths that are represented, for example, a fifth or an octave above or below the value we perceive in the original recording. This can easily be corrected, but must be recognised as such. However, it is important to correct only those values that clearly do not represent the analyst's auditory impression of the recording.

Fourth, as human perception of pitch is not linear but logarithmic, it is helpful to choose a logarithmic representation when creating a drawing of a pitch curve. Although logarithmic perception is less relevant for speech, where relatively low pitch values are achieved, and more interesting for sound perception in music, the choice of a logarithmic drawing will nevertheless increase the visual resemblance of the pitch curve to our perception of the pitch analysed.

Finally, the pitch curve should always be aligned with the words or, even better, the syllables of the spoken text. For this, a text tier needs to be added to the pitch analysis. This is necessary, as any interested reader will want to see which pitch movements co-occur with which parts of the utterance.

Consider, for example, Extract 2.1. The participant in this conversation is talking about a degree in equine management for which she is required to take a class in blacksmithing. All analyses below have been generated by PRAAT 5.0.03.

Extract 2.1   SBC001 Actual blacksmithing   🎧

> 1 Lynne: dOwn thEre um it's MANdatory –
> 2   you have to-
> 3   to GRAduate,
> 4   you KNOW,
> 5   wEll to get the deGREE,
> 6   you KNOW,
> 7   .hh
> **8   you HAVE to tAke this ↑CLASS.**
> 9   .hh
> 10   and you can ONly ta-
> 11   if you WANT to you can only take it for
> 12   EIGHT WEEKS;

Let us assume that we want to analyse the pitch movement on the word *class* at line 8. Our first point above concerned the length of the material used for a pitch analysis. The recording of the transcribed extract is 11.9 seconds long; Figure 2.1 shows a pitch analysis of the full extract.

It is obvious from this analysis that the sheer length of the analysed material poses problems for the representation of the pitch value we are interested in. Individual pitch patterns cannot be shown in great detail, and the space does not allow for a matching of words in the text tier with points in the pitch curve. There are also a number of stray values. The figure shows pitch candidates at around 100 Hz and at around 500 Hz, which are clearly not in line with the rest of the pitch curve. Furthermore, Figure 2.1 contains a non-logarithmic representation.

In contrast, Figure 2.2 contains an analysis of the pitch movement we are interested in and its immediate context, that is the phrase *you have to take this class* (line 8). All other preceding and following talk has been removed from the sound file, including the speaker's in-breaths (lines 7 and 9). The pitch movement on *class* is now clearly visible, and the text fits comfortably into the text tier, which allows the reader to see which syllables correspond to which pitch event. The representation is a logarithmic one, representing more clearly a human perception of the pitch curve in question.

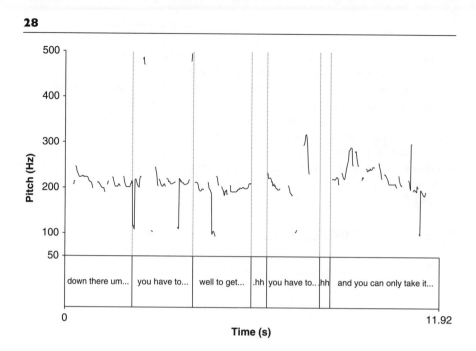

Figure 2.1   Pitch analysis of Extract 2.1

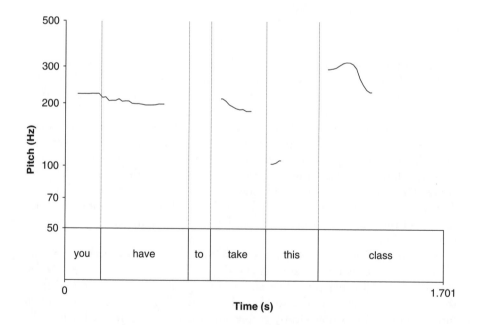

Figure 2.2   Pitch analysis of line 8 in Extract 2.1

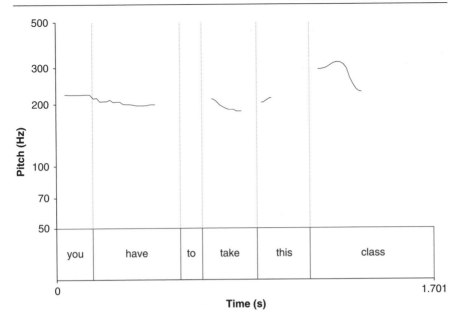

Figure 2.3   Final pitch analysis of line 8 in Extract 2.1

The only remaining correction to be made in this analysis is a stray value at around 100 Hz. Thanks to the alignment of pitch to syllables, we can detect this value as the pitch path on the word *this*. Listening to the recording, we can hear clearly that the pitch value we perceive is in fact slightly higher than the preceding one on *take*, not lower, as indicated by the path in the analysis. And indeed, when we move the value up by an octave, it represents our perception. In order to be certain that we have correctly changed the path it is helpful to listen to the pitch value we have created and compare it with the original sound file. Figure 2.3 shows the corrected analysis.

The points mentioned above are just some of the issues surrounding the use of speech analysis software, and we have only touched upon them very briefly. Most importantly, we must remember that in analysing conversation we are most fundamentally interested in participants' organisation and negotiation over talk. We therefore must keep our analyses and interpretations relevant to participant action; and in particular to the actions we are currently investigating. This sometimes means resisting the temptation to represent all the phonetic and prosodic details that the software makes available to us, and instead limit our analyses to those aspects that are likely to be relevant to the participants involved in the interaction.

Pitch: Intonation

This chapter introduces the basic ground rules for an analysis of intonation in natural talk. As pitch constantly changes during speech, it is important to focus only on those changes that are relevant to interaction. Section 3.1 presents the most important intonational contrasts: pitch accents, intonation contours and intonation phrases. Section 3.2 introduces a longer data extract, and provides a step-by step analysis that shows how participants orient to intonation during an interaction. The section also provides a number of exercises to practice analytical skills. Section 3.3 presents research that has identified, described and analysed how intonation works in certain discourse environments. Couper-Kuhlen (2004) shows that new sequences are typically begun with a high-pitched onset syllable; I (2006) describe the interactional role played by a specific intonation contour.

3.1 Contrasts in intonation

In some approaches to phonology the term intonation is used to cover all linguistically relevant suprasegmental aspects of speech. In those fields, 'intonation' refers to a number of prosodic features, including pitch, stress and rhythm. In this book, the term intonation is limited to *pitch*, and specifically to *pitch movement*; rhythm and loudness are treated as separate prosodic features, and introduced in Chapters 7 and 9.

I define 'intonation' simply as 'emerging pitch movement during voiced talk'. Such a minimal definition gives us the freedom to consider intonation without linking it from the outset to other linguistic modes, such as grammar, semantics or lexis. For example, in many phonological theories intonation is interpreted primarily as the vocal packaging mechanism for grammar and information structure. From such a perspective, the intonation of any given phrase can be predicted by the linguist if he or she knows certain variables, such as whether the information in the sentence is new or was already given; or whether a particular element of the sentence is being brought into focus. From such an approach arises an ultimately *prescriptive* view that there are correct and incorrect ways of using intonation, often immediately followed by the concession that everyday conversationalists do not always 'get it right'. Other approaches to language, including the interactional linguistic one adopted in this book, take a more *descriptive* view, that is they report back from their observations of intonation-in-use and show how pitch patterns are employed by participants in discourse. From this perspective, intonation is not assumed to have any a priori meanings or functions, but its handling by participants in conversation is interpreted both in the specific context of its sequential location and in the context of other phonological, linguistic and interactional events that co-occur with intonation at that location. From such an analysis it is possible to gain insights into those intonational patterns and contrasts that are relevant to an analysis of talk-in-interaction.

3.1.1   Stress and pitch accents

When analysing intonation it makes sense to distinguish between two kinds of pitch movements: those that occur locally, across one or two syllables, and those that occur across slightly longer stretches of speech. This section focuses on local pitch movements.

Consider, for example, the phrase analysed in Extract 2.1, *you have to take this class* (line 8).

Extract 2.1   SBC001 Actual Blacksmithing   🎧

<table>
<tr><td>66</td><td>1</td><td>Lynne:</td><td>dOwn thEre um it's MANdatory –</td></tr>
<tr><td></td><td>2</td><td></td><td>you have to-</td></tr>
<tr><td></td><td>3</td><td></td><td>to GRADuate,</td></tr>
<tr><td></td><td>4</td><td></td><td>you KNOW,</td></tr>
<tr><td></td><td>5</td><td></td><td>wEll to get the deGREE,</td></tr>
<tr><td></td><td>6</td><td></td><td>you KNOW,</td></tr>
<tr><td></td><td>7</td><td></td><td>.hh</td></tr>
<tr><td></td><td>**8**</td><td></td><td>**you HAVE to tAke this ↑CLASS.**</td></tr>
<tr><td></td><td>9</td><td></td><td>.hh</td></tr>
<tr><td></td><td>10</td><td></td><td>and you can ONly ta-</td></tr>
<tr><td></td><td>11</td><td></td><td>if you WANT to you can only take it for EIGHT WEEKS; 99</td></tr>
</table>

Listening to this phrase we can hear three local pitch movements: those on *have, take* and *class*. When we compare these three words with the other words in the phrase we can hear that *have, take* and *class* are stressed, whereas the words *you, to* and *this* are not. This distinction is the first important aspect of local pitch movements: they usually occur on stressed syllables.

In English, our perception of syllables as stressed depends on a variety of factors, most importantly on their loudness, duration and pitch movement. This means that we perceive a syllable most clearly as stressed when it is louder and longer than its neighbours, and when it contains a change in pitch. These three criteria do not always coincide, and natural English conversation provides

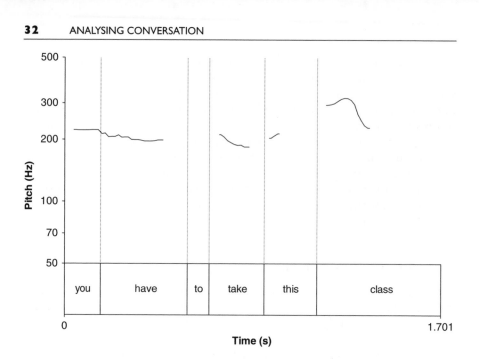

Figure 3.1   Final pitch analysis of line 8 in Extract 2.1

plenty of instances where individual syllables are, say, higher in pitch than previous ones, but not longer. However, in clear cases where several or all of the above criteria co-occur, it is usually relatively easy to distinguish stressed syllables from unstressed ones. In the phrase *you have to take this class*, for example, the unstressed syllables *you, to* and *this* are shorter than the stressed ones *have, take* and *class*, as can be seen in Figure 3.1.[1]

Amongst the three stressed syllables *have, take* and *class* we can distinguish a difference in the degree to which they are stressed. In comparison with *have* and *class*, the word *take* does not seem to be stressed as emphatically. Figure 3.1 shows that it is not as long as the other two stressed syllables; we can also hear that it is softer. In instances such as this one we describe *have* and *class* as having *primary stress* and *take* as having *secondary stress*.

In terms of analysing intonation, those syllables, or words, with primary stress are usually of the highest relevance interactionally. They carry the pitch movements that participants orient to most clearly, for example when they monitor speech for an opportunity for turn transition or when they mimic other participants' talk. A pitch movement on a stressed syllable is called a 'pitch accent'. One of the main tasks in describing naturally occurring intonation is the identification of different types of pitch accents. In the following the main types of pitch accents in standard varieties of English are introduced.

The main categories for pitch accents follow the parameters of high and low. Thus, we speak of pitch accents in terms of *rising, stepping up, falling, stepping down* and *level*, and their combinations. Sometimes it is also relevant to define *how* high or low a pitch accent is located in the context of the surrounding pitch, both in terms of how high or low it starts, and how high or low it finishes.

Rising pitch

Rising pitch involves a gradual change from low to high, during which the speaker's voice glides through all intermediate pitch values. The majority of the voiced part of the syllable is devoted to the rising movement. See, for example, the phrase *the invisible man* at line 13, Extract 3.1, from a mother–son conversation.

Extract 3.I   SBC058 Swingin' kid 🎧

```
66  1 Steven:   wAsn't there a GUY called the invisible man -
    2 Sheri:    yEs there WAS;
    3           hh.
    4 (0.48)
    5 Steven:   was HE in a MOVie,
    6 (0.15)
    7 Sheri:    YES;
    8           he WAS;
    9           hh.
   10 (0.35)
   11 Steven:   what was it CALLED;
   12 (0.23)
   13 Sheri:    the invisible MAN, 99
```

Sheri's turn at line 13 ends in a rising intonation contour, which can be seen in Figure 3.2. In this instance, the rising movement begins relatively low in the

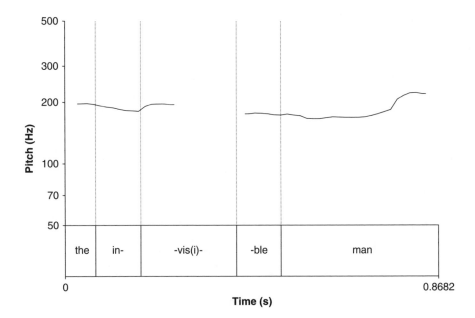

Figure 3.2 Low rise on *man*, line 13 in Extract 3.1

speaker's voice range, starting at around 165 Hz. The pitch analysis shows that while the whole phrase begins at around 200 Hz, Sheri steps down to the lower pitch for the syllable *–ble* before rising again on *man*. Such a rise is called a *low rise*: its starting point is lower than previous stressed syllables.

Rising pitch accents that begin higher than prior stressed syllables are called *high rises*. Consider, for example, the following extract, taken from a conversation between three retired women talking about their medication.

Extract 3.2   SBC011 This retirement bit 🎧

```
  1 Doris:    I'm not a very good PILL taker.=
  2           I'm re-
  3           i THINK i'm [reSENTing;
  4 Angela:              [I'm not EIther but i-
  5 Doris:    I'm reSENTing this MEDicine.
  6           and I think it's conTRIButing to my PROBlems.
  7           i REALly DO.
  8 (0.75)
  9           .h
 10           i think the (0.25) the CORtisone IS,
 11           i think the the (0.39) DIarRHETic Is, 🙶
```

The two phrases *i think the the cortisone is, i think the the diarrhetic is* (lines 10–11) end in rising intonation; Figure 3.3 represents the second phrase. In

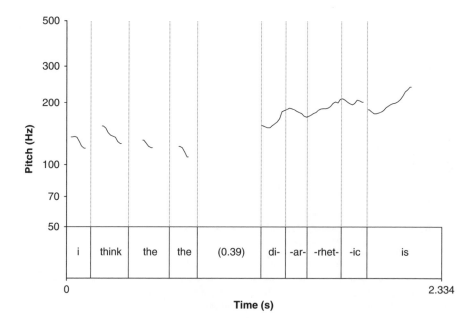

Figure 3.3   High rise on *diarrhetic*, line 11 in Extract 3.2

both cases we can hear that the beginnings of the rising pitch movements on *cortisone* and *diarrhetic* step up to a noticeably higher pitch than previous syllables.

When we compare this rising pitch accent with the phrase *the invisible man* in Extract 3.1 and Figure 3.2, the two rising movements seem to start around similar Hz values – just below 200 Hz. Therefore, considered in isolation, they could seem to be instances of the same type of pitch accent. However, when we analyse intonation, we always have to do so in the light of both the local and the global context in which they occur. Locally, the rise on *the invisible man* begins from a *lower* pitch than the beginning of the phrase, whereas the phrase *diarrhetic is* noticeably steps up to a *higher* pitch before it begins to rise. From a more global, sociolinguistic perspective, the speaker of the phrase *the invisible man* uses an overall higher voice range than the speaker of *diarrhetic is*, which is at least in part due to the age difference between the two speakers. While the participant in Extract 3.1 is a female speaker young enough to have a young child, the speaker in Extract 3.2 is in her eighties. Therefore, the same Hz value may be relatively low in the range of the first speaker, but high in that of the second one. However, it is the difference in the immediately local environment that leads us to classify the pitch accent in Extract 3.1 as a low rise, and the one in Extract 3.2 as a high rise. Note that our transcription system does not differentiate between low and high rises, but only between rise-to-mid and rise-to-high (see below).

While the terms 'low rise' and 'high rise' denote whether a speaker is rising *from* a lower or higher pitch, it is also relevant to identify where in their pitch range participants are rising *to*. Typically we differentiate between two options: rising only slightly, and rising all the way up. The rise in Extract 3.1, on the phrase *the invisible man*, is an instance of *rise-to-mid*, that is the pitch only rises to a low or medium value within the participant's pitch range, rather than all the way. In Extract 3.2, *diarrhetic is* is also an instance of a rise-to-mid: although it starts higher in the speaker's voice range, it can be heard not to rise all the way to where the participant could be rising to.

In the following extract a male speaker rises to around 200 Hz, which in his pitch range is a *rise-to-high* (see Chapter 4.1.1 for a discussion of the different voice ranges for men and women). The extract comes from a telephone conversation between a young couple. The rise-to-high occurs on the phrase *at peace with herself* (line 11).

Extract 3.3   SBC028 Hey Cutie Pie 🎧

```
 1  Jeff:   <<h> ↑GREAT.>
 2  Jill:   <<h> ↑YEAH::..>
 3  Jeff:   hOw does uhm –
 4  (0.66)
 5          tch. .hh
 6  (0.44)
 7          how's JILL;
```

```
 8              .hh
 9              hOw's her state of MIND.
10  (0.22)
11              does she seem (1.17) at PEACE with herself?
12              she HAPpy?
13  Jill:       uhU::;
14              oh YEAH::; 99
```

This pitch accent begins on the primary stress *peace*, and is carried on across the following unstressed syllables, *with herself* (see Figure 3.4). This spread of a pitch accent across a stressed syllable and the unstressed syllables that follow it is a very frequent phenomenon: unstressed syllables at the end of an intonation phrase typically continue the pitch accent begun on the last stressed syllable (see section 3.1.2 for more information on intonation phrases).

A further type of rising pitch accent is the *fall-rise*, for which, as the name implies, a speaker's pitch falls and then rises in one coherent pitch movement. Of course, during natural speech, pitch falls and rises on numerous occasions. However, we call a pitch accent a fall-rise when the falling-rising movement starts on a stressed syllable and is completed either on that same syllable or across subsequent unstressed syllables. See, for example, the phrase *he must 'a been thinking*, at line 2 of Extract 3.4. This extract comes from the same conversation as Extract 3.2; in this sequence Doris tells her friends about her meeting with a local politician.

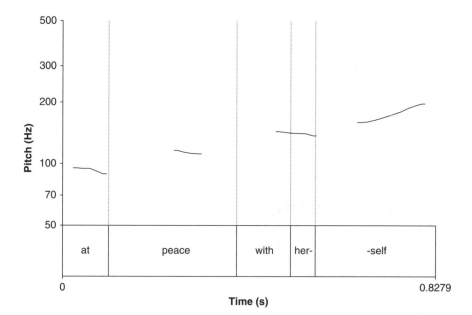

Figure 3.4   Rise-to-high on *herself*, line 11 in Extract 3.3

Extract 3.4   SBC011 This retirement bit 🎧

66 1 Doris: and you KNOW -
   2   **he MUST 'a been THINKing,**
   3 (0.74)
   4   < <all> when he sAId he wAsn't a polItical appoinTEE:;>
   5 (0.37)
   6   he MUST have been a- a- asSOciating,
   7 (0.51)
   8   his reLAtionship;
   9 (0.25)
 10   WI:TH (0.14) stEItler. 99

Figure 3.5 shows a pitch step-up from the word *been* to the syllable *think-*, and then the fall-rise: the falling movement starts on *think-*, is continued on the final syllable – *ing*, and is followed by a rising movement on that last syllable.

Stepping up

Regarding upward moving pitch accents, an important distinction must be made between a *rise* and a *step-up*. In contrast to the gradual change in pitch on the rise, the pitch step-up is a relatively abrupt change from a lower to a higher pitch at the beginning of the stressed syllable. The focus here is on the high pitch itself, rather than on a gliding change in pitch. In the previous phrase *he must 'a been been thinking*, for example, (Extract 3.4, line 2), the pitch movement

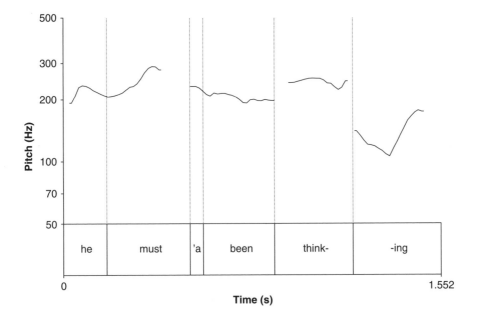

Figure 3.5   Fall-rise on *thinking*, line 2 in Extract 3.4

from *been* to *think-* is a step-up, that is it changes from a lower to a higher pitch without gliding through the intermediate pitch values; this is in contrast to the final movement on *–ing*, a rise, for which the voice glides through all intermediate pitches as it moves from the lower to the higher level.

Falling pitch

Falling pitch accents involve a gradual change from high to low. As with rises, the voice glides through all intermediate pitch values, with the main focus on the gradual change throughout the syllable. Once again, we can describe falls in terms of where they are falling from, and where they are falling to. See, for example, Extract 3.5, taken from a lecture on Martin Luther. In this short extract, all phrases end in falling pitch accents. Figure 3.6 shows the phrase *God alone is salvation*, with falling pitch accents on *alone* and *salvation* (line 1).

Extract 3.5   SBC025 The egg which Luther hatched 🎧

❝1 Foster: GOD aLONE is salvAtion.
2   (0.56)
3   GOD aLONE measures gUIlt.
4   (0.48)
5   hE alone conDEMNS.
6   hE alone GRANTS GRACE. ❞

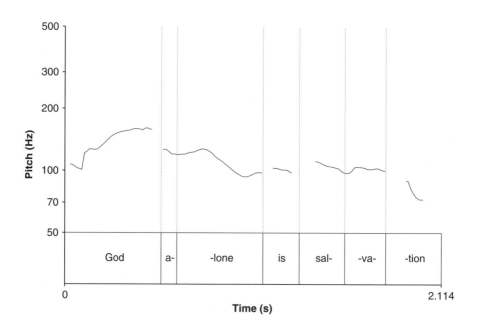

Figure 3.6   Low fall on *salvation*, line I in Extract 3.5

After a high onset on the word *God* the speaker's pitch falls on *–lone*, then remains at a roughly similar pitch level until the final fall on the syllable *–tion*. This second fall on the word *salvation* is called a *low fall*, as it starts from an initial pitch value that is lower than the previous stressed syllable *-va-*. In this case the low fall continues a declining pattern that is apparent throughout in the intonation contour.

In contrast to low falls, *high falls* are falling movements that begin high in the speaker's current pitch range, often preceded by a pitch step-up. Consider, for example, the phrase *but at least she wasn't disapproving*, taken from Extract 3.6, line 10, where the final syllables *-approving* are clearly falling from a higher pitch on *dis-*. This extract comes from the same conversation as 3.4.

Extract 3.6   SBC011 This retirement bit   🎧

66 1 Doris: sO when hE Opened UP on tha:t.
2   and SHE followed THROUGH;
3   and tOld about her HUSband.
4 (0.93)
5   you KNOW,
6 (0.8)
7 ((door))
8   nOt necessArily that shE would apPROVE of it,
9 (0.67)
10   but at lEAst she wAsn't ↑DISapprOving.
11 (0.29)
12 Angela: yeah.
13 (0.15)
14 Doris: of it.
15 Angela: yeah. 99

We can clearly hear, and see in Figure 3.7, that the participant steps up sharply on the syllable *dis-*, before beginning the fall on that same syllable and continuing to fall on all subsequent syllables. The high fall clearly starts on a higher pitch level than previous stressed syllables.

As in the case of rising pitch accents, it can be relevant for our analysis to identify where a falling pitch accent is falling *to*, that is how low the fall reaches, both in the speaker's pitch range and in comparison to previous pitch movements. Again, it is only this distinction that is relevant for our transcription notation. Both of the falls described above are *falls-to-low*. This means they fall down to the bottom of the speaker's pitch range, or at least to a pitch value that is noticeably lower than any previous values in the same speech environment. The middle-aged male speaker of *God alone is salvation* ends on 72 Hz, the elderly female speaker of *but at least she wasn't disapproving* ends on 100 Hz. Both speakers can clearly be heard to be reaching the lower sections of their voice range.

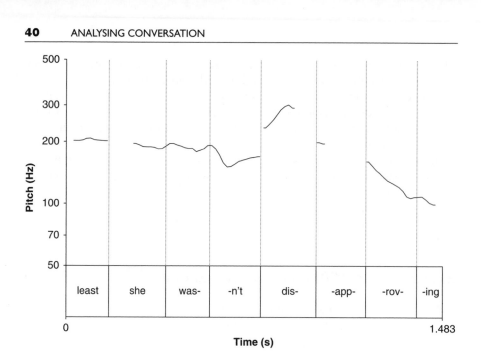

Figure 3.7   High fall on *disapproving*, line 10 in Extract 3.6

Falls that are truncated, such that they reach a pitch value that is clearly not near the bottom of a given speaker's pitch range, are *falls-to-mid*. Consider, for example, Extract 3.7, in which two women are talking about ash being blown across the room by the air conditioning system. The phrase but *look at your cigarettes* (line 13) can be heard as a fall-to-mid (see Figure 3.8).

Extract 3.7   SBC001 Actual blacksmithing 🎧

```
 1  Lenore:   it's like A:SH.
 2            is it from-
 3            that must be from the FIRES or WHAT.
 4  (0.61)
 5  Lynne:    you know mAYbe it IS.
 6  (0.51)
 7            <<all> maybe it IS;>
 8  (0.36)
 9  Lenore:   [uhm;
10  Lynne:    [cause that One that whole day you couldn't even SEE or anything,
11            from-

12            .hh
13            but lOOk at your CIGarettes;
14  (0.73)
15            just [SITting there -
16  Lenore:        [oh YEAH:; 
```

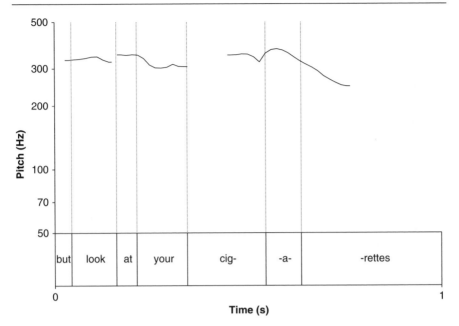

Figure 3.8   Fall-to-mid on *cigarettes*, line 13 in Extract 3.7

At the end of this phrase, Lynne's pitch can clearly be heard to be falling only to a mid-value, rather than down to the bottom of her pitch range.

A last type of falling pitch accent included here is the *rise-fall*. For this accent, pitch has to rise and then fall again, with the rise starting on the stressed syllable – and being completed across that syllable and any potential subsequent unstressed syllables. It is not always easy to distinguish a rise-fall from a high fall preceded by a pitch step-up; however, in the latter case we do not perceive an initial rising movement on the stressed, falling syllable. A further complication can arise if pitch plots show step-ups as rises (see Figure 3.7, step-up on *-dis*); this can occur because even a step-up may contain a brief moment of rising vocal adjustment to the final pitch. The main criterion here is our perception of an immediate change from a lower to a higher pitch (step-up) compared with a gradual movement (rise). For the rise-fall, there should be a rising-falling movement perceptible on the stressed syllable itself. Consider, for example, the phrase *maybe it is* in Extract 3.7, line 5. The pitch on the word *is* can clearly be heard to rise and then fall again on the same syllable. Note the extended window in Figure 3.9 to accommodate the high pitch range used by this speaker, reaching up to 700 Hz.

Level pitch

Finally, pitch on a stressed syllable can remain relatively unchanged. This type of intonation is called *level pitch*, a term which describes our lack of perception of any pitch movement. Consider, for example, the following extract, in which a couple is discussing life after death. The phrase *saw relatives coming for them* (lines 6–8) is delivered at relatively level pitch throughout.

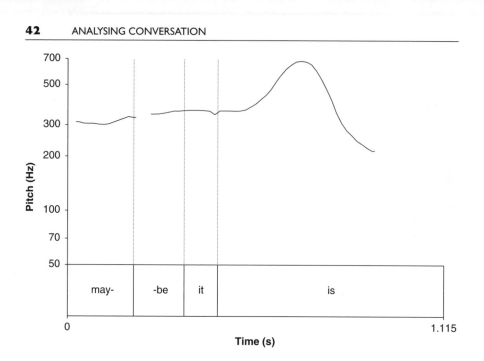

Figure 3.9   Rise-fall on *is*, line 5 in Extract 3.7

Extract 3.8   SBC007 A book about death 🎧

66 1 Pamela: people who (0.11) HAD (1.0) TECHnically died;
  2   and thEn had been reVIVED;
  3 (0.3)
  4   .hh
  5 (0.4)
  6   SAW -
  7 (0.18)
  8   RELatives COMing for them –
  9 (0.29)
10 Darryl: ts i've READ THAT,
11 (0.64)
12 Pamela: .hh
13   ↑cOUrse ↑THAT may be what hAppen:s: –
14 (0.23)
15   PRIor to the bIgʰ –
16 (1.81)
17   the BIG NOTHing. 99

Figure 3.10 shows that the term 'level pitch' is a misnomer of sorts: pitch is never entirely level, given the nature of voice production through continuous vibration of the vocal folds. Furthermore, each new syllable is likely to contain a degree of pitch variation due to the pulse of energy initiating its production.

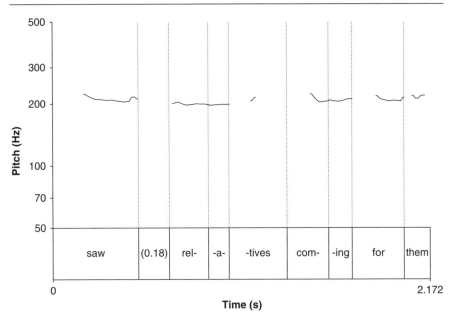

Figure 3.10   Level pitch on *saw relatives coming for them*, lines 6–8 in Extract 3.8

However, what is relevant here is our perception of certain pitch movements as level, in contrast to other clearly perceptible movements as rising or falling.

3.1.2   Intonation contours and intonation phrases

Listening to the recorded examples of talk-in-interaction in this section we can hear that the defining individual pitch movements are located on, or start on, stressed syllables. However, individual pitch accents are typically part of a larger overall intonational movement or *contour*. As participants produce talk on a moment-by-moment basis, they routinely divide their speech into short phrases, such that emerging turns-at-talk are produced phrase by phrase, chunk by chunk. Defining these phrases, or chunks, is notoriously difficult, as they do not necessarily follow syntactic phrase rules, nor are they necessarily semantically or pragmatically defined. However, one thing that is almost always present is one or more pitch accents and an overall intonation contour. Therefore these short phrases are referred to as *intonation phrases*.

In phonological literature, there are a variety of other terms in use, such as intonation unit, intonation group, tone group, tone unit, rhythm phrase or breath group. Phonologists who work in the field of intonation consider the intonation phrase a phonological phrase defined by phonological criteria such as pitch accents and prosodic boundaries, whereas conversation analysts often speak of the intonation phrase as a discourse unit, containing chunks of ideas or (parts of) turn constructional units (TCUs). Both approaches take the view that any longer stretch of speech is divided – at least in English – into shorter phrases and packaged by intonation into coherent pitch contours. Participants typically produce these more global pitch melodies across a number of stressed syllables, with one pitch accent often taking centre stage as the most prominent. This major pitch accent is traditionally referred to as the *nucleus*, and the pitch movement on it as the *nuclear pitch accent*.

Participants in spontaneous conversation are very flexible in the ways in which they package their talk. They can sometimes be found to use very short phrases that contain only the nucleus and no other pitch accents; at other times they may use more than one very prominent pitch accent per intonation phrase. What is most important here is that these short chunks of speech that participants use as building blocks for their turns and TCUs are held together by coherent intonation contours.

In listening to spontaneous speech, while it is relatively easy to make out speakers' overall tendency to divide longer utterances into shorter chunks, it can be difficult to point to the exact location where one intonation phrase ends and another one begins. The literature on intonation phrases therefore defines a number of so-called 'boundary signals', that is prosodic events that often co-occur with the transition from one intonation phrase to the next. The most frequent boundary signals are

- pauses before and after each intonation phrase;
- a change in pitch from the end of one intonation phrase to the beginning of a subsequent one, even on unstressed syllables;
- lengthening on the final syllable of an intonation phrase, irrespective of its stress;
- reduction in loudness on the final syllable;
- fast delivery of unstressed syllables preceding the first pitch accent of a new intonation phrase (*anacrusis*).

All of the phrases analysed above are also intonation phrases. Typical examples are Extract 3.4, line 2 *he must have been thinking*; Extract 3.5, line 1 *God alone is salvation*; Extract 3.6 line 10 *but at least she wasn't disapproving*; Extract 3.7, line 13 *but look at your cigarettes* and line 5 *you know maybe it is*. However, spontaneous speech is rarely an uninterrupted string of intonation phrases. Participants in natural talk may produce stretches of talk that contain no pitch accent at all, or they may abort an intonation phrase while it is underway.

For an initial example of very clear division of speech into intonation phrases, consider Extract 3.9, an extended transcript of 3.5. The majority of this extract from a theology lecture is read aloud speech.

Extract 3.9   SBC025 The egg which Luther hatched   🎧

> 1 Foster: for HOW can a PERson;
> 2 (0.41)
> 3   be reSPONsible for his DEE:DS;
> 4 (0.08)
> 5   if he posSESSes no free WILL.
> 6 (0.62)
> 7   this is what erasmus ASKED.

```
 8  (0.52)
 9            ts hOw can he decIde between good and Evil.
10  (0.74)
11            sO reasoned eRASmus.
12  (0.6)
13            sUch ARguments;
14  (0.42)
15            LO:NG known to LUther;
16  (0.44)
17            and MANy times;
18  (0.12)
19            preSENTed to him;
20            imPRESSED him;
21  (0.28)
22            NO:T in the lEAst.
23  (0.69)
24            GOD aLONE is salvAtion.
25  (0.56)
26            GOD aLONE measures gUIlt.
27  (0.48)
28            hE alone conDEMNS.
29            hE alone GRANTS GRACE.
30            JUStifies.
31            and SAVES.
32            WHEN he will;
33            and WHOM he will. 🟊
```

The lecturer in this extract clearly divides his speech into small phrases of coherent intonation contours, thus producing a string of intonation phrases. Identifying and describing the intonation phrases in this extract is relatively easy: except for lines 7 and 11, all intonation phrases begin by a perceptible step-up in pitch on the first stressed syllable; and many are preceded and followed by pauses. For example, take the sentence *for how can a person be responsible for his deeds if he possesses no free will* (lines 1–5). The speaker divides this utterance into three chunks:

for how can a person
be responsible for his deeds
if he possesses no free will.

Note that the boundary between the first and the second intonation phrase does not coincide with a straightforward syntactic boundary: both intonation phrases together form a single clause. Instead, the packaging seems to follow a rhythmic pattern. Each intonation phrase has a first pitch accent, and a final one:

for HOW can a PERson
be reSPONsible for his DEEDS
if he posSESSes no free WILL

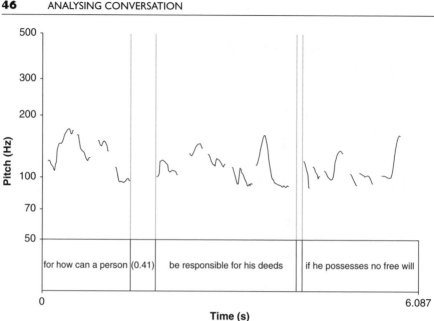

Figure 3.11   Intonation phrases, lines 1–5 in Extract 3.9

In addition, each new intonation phrase steps up to a higher pitch level than that which completes the previous contour, as can be seen in a pitch analysis of the whole utterance (see Figure 3.11).

There is a pitch step-up on *how*, a new step-up on *–spon-* in *responsible*, and a third one on *–sess-* in *possesses*. In each case, there is an overall pitch decline from the pitch of the first step-up to the final pitch value at the end of each intonation phrase; the rising-falling pitch accents on *deeds* and *will* each fall below the onset pitch.[2]

The individual intonation contours are better studied on their own. Consider, for example, the first one, *for how can a person*.

The pitch analysis in Figure 3.12 shows the stepping up and then declining pitch movement on this contour: *how* is the main step-up, followed by falling pitch on the following unstressed syllables *can* and *a*. On the word *person* the speaker steps-up on the first syllable *per-*, and then falls-to-mid on the final syllable *-son*. In this intonation phrase the main pitch accent, or nucleus, is on the word *how*. This accent can be heard and seen in the frequency analysis to be the most prominent local pitch movement.

The second intonation phrase is of a different type.

In Figure 3.13, the main pitch movement, and thus the nuclear pitch accent, occurs on the final syllable, *deeds*; while the first step-up on *-spon-* remains slightly lower. Once again, the final syllable ends in a fall-to-mid.

The third intonation phrase, *if he possesses no free will*, follows the same pattern, with a low-falling nucleus on the word *will* (see Figure 3.14).

One advantage of describing conversational intonation in terms of intonation phrases is that the pitch movement at the end of an intonation phrase often tells

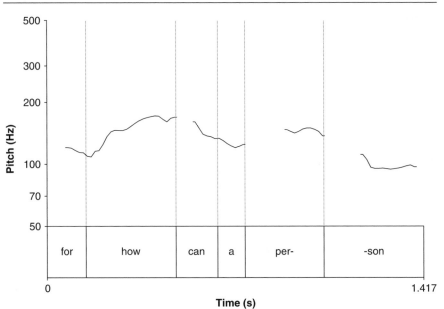

Figure 3.12 *For how can a person*, line I in Extract 3.9

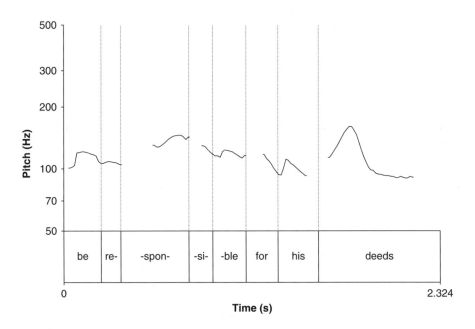

Figure 3.13 *Be responsible for his deeds*, line 3 in Extract 3.9

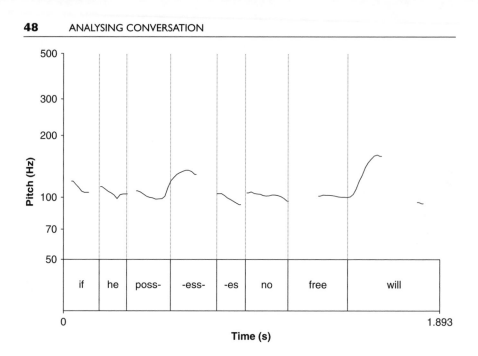

Figure 3.14 *If he possesses no free will*, line 5 in Extract 3.9

us a lot about the interactional status of the talk being delivered. In particular, final pitch movements show how participants contextualise their talk in relation to surrounding talk by themselves and other participants. For example, the pitch movement at the end of an intonation phrase can be part of a participant's turn design as projecting more talk to come, or as completing a conversational turn or activity currently in progress. Thus, for example, a phrase-final pitch movement can help other participants interpret a current intonation phrase as internal to an emerging turn – in which case more talk from the same participant can be expected – or as the last intonation phrase of a turn – in which case a potential place for turn transition is imminent. In the three intonation phrases above, final pitch movements package the speech in such a way that as listeners we know whether to expect a continuation of the activity currently in progress or a new activity. Listen, for example, to the first intonation phrase *for how can a person*. The last word *person* ends in a fall-to-mid, with lengthening on the final syllable (see Figure 3.12); the phrase is not syntactically complete. Similarly, the last word *deeds* in the second intonation phrase ends in a truncated fall, with lengthening of the final pitch value (Figure 3.13); note that this phrase does end in potential syntactic completion. In spite of the differences in syntactic endings, both phrases end in intonation contours that signal continuation by the speaker. In contrast, the last word of the third intonation phrase, *will*, falls below previous pitch levels, ending in a low fall (Figure 3.14). The creaky voice quality at the end of the low fall shows it has reached the bottom of the speaker's voice range (see Chapter 5). This pitch movement coincides with the end of the sentence and the idea currently in progress: *For how can a person be responsible for his deeds if he possesses no free will.*

This co-occurrence of low falling intonation with completion on another level – be it syntax, semantics, narrative or turn-related – is extremely frequent in spoken English. We can therefore safely assume that low falling pitch is used by participants to design certain aspects of talk as complete. *What* is being completed – whether it is a sentence, a turn constructional unit, a turn, a section of a longer narrative or the first in a string of arguments – is an entirely different question. Intonation does not tell us anything about the *type* of activity that is being packaged in this way, only how that activity can be interpreted in relation to the talk that came before and the talk that is coming afterwards.

While Extract 3.9 is a good example of a speaker dividing his or her speech into intonation phrases, it is not necessarily a representative example when it comes to spontaneous talk. As participants negotiate next actions on a moment-by-moment basis, and as they plan their own immediately next words only split-seconds prior to their vocalisation, the intonational delivery of turns emerges as, and is designed as, a local product of these processes. While participants orient to intonation phrases as ways of packaging stretches of speech within turns, their delivery is not always as clear-cut as that of read-aloud, or prepared, speech. Consider, for example, Extract 3.10(a), transcribed without intonation phrase boundaries. This longer sequence is an expanded version of Extracts 3.4 and 3.6; Doris is talking about a local politician.

Extract 3.10(a) SBC011 This retirement bit 🎧

```
 1  Doris:    sO when hE Opened UP on that and SHE followed THROUGH and tOld
 2            about her HUSband (0.93) you KNOW (0.8)
 3  ((door))
 4            nOt necessArily that shE would apPROVE of it (0.67) but at lEAst she
 5            wAsn't ↑DISapprOving
 6  (0.29)
 7  Angela:   yeah
 8  (0.15)
 9  Doris:    of it
10  Angela:   yeah
11  (0.39)
12  Doris:    ((sniff)) (0.24) AN:D uh (0.85) course duVALL might- (0.38) and I- I
13            canNOT get Over this (0.22) thAt MAN (0.11) i REALly CANNOT (0.6)
14            and you KNOW he MUST 'a been THINKing
15  (0.74)
16            <<all> when he sAId he wAsn't a polItical appoinTEE:> (0.37) he MUST
17            have been a- a- asSOciating (0.51) his reLAtionship (0.25) WI:TH (0.14)
18            stEItler
```

This extract is a typical example of everyday speech, where language, and in particular intonational chunking, evolve locally through time, rather than arriving as a prepackaged product. As can be heard on the recording, it is much more difficult than in the read-aloud speech to say with certainty where intonation phrases begin or end. For example, at the beginning of the extract, the speaker

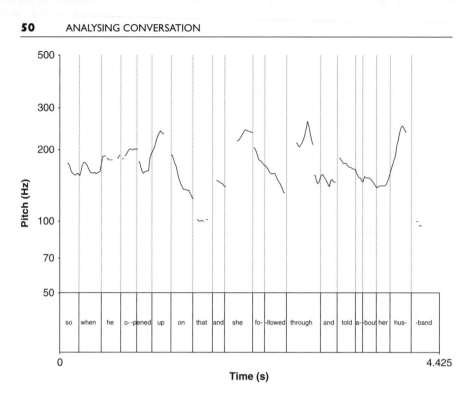

Figure 3.15   Intonation phrases, lines 1–2 in Extract 3.10(a)

does not pause throughout the first stretch of speech *so when he opened up on that and she followed through and told about her husband*. Nevertheless, we can hear that she is using prosodic phrasing mechanisms within this utterance; some of them can be seen in Figure 3.15. In the phrase *so when he opened up on that*, we can hear that the final word *that* is lengthened. The next word, *and*, steps up to a higher pitch, although it is not stressed. It can therefore be heard as the beginning of a new intonation phrase. In this second phrase, *through*, with its fall-to-mid pitch movement, is the final pitch accent: it is slightly lengthened, and the next word *and* is delivered quickly, which means we can consider it the beginning of the third intonation phrase. The subsequent stressed syllable *told* steps up to a noticeably higher pitch, clearly signalling the beginning of a new phrase. Such an analysis renders the following transcription:

1 Doris: sO when hE Opened UP on tha:t.
2   and SHE followed THROUGH;
3   and tOld about her HUSband.

Extract 3.10(a) also shows that, just as not all intonation phrases are followed by pauses, not all short chunks of speech followed by pauses, or other separating speech events, are necessarily full intonation phrases. Consider, for example, lines 4–7. Doris's phrase *not necessarily that she would approve of it* is followed by a pause of 0.67 seconds, and can be heard as an intonation phrase. This is followed by a next intonation phrase, *but at least she wasn't disapproving*. At the end of this phrase two cues speak for intonation-phrase completion: Doris herself produces a marked high falling pitch pattern on the word *disapproving* (Figure 3.7), ending in a fall-to-low; and co-participant Angela comes in with an acknowledgement token *yeah* (line 7), showing that she also considers this to be a completion point of some sort. However, following Angela's reply Doris continues her previous utterance by producing a short increment: *of it* (line 9). *of it* carries no pitch accent as it contains no stressed syllable and therefore cannot be considered an intonation phrase in its own right. Instead, it is designed by Doris as a late continuation of her previous phrase. Thus, even an utterance preceded and followed by talk from other participants is not necessarily a full intonation phrase, if it is not designed as one by the speaker herself.

Line 12, too, shows an instance of an utterance that is neither a full intonation phrase of its own, nor part of one. The phrase *course Duvall might-* is preceded and followed by pauses; however, its lack of lengthening of the final syllable shows it to be broken off before reaching completion. Notably, the preceding phrase *and uh* can clearly be heard as an intonation phrase of its own, irrespective of the small amount of lexical content.

The transcript below shows the intonation phrase boundaries for Extract 3.10(a).

Extract 3.10(b)   SBC011 This retirement bit 🎧

```
 1 Doris:    sO when hE Opened UP on tha:t.
 2           and SHE followed THROUGH;
 3           and tOld about her HUSband.
 4 (0.93)
 5           you KNOW,
 6 (0.8)
 7 ((door))
 8           nOt necessArily that shE would apPROVE of it,
 9 (0.67)
10           but at lEAst she wAsn't ↑DISapprOving.
11 (0.29)
12 Angela:   yeah.
13 (0.15)
14 Doris:    of it.
15 Angela:   yeah.
16 (0.39)
17 Doris:    ((sniff))
18 (0.24)
19           AN:D uh;
20 (0.85)
21           course duVALL might-
```

```
22  (0.38)
23          and I-
24          I canNOT get Over this.
25  (0.22)
26          thAt MAN.
27  (0.11)
28          i REALly CANNOT.
29  (0.6)
30          and you KNOW -
31          he MUST 'a been THINKing,
32  (0.74)
33          <<all> when he sAId he wAsn't a polItical appoinTEE:;>
34  (0.37)
35          he MUST have been a- a- asSOciating,
36  (0.51)
37          his reLAtionship;
38  (0.25)
39          WI:TH (0.14) stEItler. 🙴
```

Extracts 3.10(a) and (b) show, first of all, that it is not possible to predict how speakers package turns into intonation phrases, neither for prepared nor for spontaneous speech. It is always necessary to listen closely to what speakers are doing intonationally, relying as little as possible on preconceived expectations of how a given utterance might, or should be, produced. Second, intonation is only one of several interactional modes at play at any given moment in conversation. In transcribing talk as a succession of intonation phrases, the analyst separates out audible signals in the speech stream, which can be extremely helpful for an analysis of prosody. For example, intonation phrases can be instrumental in revealing which chunks of talk participants are orienting to. However, as participants are simultaneously involved in other linguistic and interactional modalities, we cannot automatically assume that there is a one-to-one relation between intonation phrases and interactional units. At present, the interface between intonational and interactional boundaries remains a complex one and is still little understood.

3.1.3 Summary

The main points to take away from this section are:

* Intonation is emerging pitch movement during voiced talk.
* Pitch accents in English may rise, fall or remain level.
* Rising pitch involves a gradual change from low to high.
* Types of rises are

   o low rise: starting lower than previous stressed syllables and typically located low in a speaker's pitch range;

- high rise: starting higher than previous stressed syllables and typically located high in a speaker's pitch range;
- rise-to-mid: rising to mid in a speaker's pitch range;
- rise-to-high: rising to high in a speaker's pitch range;
- fall-rise: pitch falls, then rises, starting on a stressed syllable.

- Falling pitch involves the gradual change from high to low.
- Types of falls are

  - low fall: starting lower than previous stressed syllables and typically located low in a given speaker's pitch range;
  - high fall: starting higher than previous stressed syllables and typically located high in a given speaker's pitch range;
  - fall-to-mid: falling to mid in a given speaker's pitch range;
  - fall-to-low: falling to low in a given speaker's pitch range;
  - rise-fall: pitch rises, then falls, starting on a stressed syllable.

- Level pitch involves little perceptible pitch change throughout a stressed syllable and any following unstressed syllables.
- Local pitch movements on, or originating on, stressed syllables are called pitch accents.
- Pitch configurations across longer stretches of talk are called intonation contours.
- Intonation contours often form intonation phrases.
- Intonation phrases have at least one pitch accent.
- The boundaries of intonation phrases may be created by

  - pauses;
  - a change in pitch on unstressed syllables;
  - lengthening;
  - reduction in loudness on the final word or syllable;
  - anacrusis.

3.2 Analysing intonation

After the introduction to the main intonational contrasts in the previous section, we now take a look at a longer extract of talk to show how intonation can be analysed step-by-step as a relevant component of an emerging interaction. Along the way some frequent pitfalls and common misconceptions are pointed out. The two most important aspects of intonation analysis are the practical training of our ears and the analytical training of our interpretive skills in focusing on what is treated by participants as interactionally relevant. Both can be practised with the exercises provided at the end of this section.

The extract below is taken from the same conversation as Extracts 3.2, 3.4, 3.6 and 3.10. Angela, aged 90, is visiting her friends Doris, aged 83, and Sam, aged 72. The recording begins with the introduction of a new conversational sequence by Angela.

Extract 3.11   SBC011 This retirement bit 🎧

```
 1  Angela:   I STILL haven't found Anybody that wAnts to –
 2  (1.41)
 3            lEt me pay a little FEE (0.1) and then;
 4  (1.87)
 5            CALL them Every mOrning –
 6  (0.99)
 7            that i'm (0.25) UP and aROUND.
 8  (0.54)
 9  Doris:    <<all> what what what - >
10            bAck UP a minute.
11            DO WHAT,
12  (0.35)
13  Sam:      hh.
14  (0.67)
15  Doris:    [YOU'LL PAY –
16  Angela:   [.hh I've –
17  Doris:    [<<p> to be CALLED ->
18  Angela:   [I've been lOOking for SOMEbody,
19            who will sIt by the PHONE;
20            in the MORning,
21  (1.02)
22            and-
23  (0.73)
24            and CLIENTS will cAll in and say;
25            good ↑MORning -
26            I'm ↑UP –
27  (0.65)
28            hehe -
29  (0.79)
30            and so that-
31  (0.31)
32            they're THROUGH for the DAY then.
33  (0.58)
34            I'm UP.
35  (0.46)
36            if I DON'T call In by say:;
37            NINE o'CLOCK;
38  (1.1)
39            [then-
40  Doris:    [well I'll be GLAD to do that for a FEE:,
41  (0.55)
42  Angela:   you WILL?
43  (0.34)
44            [how mUch is the F[EE: thOUgh;
45  Doris:    [ehhhh            [hehehehehehehehe
46  Angela:   he[hehehehe
47  Sam:        [ehehe
48  (0.78)
49  Doris:    (Angela) does thAt-
```

50		does it rEAlly BOTHer you,
51	(0.91)	
52	Angela:	.h I'D like to have somebody i can call into;
53		EVEry MORning.
54	(0.55)	
55	Doris:	YOU cAll In -
56		or I cAll In.
57	Angela:	.h I call in let y-
58	(0.44)	
59		whOever it IS,
60	(0.32)	
61		know i'm ↑UP –
62	(0.57)	
63	Sam:	WELL,
64		you can do that with US,
65		WE'RE [up;
66	Doris:	[YOU can do with that-
67		YOU can do that with US.
68	(0.79)	
69		sOmetimes wE're up at fOUr o'↑CLOCK.
70	Angela:	ehe[hehehehe
71	Doris:	[hehehehehehehe
72	Sam:	((throat))
73		wE're up [EARly.
74	Angela:	[hehehehe
75	(0.42)	
76		.hh
77	(0.42)	
78		WELL,
79		I would like to hAve it on a BUSIness BAsis with [sOmebody.
80	Doris:	[Oh well ALL RIGHT;
81		WE'LL put it on a bUsiness bAsis?
82	(0.25)	
83	Angela:	you WILL?
84	Doris:	↑YEAH.
85	(1.22)	
86		it's on [a BUSIness BAsis.
87	Angela:	[WELL,
88	Doris:	RIGHT now.
89		we [jUst formed a cOrpoRAtion;
90	Angela:	[i-
91		i'll DRAW up the pApers.
92	Doris:	YOU DO [thAt.
93	Sam:	[ehehe
94	Doris:	[YOU DO thAt.
95	Angela:	[ehe
96	Doris:	we'll have them WITnessed,
97	(0.62)	
98		A::ND –
99	Angela:	ehehe
100	(0.28)	
101	Doris:	w- we're in ↑BUSIness.

```
102  Angela:    should we have an atTORney to adVISE us,
103  (0.62)
104  Doris:     ↑Oh i thInk it can DO tha:t;
105  Angela:    hahahaha
106  Doris:     mhmhm
107  (0.58)
108  Angela:    ((sniff))
109             ehe
110  (0.64)
111             aw:::;
112  (1.68)
113  Doris:     hehehehehehe 🙴
```

3.2.1 Intonation phrases

The first step in any initial prosodic analysis of a longer extract of talk is the identification of intonation phrases and pitch accents. Intonation phrases display how a given participant has chosen to package his or her spoken material, while pitch accents show how specific words or syllables are ranked in prominence by speakers in relation to surrounding words and syllables. However, we should retain an awareness that while pitch accents can often be clearly defined as rising, falling, etc., intonation phrases are a more evasive category. As analysts we always come to a conversation 'after the fact', and from this perspective of temporal distance it can be tempting to superimpose phonological boundaries on the grounds of what a given utterance could have sounded like, had it been prepared in advance. This pitfall can easily be experienced by any analyst reproducing a short utterance only moments after hearing its original recording. The intonation phrase boundaries of the reproduction will always sound more clear-cut, as the analyst is not at the same time engaged in online processing and interactional negotiation, but is able to deliver a phrase that is ready for intonational packaging as a single chunk of speech.

In the above extract we encounter some of these complications. We focus for now on lines 1–7 in the transcript: *I still haven't found anybody that wants to let me pay a little fee and then call them every morning that I'm up and around.* Starting with the question of how the participant has intonationally packaged her material, the first difficulty the analyst faces in this utterance is over the initial intonation phrase boundary. In our transcript the author has decided that the utterance is best represented by showing a boundary after the word *to*, thus showing the word *let* as the beginning of a new intonation phrase. However, the whole utterance *I still haven't found anybody that wants to let me pay a little fee* could also be heard as one coherent phrase. This is the case because according to our linguistic expectations the gap after *to* is an unlikely place to stop; in terms of syntax, it is the middle of an infinitive phrase. Therefore we are inclined to project more talk to come in the 'same breath', and we interpret the pause as the speaker breaking off, rather than chunking speech coherently. However, in reality the participant produces stress and lengthening on the word *wants*, stays on the same low pitch for *to*, leaves a pause of 1.41 seconds and then steps up to a new higher pitch on *let* (see Figures 3.16 and 3.17). The high

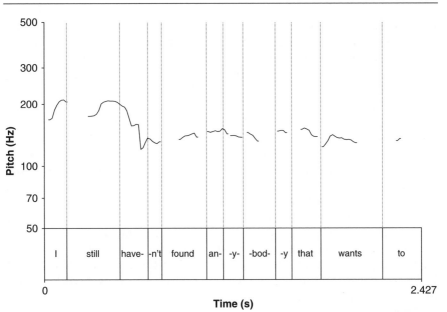

Figure 3.16 *I still haven't found anybody that wants to,* line 1 in Extract 3.11

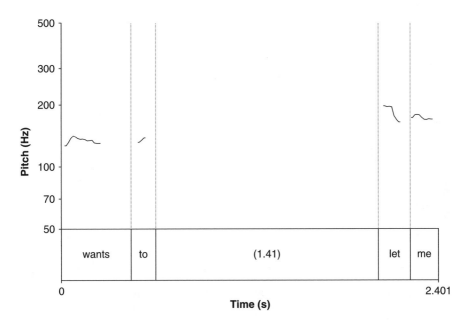

Figure 3.17 *Wants to let me,* lines 1–3 in Extract 3.11

pitch on *let* shows a new beginning. Therefore, if we want to be true to what the speaker is actually doing, rather than rely on our own preconceptions, we have to place an intonation phrase boundary between *to* and *let*. This practice of incorporating and taking seriously the participant's speech production is the only way of making linguistic categories such as the intonation phrase relevant for naturally occurring language.

A similar problem arises at the next boundary, although this one is intonationally less clear-cut. Syntactically, the sentence in progress ends with *fee*, and a prepared speaker could be expected to place a boundary after that word, before going on to the following main clause *and then call them every morning*. However, this participant chooses to attach the beginning of the new clause, the two unstressed syllables *and then*, to the intonation contour in progress. She leaves a substantial pause of 1.87 seconds and subsequently starts a new intonation phrase *call them every morning*, with a clear high onset pitch on *call*. However, the two unstressed syllables *and then* don't continue the pitch pattern begun on *fee*, but perceptibly step down to a lower pitch (see Figures 3.18 and 3.19). Unlike the previous intonation phrase, where the final unstressed syllable *to* continues roughly the same pitch level as the previous stressed syllable *want*, here we have the type of pitch change on unstressed syllables often associated with the beginning of a new intonation contour and phrase. If we took this stance, then our transcription would have to be:

```
3  Angela:   lEt me pay a little FEE –
4  (0.1)
5             and then (1.87) CALL them Every mOrning –
```

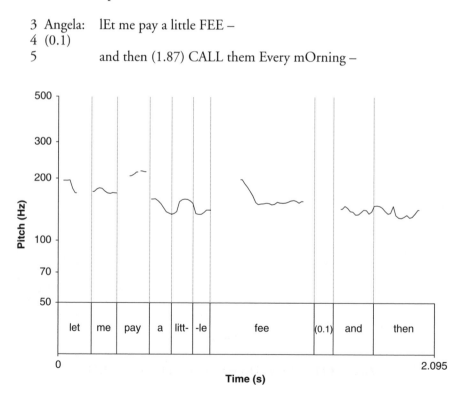

Figure 3.18 *Let me pay a little fee*, line 3 in Extract 3.11

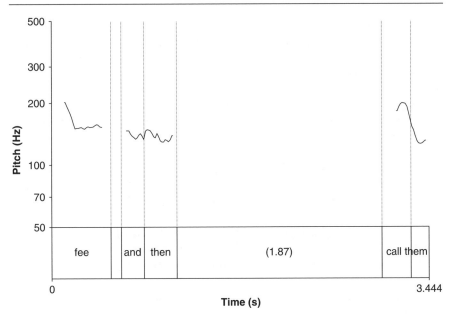

Figure 3.19 *Fee and then call them*, **lines 3–5 in Extract 3.11**

On the other hand, we could make a different decision based on the long pause and the pitch step-up on *call*, in which case our transcript would be the one we have adopted:

3 Angela: lEt me pay a little FEE (0.1) and then;
4 (1.87)
5   CALL them Every mOrning –

This short utterance represents a frequently encountered difficulty in the allocation of unstressed syllables occurring near intonation phrase boundaries. However, while for the analyst the challenge is to decide which intonation phrase the unstressed syllables *and then* might belong to, for the participant this is simply a result of the nature of talk as locally emerging. The precise location of the intonation phrase boundary is clearly not an issue that is of primary relevance to participants themselves – otherwise we would not find so many unclear instances involving unstressed syllables in spontaneous talk. Thus, this extract shows once again that while participants are indeed orienting to an intonational packaging strategy as such, this strategy is evolving with speech, rather than being pre-existing. After-the-fact discussions over boundary locations must take into account that these boundaries originally emerged *in situ*, and that as a result there may not be a clear-cut solution. Similar to grammatical pivots (Walker, 2007), unstressed syllables in intonation may at times emerge as simultaneously belonging to a prior, and a subsequent, intonation phrase.

The boundary between the next two intonation phrases at *morning* and *that* (lines 5–7) shows the same difficulty. We can hear clearly that in the utterance *call them every morning that I'm up and around* (lines 5–7) there is an intonation phrase boundary somewhere between the pitch accents on *call* and *up*. The intervening words *them every morning that I'm* carry little stress, and in particular the unstressed words *that I'm* could be heard as belonging either to the end of the previous intonation phrase or to the beginning of the next one. This is the case particularly because they continue the pitch level of prior words, rather than stepping up to a new beginning. A decision has been made here on the basis of the length of the preceding pause, resulting in the transcription above:

```
5 Angela:   CALL them Every mOrning –
6 (0.99)
7                      that i'm (0.25) UP and aROUND.
```

However, as in the previous case, the words could also have been heard as attached to the prior phrase or even considered to be free standing unstressed words. In these cases the transcripts would have shown either:

```
5 Angela:   CALL them Every mOrning (0.99) that i'm;
6 (0.2)
7                      UP and aROUND.
```

or:

```
5 Angela:   CALL them Every mOrning -
6 (0.99)
7                      that i'm
8 (0.2)
9                      UP and aROUND.
```

While we have so far taken seriously the speaking participant's perspective on the intonational packaging of this utterance, this extract also allows us to analyse the next participant's turn as related to its intonational delivery. Doris's repair initiation *what what what back up a minute do what you'll pay to be called* (lines 9–17) highlights a major trouble source in Angela's turn. While the phrase *do what* seems to question the overall activity Angela has been describing, *you'll pay to be called* defines the problem over the specific activity of calling, a matter that is still not resolved later on when Doris asks *you call in or I call in* (lines 55–56). The misunderstanding over who is calling whom is most probably related to Angela's intonational packaging of the utterance containing that information. Her sentence *I still haven't found anybody that wants to let me pay a little fee and then call them every morning* (lines 1–5) is grammatically slightly complex, as the subclause *call them every morning* is dependent on *let me*; i.e. 'let me pay a little fee and then (let me) call them every morning'. The connectors *and then*, and the following substantial pause of 1.87 seconds, strongly suggest a new main clause, and the high pitch onset on the next word *call* seems to confirm that expectation, only to be then seemingly lacking a subject noun phrase. Therefore, in this instance, the packaging of a turn into chunks of speech that are not grammatically separate is treated by a next participant as a problem. This is evidence from the participants involved that intonational packaging is indeed relevant for interaction and that it can be the source of difficulty, not only for analysts, but also for conversationalists themselves.

3.2.2   Pitch accents

Having identified the way a participant has packaged his or her speech into intonation phrases, the second important step is to identify the kind of pitch movement that has been used on the stressed syllables. Once again, we have to be careful not to hear what we expect to hear, but to describe what a partici- pant is really doing. Some conversational contexts raise certain expectations in terms of what kind of pitch accents are most likely to be used. For example, a participant may be engaged in a conversational list, and we may expect to hear slightly rising intonation at the end of every list item. However, speakers in nat- urally occurring talk do not always comply with those expectations and may be using different pitch accents instead. In addition, some inherent phonetic features such as vowel quality can influence our initial auditory impression of a pitch movement. For example, high vowels such as [i] can lead to a hearing of the pitch as 'high', when the actual Hz value is not. Furthermore, the very nature of high pitch leads some listeners to assume that intonation is rising, when it may in fact be stepping up instead.

A clear example of a pitch accent in an environment where we would indeed expect it is Angela's final fall-to-low on her phrase *that I'm up and around* (line 7, Figure 3.20). We can clearly hear her pitch dropping lower than any previous

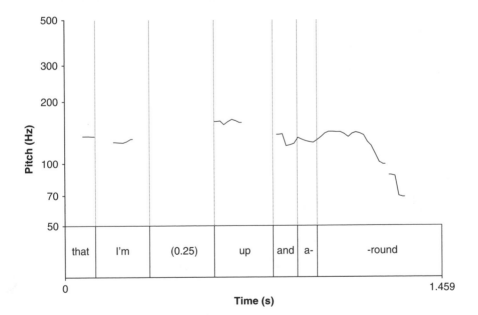

Figure 3.20   *Up and around*, line 7 in Extract 3.11

pitch levels in her current turn. In her next turn, Doris shows that she treats Angela's turn as completed, by coming in to speak.

As mentioned above, in standard varieties of British and American English pitch accents that fall to low are often associated with the concept of 'completion', either of a speaking turn or other sequential projects. In our example, we can see the same pattern in line 53, where the phrase *every morning* receives a fall-to-low and is followed by a turn transition; similarly in lines 56, 91 and 101. All these instances show that in certain sequential contexts participants treat pitch accents that fall to low as cues that a current speaker has arrived at a point of possible turn completion. Another strong piece of evidence for this type of pitch accent to be treated as a cue for some form of finality is Doris' interruption of Angela's turn in lines 79–81:

79 Angela: I would like to hAve it on a BUSIness BAsis [with sOmebody.
80 Doris: [Oh well ALL RIGHT;
81   WE'LL put it on a bUsiness bAsis,

Listening to the recording we can hear that Angela has reached a fall-to-low after her final stressed word *basis* (Figure 3.21). This location is treated by Doris as a place for turn transition. Although Angela has not finished yet, her intonational delivery has provided a cue for Doris to come in.

The extract also shows how falls-to-low are used to structure other aspects of talk besides turn endings. For example, Doris's utterance *back up a minute* (line 10) receives a fall-to-low, but is not followed by a speaker change. However, it is followed by a new conversational activity: while the phrase *what what what back up a minute* accomplishes the first part of the repair initiation in

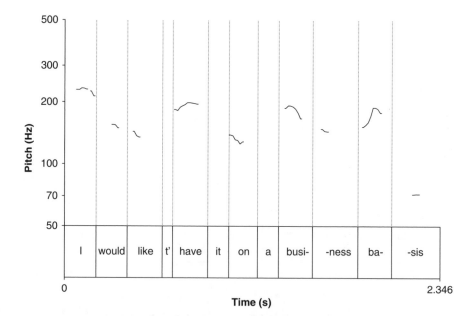

Figure 3.21 *I would like to have it on a business basis*, line 79 in Extract 3.11

which Doris designs her turn as bringing Angela's turn to a halt, the subsequent part *do what* (line 11) targets the actual trouble source. Similarly, Angela uses falls-to-low on her phrases *they're through for the day then* (line 32) and *I'm up* (line 34) before she continues with the next element of her argument *if I don't call in by say nine o'clock*. Such uses of falls-to-low show that participants – both those currently speaking and incoming next speakers – treat this type of pitch accent as a structuring cue for the completion of a variety of conversational actions.

At times, conversational contexts suggest falls-to-low, but participants use different pitch patterns instead. In those cases we must be careful to hear what speakers are actually doing, rather than what we would expect them to do. With this in mind, however, small prosodic differences are not always treated as interactionally relevant differences by participants themselves. We have to distinguish, on the one hand, between those contrasts that are made relevant by speakers and, on the other hand, instances in which participants deliver a pitch pattern as a version, or *token*, of a certain *type* of pitch accent, but for immediate articulatory reasons do not accomplish the entire pattern. The following two extracts show examples of pitch patterns that are different to our expectations. In the first instance, the pitch pattern is nevertheless treated by participants as a token of the expected pattern; in the second example, the unexpected pattern does make an interactional difference.

Towards the end of our data extract, Doris and Angela playfully engage in the idea of setting up a business. This non-serious sequence begins with Doris's turn *oh well all right we'll put it on a business basis* (lines 80–81) and continues until her exclamation *we're in business* (line 101):

```
 80  Doris:    oh well ALL RIGHT;
 81            WE'LL put it on a bUsiness bAsis,
 82  (0.25)
 83  Angela:   you WILL?
 84  Doris:    ↑YEAH.
 85  (1.22)
 86            it's on [a BUSIness BAsis.
 87  Angela:           [WELL,
 88  Doris:    RIGHT now.
 89            we [jUst formed a cOrpoRAtion;
 90  Angela:      [i-
 91            i'll DRAW up the pApers.
 92  Doris:    YOU DO [thAt.
 93  Sam:             [ehehe
 94  Doris:    [YOU DO thAt.
 95  Angela:   [ehe
 96  Doris:    we'll have them WITnessed,
 97  (0.62)
 98            A::ND –
 99  Angela:   ehehe
100  (0.28)
101  Doris:    w- we're in ↑BUSIness.
```

At the core of this sequence is a series of intonation phrases that all seem to end in falls-to-low: *it's on a business basis. / right now. / we just formed a corporation. / I'll draw up the papers. / you do that. / you do that.* Their repetitive nature creates an expectation that each of these pitch accents follows the same pattern. However, if we listen closely, we can detect that one of them does not fall to low: Doris's phrase *we just formed a corporation* does not reach the same low pitch as surrounding phrases. When we analyse the phrases preceding and following this utterance, *right now* and *I'll draw up the papers*, we can see that they end considerably below 100 Hz (due to their creaky voice quality, see Chapter 10), whereas *corporation* ends just above at 112 Hz (Figures 3.22, 3.23 and 3.24).

In this instance both participants involved in the sequence treat the phrase *we just formed a corporation* as of the same type as surrounding phrases. Doris herself continues with this turn a previously begun list of turns that playfully accomplish the performative action of setting up the business (*it's on a business basis / right now / we just formed a corporation*). Co-participant Angela treats it as a cue for speaker change, and she also repeats the fall-to-low on her next turn *I'll draw up the papers*, a turn in which she further continues the local conversational activity.

Truncated falls like the one on *corporation* can be treated by participants as one of two options. They can be tokens of falls-to-low that are not fully realised, but treated by participants as versions of the fall-to-low type. On the other hand, they can be specifically designed as truncated falls, rather than as falls-to-low, and treated as different patterns by participants. For the second possibility we turn to Angela's intonation phrase *nine o'clock* at line 37 in the transcript. Angela

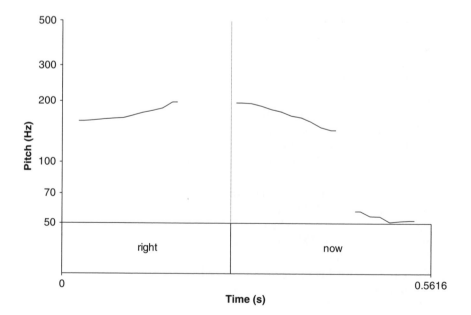

Figure 3.22   *Right now*, line 88 in Extract 3.11

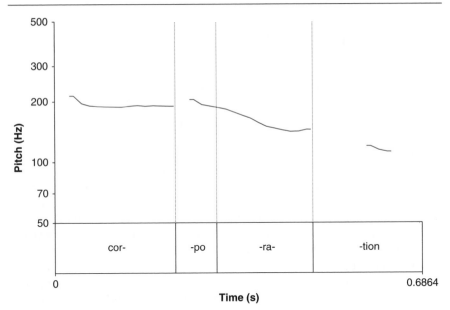

Figure 3.23 *Corporation*, line 89 in Extract 3.11

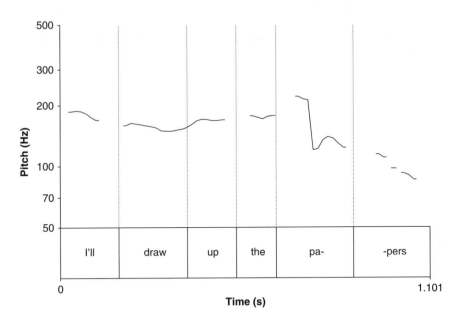

Figure 3.24 *I'll draw up the papers*, line 91 in Extract 3.11

has presented a scenario in which she calls somebody and lets them know that she has got up. From this she has moved to a description of a second scenario in which she does not make the call. She begins this scenario with an if-clause: *if I don't call in by say nine o'clock.*

36   if I DON'T call In by say:;
37   NINE o'CLOCK;
38 (1.1)
39   [then-
40 Doris: [well I'll be GLAD to do that for a FEE:,

The last stressed syllable *clock* ends in a fall-to-mid, which in combination with the unfinished grammatical *if X, then Y* construction clearly projects further continuation from Angela (Figure 3.25). And indeed, Angela later briefly continues with an aborted intonation phrase *then-* at line 39. However, before she does so, she leaves a pause of 1.1 seconds. This sequential location is treated by Doris as an opportunity for turn transition: she comes in with her turn *well I'll be glad to do that for a fee*, which refers back to Angela's turn prior to the aborted *if*-construction (lines 18–34), in which she described the first, default scenario of getting up and making the phone call.

The beginning of a next turn by Doris at this point is relevant precisely because it is placed at a – grammatically and intonationally designed – non-completion location. The turn that Angela has embarked on with her *if*-construction is one that projects a scenario that has remained implicit throughout the sequence and would be implied by Angela's failure to call: a potential injury or worse that may prevent her from reaching the telephone. Doris's early incoming with a playful remark shows her orientation to the tacit agreement that such a scenario must remain unspoken. The non-serious sequence that emerges shows all participants' orientation to this avoidance strategy.

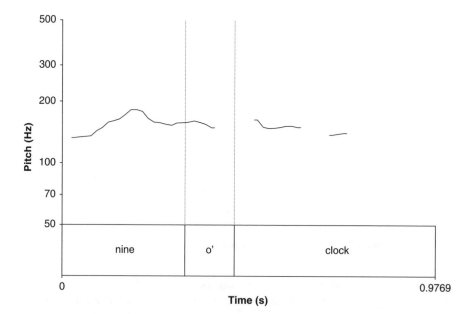

Figure 3.25   *Nine o'clock*, line 37 in Extract 3.11

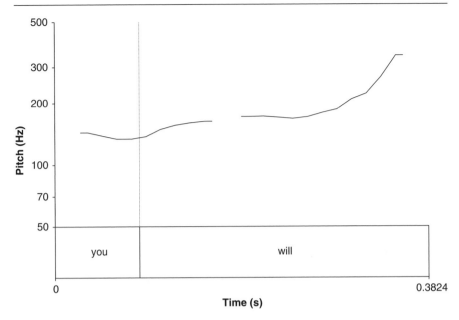

Figure 3.26   *You will*, line 42 in Extract 3.11

Regarding rising pitch accents, Angela's repair initiations *you will* (lines 42 and 83) are good examples of rises-to-high. Figure 3.26 shows an analysis of line 42. In both instances, the end Hz values are noticeably higher than any of Angela's previous pitch values. Both rises-to-high and rises-to-mid can be treated by next speakers as potential opportunities for turn transition. For example, Angela's repair initiation *you will* is responded to by Doris with *yeah* (line 84). Turn transitions after rises also occur after Doris's turn *well I'll be glad to do that for a fee*, ending in a rise-fall-rise (line 40); after Doris's question *does it really bother you*, ending in a rise-to-mid (line 50, Figure 3.27); and after Angela's turn *should we have an attorney to advise us*, also ending in a rise-to-mid (line 102).

Rises, particularly those that do not reach high end pitch, are often interpreted as signalling that a participant has not yet finished speaking. While this interpretation may be based on a valid intuition concerning the vague 'meanings' of intonation contours, the above examples clearly show that participants treat at least some turns ending in rises-to-mid as complete in terms of turn structure. Whether there are other aspects of talk that are incomplete, and designed as such through the rising pitch accent, is another question. As in the case of falling intonation, which elements of talk are being completed, or left incomplete, may vary across contexts. We must not assume that one interpretation fits all instances of a certain intonation pattern.

However, the notion of incompleteness regarding rising intonation is indeed exploited by participants in some contexts. For an example of pitch accents in turn continuing position, that is at a location where a rising pitch accent co-occurs with a turn that is designed as continuing beyond the currently emerging intonation phrase, we can examine Angela's utterance (*I've been*

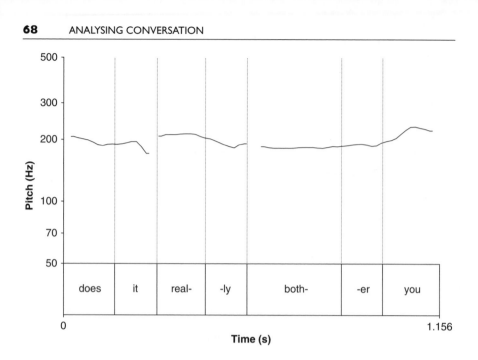

Figure 3.27 *Does it really bother you*, **line 50 in Extract 3.11**

looking for) somebody who will sit by the phone in the morning (lines 16–20). The beginning of this utterance is produced in overlap with Doris's turn *you pay to be called*, but from the word *somebody* Angela's turn is in the clear. This short extract contains three words carrying primary stress (*somebody, phone* and *morning*), all of which occur at the end of their respective intonation phrases. Each phrase projects more talk from Angela, as she is in the process of providing a description of the type of service she is looking for. In two out of the three cases, she uses slightly rising intonation: *somebody* ends in a rise-to-mid, *phone* in a fall-to-mid and *morning* in another rise-to-mid (see Figures 3.28–3.30).

```
18 Angela:   been lOOking for SOMEbody,
19           who will sIt by the PHONE;
20           in the MORning,
```

While the first and the third of the above intonation phrases show the rise-to-mid on intonation phrases that project more talk from the same speaker, the second intonation phrase shows the same interactional location for a fall-to-mid. An initial hearing of this short extract may raise expectations that all pitch accents involved end in the same pitch pattern, a slight rise; however, once again it is important to listen out for what the participant is actually doing prosodically. Interactionally the two pitch patterns rise-to-mid and fall-to-mid are used interchangeably in this particular instance by this participant. This may be the case because both patterns carry the potential to be employed for incomplete interactional projects. This does not mean, however, that they are always used interchangeably or that they always signal 'incompletion'.

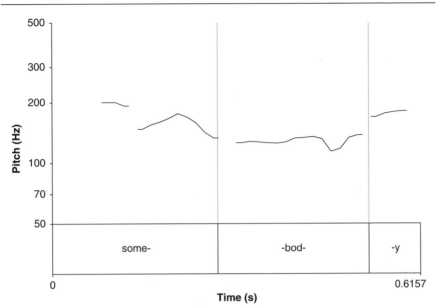

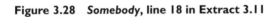

Figure 3.28   *Somebody*, line 18 in Extract 3.11

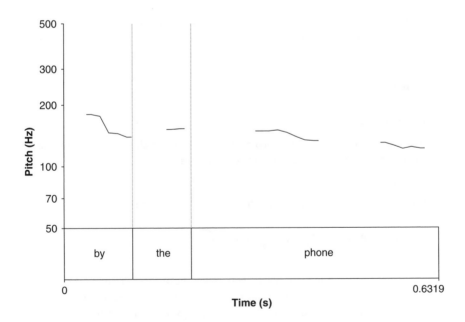

Figure 3.29   *By the phone*, line 19 in Extract 3.11

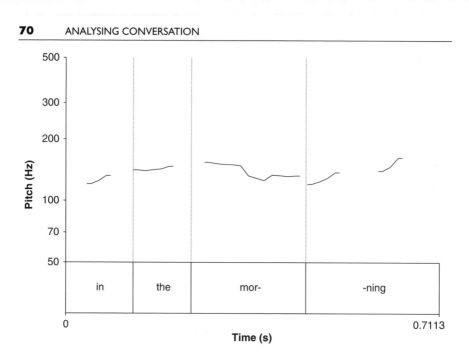

Figure 3.30 *In the morning*, **line 20 in Extract 3.11**

3.2.3 Exercises

Keeping in mind the criteria for analysing intonation outlined above, the following exercises provide opportunities to practise aural skills regarding intonation phrases and pitch accents.

EXERCISE 3.1

Intonation phrases

Listen to the following extract from an undergraduate chemistry lecture and indicate the speaker's intonation phrase boundaries.

Example

Phil: I would like to / talk to you about / these three items . . .

SBC027 Atoms hanging out 🎧

> Phil: I would like to talk to you about these three items I have here some ice in a pan water in this glass and steam rising from this pot now I would like to ask you how these three things tell me please how are they all alike these three things this ice here in this pan this water in this glass and the steam rising from this pot just yell it out we are informal here yes correct they are all forms of water this ice here of course is water I told you there was water in this glass and you have all seen water boil at home so you are familiar with steam

EXERCISE 3.2

Stressed syllables

Listen to the same extract again and decide which syllables the speaker stresses. Underline the stressed syllables in the text.

Example

Phil: <u>now</u> I would like to <u>ask</u> <u>you</u>

66 Phil: I would like to talk to you about these three items I have here some ice in a pan water in this glass and steam rising from this pot now I would like to ask you how these three things tell me please how are they all alike these three things this ice here in this pan this water in this glass and the steam rising from this pot just yell it out we are informal here yes correct they are all forms of water this ice here of course is water I told you there was water in this glass and you have all seen water boil at home so you are familiar with steam 99

EXERCISE 3.3

Pitch accents

Listen to the same extract and decide which pitch accents the speaker chooses for his stressed syllables, in particular those with primary stress. Indicate the pitch accents at the end of intonation phrases with symbols such as

- question mark (?) for a rise-to-high;
- comma (,) for a rise-to-mid;
- dash (-) for level pitch;
- semicolon (;) for a fall-to-mid;
- full stop (.) for a fall-to-low.

Example

Phil: <u>now</u>. i would like to <u>ask</u> <u>you</u>.

66 Phil: I would like to talk to you about these three items I have here some ice in a pan water in this glass and steam rising from this pot now I would like to ask you how these three things tell me please how are they all alike these three things this ice here in this pan this water in this glass

EXERCISE 3.3

(Continued)

and the steam rising from this pot just yell it out we are informal here yes correct they are all forms of water this ice here of course is water I told you there was water in this glass and you have all seen water boil at home so you are familiar with steam 💬

EXERCISE 3.4

Stress and pitch accents

Listen to the following sequence from a conversation involving two participants, cousins Fred and Richard. Fred is telling Richard about an experience at work. Decide which syllables receive primary stress and what their pitch accents are. Underline the stressed syllables, and indicate pitch accents using the symbols above.

SBC047 On the lot 🎧

1	Fred:	and on my production card
2	(0.8)	
3		see
4	(0.31)	
5		the day before yesterday
6	(0.14)	
7		i did ice cream
8	(0.15)	
9		right
10		balian
11	(0.28)	
12	Richard:	uhu
13	(0.17)	
14	Fred:	and you gotta pack those
15		in cases
16	(0.24)	
17		.hh
18	Richard:	ri[ght
19	Fred:	[and so like
20		i didn't put that down on my production car[d
21	Richard:	[how many cases
22		you packed

EXERCISE 3.4

(Continued)

23	Fred:	.hh
24		i don't know man
25	(0.3)	
26		i packed two pallets
27	(0.37)	
28		you know
29	(0.43)	
30		i don't know how many (0.12) cases [that is but
31	Richard:	[(uh)
32	Fred:	.hhh
33		you know that
34	(0.3)	
35		that shit was heavy man ”

3.3 Research on intonation in natural conversation

Research in the area of prosody in conversation has brought to light many ways in which participants make intonational patterns relevant. In this section two examples from the literature on intonation in spontaneous interaction show how intonation can be identified, described and analysed in certain conversational environments. When studying intonation, or any other prosodic aspect of talk, as part of natural interaction, most analysts make a choice from one of two possible starting points. The first, more common, option is to begin with an interactional phenomenon, for example the way in which participants end one part of their turn and begin a new part. A first step in such a study is the collection of instances of this phenomenon, its description, definition and delimitation from similar phenomena. In studying such a conversational activity, analysts may then find that prosody plays an important part in its achievement, and their research leads them to identify, describe and analyse certain prosodic patterns as ways of accomplishing certain conversational practices. The findings of such a study contribute to a better understanding of participants' handling of conversational sequences and actions. Our first example below, Couper-Kuhlen (2004), takes such an approach.

The second option is to start with an intonational phenomenon, say, for example, a certain kind of intonation contour, and examine how it is employed by participants in natural talk. In this case, the analyst first collects instances of the intonational phenomenon and subsequently describes and defines its prosodic characteristics. In a second step, the researcher then looks at the interactional context in which this phenomenon occurs and from a close analysis of the whole collection identifies typical sequential environments for this specific pattern. Findings from such a study contribute to our knowledge of the prosodic repertoire participants employ in natural interaction. Our second example from Szczepek Reed (2006) demonstrates this second approach.

3.3.1 Elizabeth Couper-Kuhlen (2004): Prosody and sequence organization in English conversation: the case of new beginnings

Couper-Kuhlen (2004) takes as a starting point the conversational phenomenon of participants' display of the beginning of a new sequence. The chapter begins by explaining the interactional need for such a practice: as next turns are by default heard as continuing what was previously in progress, they have to be clearly marked as new if they are not a continuation of prior talk. An example is used to demonstrate the transition from a telephone opening sequence to the reason-for-the-call, and to introduce the characteristics of the beginning of that new sequence. It is noted that the new sequence is delivered as disjunct from the prior turn in several ways: for example, there is a temporal distance as the participant breathes in a number of times before he begins to speak, and the turn is preceded by several prefaces such as *hey* and *uh*. The first stressed word of the new turn also steps up to a high pitch accent and is followed by another high accent at the beginning of the second intonation phrase. It is this prosodic aspect that is explored further.

After describing the high pitch accents that introduce the new beginning, Couper-Kuhlen notes another pitch-related finding: not only do the first stressed syllables of new sequences carry high pitch accents, but preceding unstressed syllables in those turns are also delivered with higher pitch. For example, in one of the extracts the phrase *oh honey that was a lovely luncheon*, in which *hon-* is the first stressed syllable, the intonation phrase starts with high pitch on the unstressed word *oh*.

The study then shows examples in which this combination of intonational factors is oriented to by participants as doing new beginnings; for example, in one extract a participant apologises for 'changing the subject' in the same turn in which she also uses the prosodic patterns for new beginnings. The chapter goes on to provide more examples of new sequential beginnings, always pointing out not only the intonation pattern in question – the high pitch accent, potentially preceded by high pitched unstressed syllables – but also other interactional practices that accompany the phenomenon, such as lexical signs of disjunction, temporal gaps and in-breaths, and an increase in loudness co-occurring with the pitch step-up.

In a next step, the study provides further evidence for high pitch accents as signals for new beginnings by showing that participants do not use the same prosodic cues when they expand on a sequence. The chapter shows that if at points of potential sequence closure participants choose to expand the sequence-in-progress, they may employ temporal gaps and similar lexical items, but they do not use the marked step-up in pitch that is characteristic of new beginnings.

The final part of the chapter provides evidence for intonation as the defining cue for participants when it comes to turns following potential sequence closings. The cited examples show that in cases where there are no lexical or syntactic indications as to whether a next turn after a potential sequence closing is a continuation of that sequence, or the beginning of a new one, prosody alone is treated by speakers as the defining signal.

This study is a prime example of the way in which the role of intonation for a specific interactional activity can be investigated. After identifying a precise conversational action and location (beginning a new sequence, after a previous one has come to a potential close), participants' practices for that action are identified (lexical items, temporal gaps, high pitch accents). The study then shows that it is the prosodic practices that are most significant for participants' treatment of a next turn as new or continuing.

3.3.2 Beatrice Szczepek Reed (2006, pp. 111–19, 127–30): Marked prosody: declining intonation contours with lengthening and portamento

In this book I investigate the phenomenon of prosodic orientation, that is participants' display of awareness of each others' prosodic patterns. One form of prosodic orientation is prosodic matching, i.e. the repetition of a prosodic pattern by a previous speaker. One of several prosodic patterns that are frequently matched by next speakers are intonation contours. The section we are interested in here takes a specific type of intonation contour as its starting point: a steadily falling contour, gliding from a high onset pitch to lower pitch through all intermediate pitch values (referred to as 'portamento'). The words on which this intonation contour is used are frequently extremely lengthened. The study begins by describing the intonational phenomenon in question and providing a typical example. The example comes from the Santa Barbara Corpus of Spoken American English; the extract is taken from a birthday party. Immediately prior to the transcribed sequence, Kendra has opened her birthday present, a baking set:

Extract 3.12   SBC013 Appease the monster   🎧

```
 1 KA:    <<musical interval> OH [oh:: - >
 2 KE:                        [<<portamento> Oh:::::> yeah;
 3 KA:    we're TALKin;
 4        BAKing MONster.
 5 KV:    [<<singing> TOLL: HOUSE MORsels>
 6 MA:    [it's definitely more than a PAIR and a SPARE.
 7 KA:    ↑COOKie mOnster:;=
 8        apPEA:SE the mOnster:;
 9        HO::L[Y                    [<<portamento> CO:::W;>
10 KE:         [<<portamento> OH[:::;
11 KV:                            [<<portamento> YAY:::::;>
12        [HOly COW;
13 KA:    [cOOkie BAKing set.
14 MA:    [<<portamento> alRI:::GHT;>
```

```
15           <<portamento> alRI:::GHT.>
16 KA:       <<portamento> mmm:::::::::[:::::::;>
17 KV:                                 [RUBb[er <<portamento> MAI::D;>
18 MA:                                      [oh;
19           [let me SEE it.
20 KV:       [<<f> you CAN'T SQUASH it;>
21 KA:       <<portamento> mm::::::;>
22 MA:       [oh: NEA:T.
23 KA:       [RUBber <<portamento> MAI:::D;>
24 KV:       TWELVE      ['PIECes;
25 KA:                   [yay;
26 KV:       ((gasp))
27 KA:       [that's-
28 MA:       [oh that's-
29 KA:       [<<portamento> WO::W;>
30 KV:       oh that inCLUDES all the TEA spoons; 🙶
```

Figure 3.31 shows the lengthened, declining intonation contour in Kendra's *mm* (line 21).

More examples of this intonation contour are provided from a variety of conversational settings. Subsequent to describing other types of prosodic orientation, the chapter then moves on to the interactional roles of the described phenomena. Analysing the long declining intonation contour in the context of its interactional occurrences, I find that it is used by participants to display appreciation of physical or conversational objects. The sequential location for the contour is shown to be following the presentation of a linguistic or physical item for which admiration has been invited. Lengthening of sounds and syllables is identified as an iconic representation of approval.

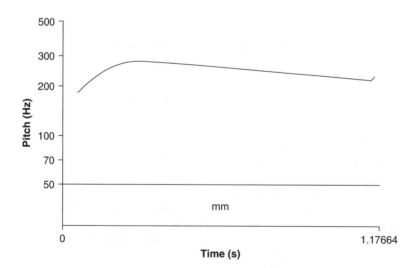

Figure 3.31   *mm*, line 21 in Extract 3.12

An approach such as this one, that starts with a prosodic phenomenon and only later interprets it in its interactional context is rather rare, and mostly reserved for prosodic events that are in some way perceived as out of the ordinary. The more frequent approach to analysing prosody in conversation begins with a conversational location or activity, finds prosody to be playing an important part, and subsequently describes and analyses the precise nature of the prosodic pattern, and its interactional role.

FURTHER READING

For a deeper insight into the phonological issues of intonation, see, for example, Couper-Kuhlen (1986, pp. 63–208), Cruttenden (1997) and Wells (2006), all of whom follow the so-called 'British school' of intonation research we have loosely adopted in this book, with a focus on intonation phrases and pitch accents. Precursors of this approach are O'Connor and Arnold (1973), Crystal (1969, pp. 195–252), Halliday (1967, 1970), Schubiger (1958) and Kingdon (1958).

For a good introduction to another important research method of studying intonation, auto-segmental metrical phonology, see Ladd (1996). The original development of this approach can be found in Pierrehumbert (1980).

Intonation has been described and studied with a perspective on ordinary conversation in Couper-Kuhlen (1983, 1996b, 2001a, 2003, 2004); Couper-Kuhlen and Selting (1996a); Cutler and Pearson (1986); Fox (2001); Günthner (1996); Johns-Lewis (1986); Ogden et al. (2004); Selting (1992a, 2004); Szczepek Reed (2004); Wells and Macfarlane (1998); Wennerstrom (2001) and Wichman (2000).

For an overview of intonation systems across languages, see Hirst and Di Cristo (1998).

Pitch: Range and Register

This chapter explores the analysis of pitch in terms of the overall vocal range employed by participants. Rather than focusing on the continuously emerging melody of intonation, this chapter deals with the issue of pitch from a more global perspective and the question as to whether speakers are using it in a high, medium or low pitch setting.

When identifying a voice as high or low we distinguish between a speaker's overall vocal settings – as higher or lower compared with other speakers' voices – and a speaker's immediately local choice in delivering a specific phrase or turn with higher or lower overall pitch. These two possibilities are introduced as pitch range (section 4.1.1) and pitch register (section 4.1.2). Section 4.2 takes a closer look at a longer extract from naturally occurring conversation and shows how pitch register is oriented to by participants as interactionally relevant during talk-in-progress. The section also provides a number of exercises. Section 4.3 gives two examples of research on pitch range and register in conversation: Couper-Kuhlen (1996a) shows how participants orient differently to other speakers' repetition of their turns, depending on the pitch register of that repetition and where it is located in a given speaker's pitch range. Klewitz and Couper-Kuhlen (1999) show how pitch register is relevant in instances of reported speech.

4.1 Contrasts in pitch range and register

Changes in pitch do not only occur moment-by-moment as speakers create intonational patterns. They also occur as a speaker's overall pitch span changes throughout life, throughout the course of a day and throughout the course of a single conversation. These changes can be physiologically or interactionally motivated: for example, typically a child has a higher overall voice range than an adult, based on physiological differences in the vocal tract; interactionally, a speaker may choose to use a higher voice during the opening part of a telephone call, than when muttering a side comment in the middle of a conversation. For the analysis of talk-in-interaction, those changes in pitch span which are interactionally motivated; are most interesting however, physiological changes can also become relevant in the course of a conversation. Participants' local choices in overall pitch are distinguished below from their global voice settings, as it is necessary when conducting a prosodic analysis to interpret the former in terms of the latter.

4.1.1   Pitch range

Pitch range can be roughly defined as a speaker's overall speaking range during a given conversation. To a certain degree, pitch range is physiologically determined by a speaker's *voice range*: the longer the vocal folds, the lower the voice range. However, in standard varieties of spoken English the span of pitch values used during speech is rarely as wide as speakers' physiologies would allow; most participants do not use their full voice range in conversation. Instead, speakers *adopt a pitch range*, and they do so in orientation to sociolinguistic factors such as gender, ethnicity, linguistic variety and their immediate social circle. For example, in many Western societies it is common sociolinguistic practice for women to adopt a higher overall pitch range than men, even if they are physiologically able to speak as low as some of their male co-conversationalists. Furthermore, within these broad sociological frameworks speakers additionally adopt individual speaking habits.

However, in defining pitch range, we must not only draw into consideration the broad sociolinguistic factors that influence a speaker's pitch range in general but also their idiosyncratic way of speaking in particular. In addition, most people also use different pitch ranges for different speaking situations and sequential environments. This, too, can have both physiological and sociological explanations. For example, most of us speak in a slightly lower pitch range just after we have got up in the morning, provided we have had a good night's sleep, than in the tense situation of, say, a job interview. In the first instance our vocal folds are still relaxed after the long rest they have had over night, whereas in a mentally strenuous situation our vocal folds are often equally strained. These different settings may produce a lower or higher pitch range, respectively. On the other hand, interactional factors such as where in a given sequence a turn is produced also has implications for what kind of pitch span is employed by the participant. For the analysis of conversation, it is therefore most useful to adopt a definition of *pitch range* as *a participant's overall speaking range in a single given interaction*. Such a definition allows the analyst to define an overall pitch range for a given speaker and interpret local pitch changes in relation to that overall range; however, it also recognises the reality of pitch range as a sociolinguistic and interactional variable.

The variability in determiners for pitch range is in large part due to the close link between a speaker's pitch range and his or her identity. As participants negotiate and accomplish identity through talk, their pitch range is employed as an identity marker, as are other prosodic features. By speaking with a certain pitch range a speaker identifies him- or herself, for example, as a child or an adult, a man or a woman, a relaxed or an excited person, a doctor talking to a patient, or a customer complaining to a waiter. Whatever the conversational extract under analysis, an awareness of a participant's overall pitch range allows us to interpret other pitch events in relation to that range. For the prosodic analysis of talk-in-interaction it is therefore necessary to be able to identify a participant's speaking range as broadly high, medium or low, with respect to their baseline. Pitch range is best identified according to the lowest, rather than the highest, pitch used by a participant, because participants rarely use the top of their voice range during talk; however, they can frequently be found to use their vocal baseline.

Low pitch range

Men's and women's voice ranges vary physiologically to a certain extent and naturally have an impact on the pitch range adopted for a given interaction. The examples below provide instances of different pitch ranges adopted by both men and women. Starting with low pitch range, the following two extracts are taken from a telephone conversation between family members at Christmas. They show those instances during the conversation at which one of the participants, Cindy, reaches her highest and lowest pitch, respectively. Both values can then be taken as the pitch range she employs during this interaction. Figure 4.1 shows the point at which Cindy reaches her highest Hz values during the whole recorded interaction, 429 Hz on the word *hi*. Figure 4.2 shows her lowest Hz value during the whole interaction on the word *bad*, 139 Hz. For an adult woman this can be considered a low speaking range, as women have in the past been claimed not to reach below 170 Hz. While we found many women in our data corpus who use lower pitch values than 170 Hz, this speaker's 139 Hz is nevertheless on the low end of the spectrum.

Extract 4.1   SBC052 Oh you need a breadbox 🎧

```
66  1 Andrew:   i'm gonna let CINdy tell you.
     2           HOLD On.
     3 (0.31)
     4 Darlene:  OK;
     5 (1.54)
     6 Cindy:    HI;
     7           whO am i TALKing [to;
     8 Darlene:                   [this is darLENE -
     9 Cindy:    .hh << h > HI darlene how you DOing;>
    10 Darlene:  I'm FI:NE;
    11 Cindy:    mErry CHRISTmas;
    12 Darlene:  mErry chrIstmas [to you;
    13 Cindy:                    [Ok; 99
```

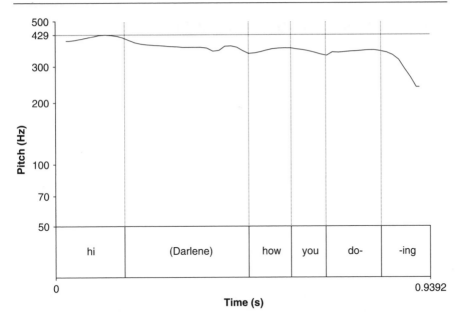

Figure 4.1   Low pitch range, female voice: highest pitch at 429 Hz

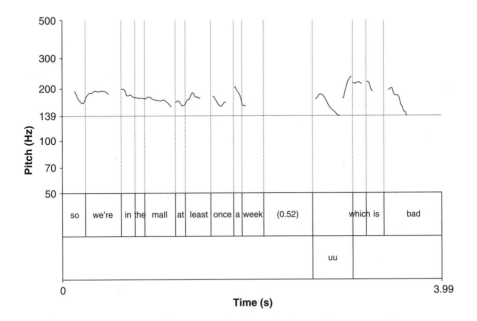

Figure 4.2   Low pitch range, female voice: lowest pitch at 139 Hz

Extract 4.2 SBC052 Oh you need a breadbox 🎧

```
 1 Darlene:    <<h> do yOU go out SHOPping very often,>
 2 (0.33)
 3             like to the MALL or anything,
 4 Cindy:      well we GO OU:T;
 5             SATurday mOrning to brEAkfast.
 6             .hh
 7             Every SATurday;
 8             and the PLACe we GO is on;
 9             .hh in the PYRamid area where they have kind of like a FOOD COURT.
10 (0.25)
11             so WE'RE in the MALL at lEAst once a wEEk.
12 (0.52)
13 Darlene:    uhu,
14 Cindy:      whIch is BA:Dh. 🙶
```

Thus, the pitch range of this female speaker during this particular interaction can be described as 139–429 Hz, with the lower end of the range being the most relevant indication for a low pitch range. Remember, this is the case because in conversation participants can be found to employ the very bottom of their voice range for a variety of interactional practices, whereas the top end is rarely used.

This participant's lowest pitch value of 139 Hz means that she is near $C\#_3$, which is C# below middle C; most women would find this to be a considerably low note if they had to sing it. However, Cindy's highest pitch of 429 Hz is located between a $G\#_4$ and an A_4, that is, G# and A above middle C, which is almost certainly not the highest note Cindy would be able to reach if she were singing. However, there are circumstances during which participants do employ the top end of their voice range; a typical instance occurs in Figure 4.7, which shows a participant reaching the top of his voice range while laughing.

Figures 4.3 and 4.4, from the following two extracts from a conversation between two friends, show the highest and lowest pitch used by a male speaker during this particular conversation.

Extract 4.3 SBC017 Wonderful abstract notions 🎧

```
 1 Jim:        an artIfIcial inTELligence personALity;
 2             that you CALL;
 3 Michael:    <<laughing> yehehe so;>
 4             if you do not lIke THIS personality,
 5             PUSH ZEro:,
 6 Jim:        [yehehe
 7 Michael:    [and a: ↑NEW personality will b' provided for you at no extra
 8             CHARGE.
 9 Jim:        m;
10 Michael:    yOU are allowed up to FIVE personalities in ONE phone call. 🙶
```

Extract 4.4   SBC017 Wonderful abstract notions   🎧

66   1 Jim: YEAH well;
      2   creAtive people GENerally DO what they LOVE to DO.
      3 Michael: ↑YEAH.
      4   RIGHT.
      5 (0.32)
      6   and thAt's pretty much the END of the TRUTHful PART of the
      7   PROCess.
      8   .hh
      9 (0.2)
     10   the REST of it is ALL: M:ARketing. 99

In Extract 4.3, speaker Michael reaches the top of his pitch range for this particular conversation at 317 Hz (see Figure 4.3), which on a musical scale would
be between a D#$_4$ and E$_4$. For a male singing voice, this would be a relatively
high note. The bottom of his pitch range in Extract 4.4 is shown to be 54 Hz
(see Figure 4.4), which is just below A$_1$, that is two octaves and a minor third
below middle C. This pitch is lower than a bass would be expected to be able
to sing.

Thus, this speaker's pitch range is 54–317 Hz for this conversation. Again, it
is the lower end that defines this speaker's pitch range as low, as men, too, rarely
use the top end of their physiological voice range during speech.

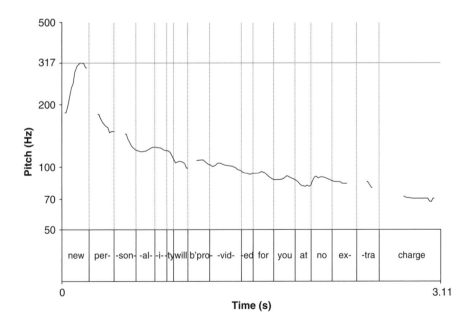

Figure 4.3   Low pitch range, male voice: highest pitch at 317 Hz

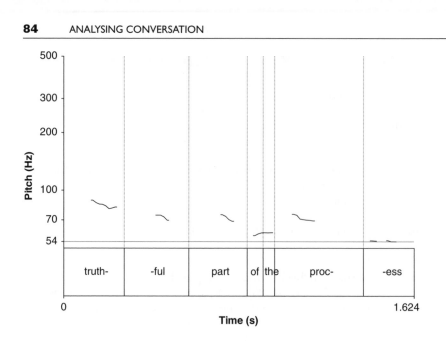

Figure 4.4   Low pitch range, male voice: lowest pitch at 54 Hz

High pitch range

The following extracts contain instances of high pitch range. Again, in spite of the focus now being on *high* pitch range, in order to determine it we are interested in the *lowest* pitch employed by a speaker. In Extracts 4.5 and 4.6 a female attorney, Rebecca, is in the process of preparing a witness for a trial. Extract 4.5 shows the context for her highest pitch during this interaction; Extract 4.6 for her lowest Hz value.

Extract 4.5   SBC008 Tell the jury that

```
 1 Rebecca:   so YOU can testify to TWO of them.
 2 Rickie:    YEAH.
 3 Rebecca:   THAT'S why i had yOU come up.
 4            becAUse[::
 5 Rickie:            [yeah;
 6 (0.39)
 7 Rebecca:   uhm;
 8 (0.72)
 9            THAT'S GREAT.
10 (0.15)
11 Rickie:    yeah;
12 (0.51)
13 Rebecca:   uhm i mean nOt for <<laughing> YOU;>
```

14	Rickie:	ehehehehe
15	Rebecca:	[but;
16	Arnold:	[hehehe[hehe
17	Rickie:	[mhmhmh
18	Rebecca:	[for US.
19		[ehehehehe
20	Arnold:	[ehehehehe
21	Rebecca:	uh:::m: -
22	(0.44)	
23		ts
24	(0.56)	
25		**in our FIRST cAse;**
26		amElia gonzAlez;
27		uh:m:
28	(0.23)	
29		THAT happened back in NINEty. 🔊

Extract 4.6   SBC008 Tell the jury that 🎧

🔊 1	Rebecca:	when a PERson;
2	(0.18)	
3		is CHARGED with multiple CRI:MES;
4	(0.34)	
5		a:nd;
6		uh:m;
7	(0.21)	
8		thEre (.) Are Other INcidences?
9		where he Acted in the same WAY?
10	Rickie:	m;
11	(0.35)	
12	Rebecca:	when WE have to prove;
13		**in THIS cAse we have to prove specIfic inTENT.** 🔊

Rebecca's highest pitch only reaches 346 Hz in this conversation (see Figure 4.5), that is just below F above middle C; not a high note in singing terms. However, the bottom of her pitch range does not reach below 174 Hz, that is F below middle C (see Figure 4.6). While this is not necessarily a note a soprano voice would be comfortable singing, during speech it is not a particularly low pitch, even for women. Therefore, Rebecca's pitch range of 174–346 Hz can be classified as high, even though she does not use particularly high pitch during the interaction. Again, the defining factor is her baseline.

Extracts 4.7 and 4.8, taken from a family birthday party, show a male speaker, Kevin, using a high pitch range. Both extracts are taken from a sequence in which Wendy, Kevin's wife, gives his sister Kendra her present. In Extract 4.7

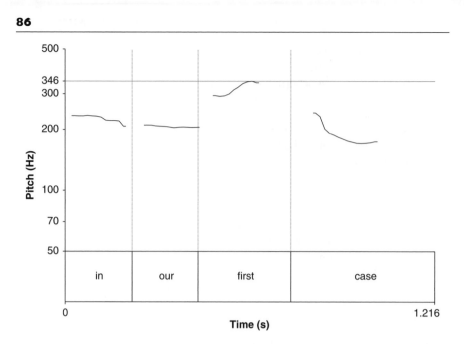

Figure 4.5 High pitch range, female voice: highest pitch at 346 Hz

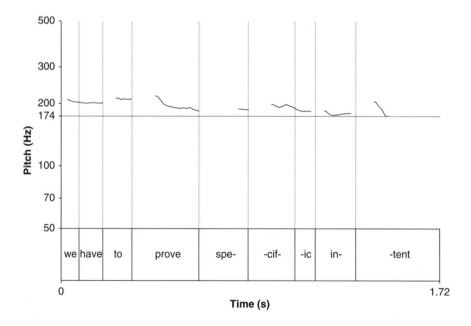

Figure 4.6 High pitch range, female voice: lowest pitch at 174 Hz

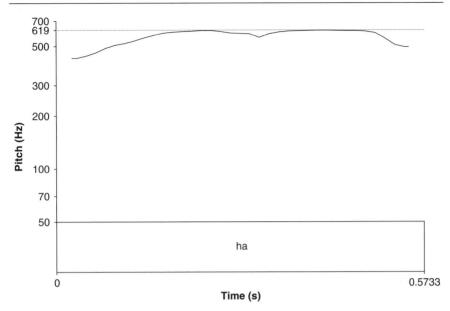

Figure 4.7   High pitch range, male voice: highest pitch 619 Hz

Kevin notices a hair of Wendy's inside the packaging. It is while laughing at this incident that he reaches a pitch value of 619 Hz, that is just below D#$_5$ (Figure 4.7). This is a very high musical note for a man; however, during laughter participants do at times employ the top of their voice range. More important for the identification of Kevin's pitch range, however, is that his lowest pitch value is only 101 Hz on a fall-to-low (see Extract 4.8 and Figure 4.8). Musically, this Hz value is somewhere between a G$_2$ and G#$_2$. This would still be heard as a low note when sung; however, for male speech it is a relatively high baseline.

Extract 4.7   SBC013 Appease the monster 🎧

```
 1  Kevin:    lOOks like wendy's HAIR is On it -
 2  (0.82)
 3  Wendy:    ↑WHERE.
 4  (0.12)
 5  Kendra:   WENDO[::,
 6  Kevin:         [is thIs your HAI:R?
 7  (0.63)
 8            SURE I[S;
 9  Kendra:         [Oh it's a piece of wendy's HAIR;
10  Kevin:    eheha [<<h> HA:: - >
```

11 Kendra: [COOL;

12 (0.38)

13 Kevin: [thAt shows SOMEbody was IN there,

14 Kendra: [and YOU can TELL; 🎤

Extract 4.8 SBC013 Appease the monster 🎧

🎤 1 Marci: HE thought your clUE was STUpid;

2   and it rEAlly WASn't.

3   WAS it.

4 Ken: [hehe

5 Kevin: [i don't think kEndy will GUESS it though.

6 (0.38)

7 Ken: ah SHE [MAY,

8 Kevin: [thAt's the-

9 (.)

10   thAt's the WHOLE POINT. 🎤

As we have seen, in order to determine a participant's pitch range it is helpful to listen to the entire conversation, with a focus on the lowest pitch values in particular. In terms of its relevance for interaction, pitch range is generally of less conversation analytic interest than pitch register, because of its global nature.

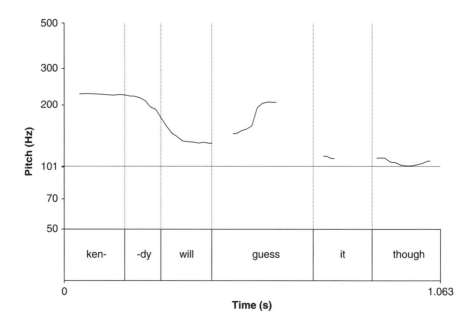

Figure 4.8   High pitch range, male voice: lowest pitch 101 Hz

The fact that pitch range spans across the entire length of a given conversation means that it is not employed at specific interactional locations and the role it plays in displaying speaker identity is therefore more fruitfully studied from a broadly sociolinguistic perspective. However, for the interpretation of pitch accents or pitch register as high or low, it is important to be able to locate them in the context of the pitch range adopted by a given participant.

4.1.2 Pitch register

In contrast to pitch range, which was defined as a speaker's overall speaking range in a given interaction, the term pitch register refers to a more local choice in terms of pitch span. In the course of a conversation, participants may change from a lower to a higher overall pitch setting by raising or lowering the baseline of their pitch span. Such changes are typically interactionally motivated and affect both stressed and unstressed syllables alike. For example, the beginning parts of conversations, so called *opening sequences*, are routinely characterised by participants' use of a higher pitch register, in which the overall pitch setting is raised. During the transition out of the opening sequence participants typically lower their register into the medium part of their pitch range. Participants may also change their pitch register for even shorter stretches of talk. For example, side comments to an ongoing turn, known as *asides*, are routinely delivered in a lower pitch register than the main body of the turn currently in progress. Pitch register is therefore continuously interactionally employed by participants for sequential organisation. In this book we define *pitch register* as a *participant's local pitch span during a given interactional sequence, turn or intonation phrase*. Thus, the domain of pitch register is considerably smaller than for pitch range: while the domain for pitch range is the entire conversation, the domain for pitch register can be as small as a single intonation phrase, but rarely larger than a single sequence.

By changing into a different pitch register, participants do not so much accomplish an overall social identity as they do in the case of pitch range; instead, they design their current talk as implementing certain conversational actions. This is, of course, accomplished in combination with other prosodic features and other linguistic and interactional practices. Like all prosodic parameters, pitch register rarely fulfils a conversational function on its own. Rather, it is an important contributor to the interactional achievement of conversational practices and actions.

Low pitch register

Broadly three types of pitch register can be distinguished: low, medium and high. However, in a transcript, we only indicate changes from a participant's medium register. Below, two examples are presented in which a female and a male speaker change into low pitch register. In Extract 4.9, from a lively family interaction, Stephanie is in the process of telling her mother about a friend's application to a college that has changed from 'liberal' to 'conservative'. The extract begins with Stephanie in a higher pitch register; later in the sequence she changes to a lower register (line 6).

Extract 4.9   SBC035 Hold my breath 🎧

```
 1  Stephanie:    <<h> THEY HA:D;
 2  (0.76)
 3                YEARS agO;
 4  (0.12)
 5                THEY HA:D;>
 6                <<l+p> the SIT I:NS - >
 7  (0.12)
 8                EVErything you know;
 9  (0.24)
10                REal LIBeral;
11  (0.17)
12                NOW they're going to conSERvative;
```

Stephanie's change into the lower register occurs only during her delivery of the phrase *the sit ins*, after which she returns to a more medium range (see Figure 4.9). Her use of pitch register is not physically or sociolinguistically motivated, but it is part of her turn design. In this instance, the phrase *the sit ins* is designed prosodically as if it were part of a list, even though there are no other list items.

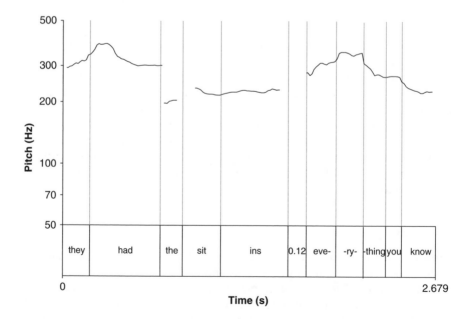

Figure 4.9   Shift to low pitch register, female voice

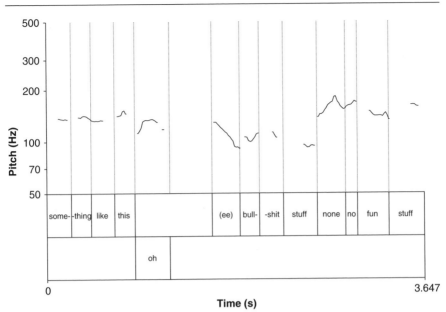

Figure 4.10   Shift to low pitch register, male voice

In Extract 4.10, from the same telephone conversation as Extract 4.1, Andrew describes a book he received for Christmas as 'bullshit stuff' (line 9), in contrast to other 'fun stuff'. His negative evaluation is delivered in lower pitch register, as can be seen in Figure 4.10.

Extract 4.10   SBC052 Oh you need a breadbox   🎧

```
 1 Darlene:   yOU said you gOt a bOOk TOO;
 2 (0.19)
 3 Andrew:    WELL:;
 4            you wOUldn't wAnna KNOW.
 5            MINE is cAlled uh uh:;
 6            S:EVen HABits of effEctive pEOple or something like this,
 7 Darlene:   <<l> Oh:;>
 8 (0.35)
 9 Andrew:    <<l> (ee) BULLshIt stuff.>
10            nOne nO FUN <<laughing> stUff,>
11 Darlene:   hehe,
12 (0.1)
13 Andrew:    MINE'S pUre wOrk. 
```

In both of the above cases, the participants' change to a lower pitch register begins on unstressed syllables (*the*; *(ee)*). This is relevant because it shows that the entire pitch span is being lowered, rather than only an individual pitch accent. The same distinction can be made between changes into high pitch register and pitch step-ups on single stressed syllables.

High pitch register

The following two extracts show examples of high pitch register produced by a male and a female participant, respectively. In Extract 4.11, Darryl argues against supernatural phenomena, and changes to a high pitch register for his final phrase *that doesn't work* (line 3). Figure 4.11 shows the pitch change from the end of the word *replacement* to the unstressed word *that*. Once again, it is the change in pitch on unstressed syllables that shows a rise in pitch register particularly clearly.

Extract 4.11 SBC007 A book about death 🎧

1 Darryl: but but to TRY and and tAlk me out of belIEving in mUrphy's LAW;
2   by Offering a MIRacle as a replAcement;
3   <<h> that doesn't ↑WORK – >
4 (0.23)
5 Pamela: well you're RIGHT;
6   i think they're prObably flip SIDES;

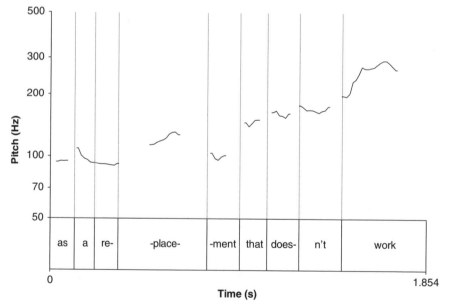

Figure 4.11 Shift to high pitch register, male voice

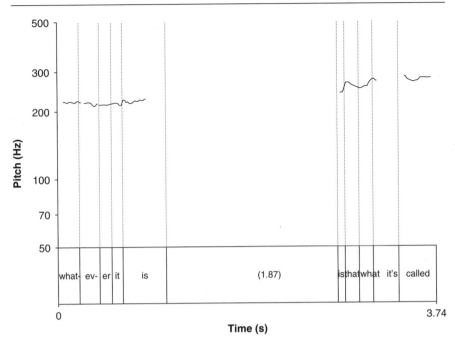

Figure 4.12   Shift to high pitch register, female voice

In Extract 4.12, speaker Lynne uses a high pitch register on a repair initiation following a lengthy silence. Figure 4.12 shows its location in a higher register compared to the previous phrase.

Extract 4.12   SBC001 Actual blacksmithing 🎧

```
  1 Lynne:     <<h> ↑I don't know what her PLANS really are;>
  2            but i thInk pretty much just gO OUt –
  3            and TAKE CARE of em and then;
  4            .hh
  5            maybe gO to that (0.51) sEAsonal DANCE,
  6            or whatEver it IS,
  7 (1.87)
  8            <<h> is thAt what it's CALLED?>
  9 (1.04)
 10 Lenore:    I don't knOw –
 11 (0.73)
 12 Lynne:     <<all+p> i don't know> what it's cAlled EIther;
```

In determining pitch register it is most helpful to focus on the point at which the overall pitch setting steps up or down from a previous setting. This typically occurs at intonation phrase boundaries. While individual pitch accents may reach very high or low pitch values, it is only if unstressed syllables, too, remain in the higher or lower range that one can speak of high or low pitch register. Changes that occur only on individual syllables are pitch accents, whereas changes in the entire intonation phrase are changes in pitch register.

As was the case for intonation, in analysing pitch register we have to remember that individual Hz values in themselves are not very meaningful. Pitch register can only ever be considered high or low in relation to prior and following talk, and can therefore not be identified and interpreted in isolation from the context in which it occurs. Pitch register must also be interpreted in relation to a speaker's pitch range, during a given interaction, and his or her overall voice range.

4.1.3 Summary

The points to remember from this section are:

- Voice range is defined as a person's physiologically determined pitch span.
- Speakers of English rarely use the top end of their voice range during speech.
- Pitch range is defined as a speaker's overall speaking range, that is the pitch span between his or her lowest and highest pitch value during a given conversation.
- Low or high pitch range is identified according to a speaker's baseline in a given interaction.
- Pitch register is defined as a participant's pitch span during a given sequence, turn or intonation phrase.
- Pitch register is employed by participants as a local prosodic resource for the accomplishment of specific interactional tasks.
- Pitch register must be interpreted in relation to a speaker's pitch range and voice range: what may be a high register for one speaker may be a medium register for another, depending on his or her overall vocal practice and physiology.

4.2 Analysing pitch register

In this section, a longer extract from a conversation among friends is analysed with respect to pitch register, and some of the issues mentioned in previous sections are explored more fully. The analysis does not include pitch range, as in the large majority of cases it is pitch register, rather than pitch range, that is employed and treated as interactionally relevant by participants.

In the face-to-face interaction represented in the transcript below three people are present: the couple Joanne and Ken, and their friend Lenore. Immediately prior to the transcribed section they have closed a sequence in which they discussed a slide show about Nicaragua. Line 1 in the transcript is Joanne's second attempt at opening up a new sequence on the topic of travel restrictions for American citizens.

Extract 4.13   SBC015 Deadly diseases 🎧

```
 1  Joanne:    it's an INteresting THING though because uhm;
 2             i'm WONdering-
 3  (0.48)
 4             you know since it is sUch-
 5  (1.28)
 6             UH::M;
 7  (0.96)
 8             it's reSTRICTed;
 9             you have to go through MEXico.
10  (1.08)
11  Ken:       tch <<h> NO;
12             I don't> [THINK so,
13  Joanne:             [Isn't nica[RAgua one of the things you
14  Ken:                          [<<h> NO;>
15  Joanne:    [places you can't go,
16  Ken:       [<<hh> I don't thInk so;
17             [NO;
18  Joanne:    [i [THINK it i:s;]
19  Ken:          [wE have->]
20             NO;
21             I don't thInk so;
22             we have f-
23  (0.24)
24             .hhh
25  (0.23)
26             <<l> TECHnically SPEAKing;
27             FULL: (0.19) diplomAtic re[lAtions with nicaragua;=
28  Joanne:                               [oh YEAH:?
29  Ken:       ↑YEAH;=
30             they have an n- an amBASsador an-
31             <<all> you know an aMERican amB[ASsador there who-
32  Joanne:                                   [<<h> I then-
33             WHY does every[body always have to go through MEXico;;>
34  Ken:                     [<<f> like a NEST of Cia spies;>>
35             .hh
36             <<h> thAt's just;
37             there there Isn't a diRECT transportation.=
38             [but there it's not->
39  Joanne:    [i thought no but i th[ought it
40  Ken:                            [.hh <<f+h> it's NOT like going to CUba.>
41  (0.14)
42  Ken:       <<h> whEre [they have to mAke connections through MEX[ico
               because->
43  Joanne:               [<<p> oh: - >
44                                                                  [<<h> I
45             knew someone who WENT to> cuba and had to go:;
46  Ken:       <<h> yeah - >
47  Joanne:    [make connEctions through me[xico -
48  Ken:                                   [THAT's because it's il<<l>lEgal for
```

49		americans to trAvel to [cUba.>
50	Joanne:	[<<h> but i WONder whether this- >
51	Lenore:	it I:[s;
52	Ken:	[<<h> YEAH;
53		it IS.
54		[((3 syll))>
55	Joanne:	[OH YEAH;
56		jUst like LEBanon just became.
57	(1.05)	
58	Lenore:	[how long-
59	Joanne:	[they say [lEbanon is Actually-
60	Lenore:	[how long's-
61	Joanne:	they i- d-
62		it just became illegal.
63		and i-
64		you KNOW,
65	Ken:	.hh
66		<<h> for a FEW YEAR[S;>
67	Lenore:	[how long
68		[has it been illegal-
69	Joanne:	[<<h+f> LIBya;
70		TOO.>
71		isn't lIbya asWELL?
72		there's QUITE a few pla-
73		LIBya,
74	(0.42)	
75	Ken:	there's Only a-
76		there's only a HAND<<l> ful [of places.>
77	Lenore:	[how long has it been illegal for amEricans
78		to [go to cuba;
79	Ken:	[<<h+f> WE[LL –
80	Joanne:	[since the
81	Ken:	it was il[LEgal;
82	Joanne:	[(since the fifties)
83	Ken:	[it was illegal:;
84	Joanne:	[or the SIXties;
85	Ken:	it was ilLEgal;>
86		you knOw from like <<l> the: tIme of CATH-
87		the CAStro revolution.= >
88		UP until:;
89		i think the EARly SEVenties;
90		the suPREME COURT;
91		.hh
92		overturned –
93	(0.29)	
94		n- TRAVel restrictions.
95		On thE: uhm –
96	(0.32)	
97		tch
98	(0.13)	
99		on the PASSport; 99

The first instance of an interactionally relevant change in pitch register occurs at lines 11–27, reproduced below. In reply to Joanne's claim that Nicaragua is *restricted you have to go through Mexico* Ken disagrees in a slightly raised pitch register: his response token *no* and the first part of his second intonation phrase *I don't* are delivered with raised pitch. For the second part, *think so*, he falls into what can be heard as his default range:

```
11  Ken:      tch <<h> NO;
12            I don't> [THINK so,
13  Joanne:            [Isn't nica[RAgua one of the things you
14  Ken:                          [<<h> NO;>
15  Joanne:   [places you can't go,
16  Ken:      [<<h> I don't thInk so;
17            [NO;
18  Joanne:   [i [THINK it i:s;]
19  Ken:         [wE have->]
20            NO;
21            I don't thInk so;
22            we have f-
23  (0.24)
24               .hhh
25  (0.23)
26               <<l> TECHnically SPEAKing;
27            FULL: (0.19) diplomAtic relAtions with nicaragua;=
```

At this point Joanne comes in with her next turn *isn't Nicaragua one of those things you places you can't go* (lines 13 and 15). Ken's next response token *no* (line 14), delivered in overlap with Joanne's ongoing turn, is produced in a high pitch register similar to that of his earlier *no* (line 11). He then replies to Joanne's turn-in-progress in overlap with her, and with a repetition of his previous phrase *I don't think so no* (lines 16–17), this time in an even higher pitch register than before. Joanne continues speaking in overlap, and for the entire time of the simultaneous talk Ken's pitch register remains raised. However, as soon as Joanne drops out, Ken's voice returns to a noticeably lower overall pitch (lines 20–22) and, once he is back on a secure footing in terms of having the floor, his register shows a marked drop to low overall pitch (lines 26–27).

In this sequence, pitch register is employed by participants as part of their handling of simultaneous talk. In their articles on prosodic features of interruptions in conversation, French and Local (1983, 1986) show that, in their data, interrupting participants use a combination of high pitch register and increased loudness when they are illegitimately coming in during another participant's turn; while participants who are legitimate turn holders raise their level of loudness, but not their pitch register (for a summary of French and Local (1986), see Chapter 9.3.1). The extract above seems to show a slightly different pattern at work. Although we can hear a minimal increase in overall pitch register in Joanne's voice when she starts up in overlap with Ken at line 13, she cannot be heard to increase her loudness. On the other hand Ken, the current turn holder, raises mainly his pitch register, while his loudness increases only slightly.

Nevertheless, pitch register is clearly modified in alignment with the occurrence of simultaneous talk.

The strategy underlying Ken's increase in pitch register in this short exchange is one of keeping the floor and with it his conversational status as legitimate turn holder. Evidence for pitch register being employed in this way is not only his raising of overall pitch following Joanne's interruption (lines 13–18), but also the immediate drop in pitch register once Joanne has stopped (lines 18–20), and his return to an authoritative low voice at line 26. This shows that in his choice of pitch register Ken is orienting to other participants' talk: while they are still speaking, he raises his overall pitch; as soon as they drop out, his vocal delivery changes to a different setting.

Subsequent sequential development shows the participants continuing to employ pitch register for turn management. See, for example, lines 26–43:

```
26              <<l> TECHnically SPEAKing;
27              FULL: (0.19) diplomAtic re[lAtions with nicaragua;=
28   Joanne:                               [oh YEAH:?
29   Ken:      ↑YEAH;=
30              they have an n- an amBASsador an-
31              <<all> you know an aMERican amB[ASsador there who-
32   Joanne:                                  [<<h> I then-
33              WHY does every[body always have to go through MEXico:;>
34   Ken:                    [<<f> like a NEST of Cia spies;>>
35              .hh
36              <<h> thAt's just;
37              there there Isn't a diRECT transportation.=
38              [but there it's not->
39   Joanne:  [i thought no but i th[ought it
40   Ken:                           [.hh <<f+h> it's NOT like going to CUba.>
41   (0.14)
42   Ken:      <<h> whEre [they have to mAke connections through MEXico because->
43   Joanne:              [<<p> oh: - >
```

Ken's low pitch register continues throughout Joanne's subsequent interruptions (lines 28; 32–33). In line with French and Local's findings, Ken slightly increases his loudness, albeit at a point when her interruption is already well under way (*like a nest of CIA spies*, line 34). On the other hand, Joanne's pitch register is noticeably raised during her interrupting turn *I then- why does everybody always have to go through Mexico* (lines 32–33).

For his turn following Joanne's interruption (*that's just there there isn't a direct transportation* lines 36–38) Ken now raises his pitch register, too. As this turn is produced in the clear, this cannot be interpreted as a turn management device, but an instance of prosodic orientation: he matches his overall high pitch register with that of Joanne's previous turn. In doing so, he designs his turn as a responding second pair part to Joanne's prior question, which was also delivered with high pitch register.

At line 39, Joanne comes in again, once more in overlap with Ken. She raises neither pitch register nor loudness. However, in his immediately next turn *it's not like going to Cuba* (line 40) Ken increases both his loudness and his overall pitch, thus clearly positioning himself as the legitimate current turn holder. Joanne's short response *oh* (line 43) is delivered as a response token, and with its decreased loudness it is not designed as competing for the floor. This prosodic delivery is in contrast to earlier and later interruptions by her, in which she uses raised pitch and loudness in combination to compete for the floor. Overlapping talk such as her response token *oh* with low pitch and loudness is designed as a minimal response. With interruptions such as these participants not only show that they do not want to grab the floor, they also confirm currently speaking participants' status as current turn holders. Low pitch register and loudness play a crucial role in the design of such short turns as non-competitive.

Immediately after the sequence discussed above, pitch register is once again employed interactionally. In response to Joanne's remark that some people have to make connections to go to Cuba, Ken delivers his turn *that's because it's illegal for Americans to travel to Cuba* (lines 48–49):

```
48  Ken:      THAT's because it's il<<l>lEgal for
49            americans to travel to [cUba.>
50  Joanne:                          [<<h+f> but i WONder whether this- >
51  Lenore:   it I:s;
```

Joanne starts up in overlap with the final part of Ken's turn *Cuba* (line 49), and she does so with increased pitch register and slightly increased loudness. Knowing what we do now regarding high pitch register and its role for interrupting turns, we can interpret this turn as being designed as an illegitimate interruption. This is interesting, because Joanne's turn overlaps only slightly with Ken's, and could be treated as turn transitional overlap, that is overlap while a prior turn is clearly being completed. Joanne does not design her turn as such, however, which shows that she is treating Ken's turn as in-progress, rather than as about-to-be-completed.

Another interactionally relevant instance of pitch register change occurs between lines 66 and 69–70. After Joanne mentions Lebanon as another country with travel restrictions for Americans (lines 56–64), all three participants initiate new turns.

```
61  Joanne:   they i- d-
62            it just became illegal.
63            and i-
64            you KNOW,
65  Ken:      .hh
66            <<h> for a FEW YEAR[S;>
67  Lenore:                      [how long
68            [has it been illegal-
69  Joanne:   [<<h+f> LIBya;
70            TOO.>
71            isn't lIbya asWELL?
```

Ken's initiation of a new sub-sequence *for a few years* (line 66) is accompanied by a higher pitch register; this is typical for new beginnings (see Couper-Kuhlen,

2004, Chapter 3.3.1 above). As such, this instance of higher overall pitch, rather than being employed for activities related to turn-taking, is made relevant for sequential organisation. Ken is interrupted towards the end of his first intonation phrase by Lenore, who initiates what is already a third attempt at a question eventually realised later, at lines 77–78: *how long has it been illegal for Americans to go to Cuba*. Her turn is delivered with default speaking volume and pitch register. She is thus heard as not directly competing for the floor. In overlap with Lenore, Joanne comes in with a continuation of the previous sequence by adding another country to the list: *Libya too* (lines 69–70). Her turn is delivered with increased overall pitch and loudness. With this prosodic design she shows herself to be grabbing the floor illegitimately; as soon as all turn competition has ceased, she returns to default pitch and loudness (line 71).

A final instance of interactionally motivated changes in pitch register occurs towards the end of the extract, between lines 79 and 88.

```
77  Lenore:   how long has it been illegal for amEricans
78            to [go to cuba;
79  Ken:          [<<h+f> WE[LL –
80  Joanne:                  [since the
81  Ken:      it was il[LEgal;
82  Joanne:           [(since the fifties)
83  Ken:      [it was illegal:;
84  Joanne:   [or the SIXties;
85  Ken:      it was ilLEgal;>
86            you knOw from like <<l> the: tIme of CATH-
87            the CAStro revolution.=>
88            UP until:;
89            i think the EARly SEVenties;
```

Lines 77–78 show Lenore's fourth attempt at her question; previous attempts occur at lines 58, 60 and 67–68. This time, both Joanne and Ken offer responses. Ken delivers his in turn-transitional overlap with Lenore, initiating his turn during the final part of her question (lines 78–79). He does so with increased pitch register and loudness. Joanne also replies to Lenore's question; she does so in overlap with Ken, however, with default loudness and pitch register. She continues talking (lines 80; 82; 84), not relinquishing the floor to Ken, but without prosodic competition for the floor. Ken's strategy is different from Joanne's: rather than delivering his whole reply in overlap, he repeats his turn initiation at raised pitch and loudness until he has gained the floor (lines 79; 81; 83); only then does he deliver his reply to Lenore's question (lines 85–99). As we have seen in previous instances, as soon as the other participants have dropped out, Ken's prosodic delivery returns to his default pitch and loudness. This final extract shows once again that high pitch register, in combination with loudness, can be employed by participants to compete for the right to speak. Turn competition is the most frequent sequential location for pitch register to be made relevant by participants: raised register typically contributes to a design of turn competition, whereas lowered overall pitch helps design a turn as non-competitive.

The two pieces of research on pitch range and register summarised in section 4.3 show other interactional locations where overall pitch has been shown to be interactionally relevant.

4.2.1 Exercises

Listen to the following extracts. Identify instances of changes in pitch register; be sure to differentiate between cases of individual high pitch accents, such as step-ups and rises, and changes in pitch register, which affect more than one syllable at a time.

EXERCISE 4.1

In the following extract, the couple Pamela and Darryl are discussing the possibilities of life after death.

SBC005 A book about death 🎧

1	Darryl:	you have NO idEa;
2		what happens beFORE or AFter.
3	(2.52)	
4		you have NO idEa.
5	(1.67)	
6		you can read BOOKS about it,
7		you can (0.4) TALK about it –
8	(1.25)	
9		but the most pragmAtic thing to DO is jUst –
10	(0.33)	
11		LIVE it.
12	(1.85)	
13	Pamela:	m –
14	(0.86)	
15	Darryl:	LEARN the RULES of the GAME,
16	(0.97)	
17		play the GAME,=
18	Pamela:	for WHAT –
19	(0.83)	
20	Darryl:	for whatEver you WANT;
21	(2.68)	
22		for whatEver you WANT.
23	(2.1)	
24		be a: DOCtor,
25		a SCREEN writer,
26		or an ACtress,
27		or a phiLANthropist,

EXERCISE 4.1

(Continued)

28		or a:n exPLORer,
29	(3.44)	
30	Pamela:	ts an exPLORer;
31	(0.78)	
32	Darryl:	do what you WANT;
33		with the time you HAVE.=
34		LEARN,
35	(0.93)	
36		GIVE,
37	(2.01)	
38		whatEVer. 🗨🗨

EXERCISE 4.2

In the next extract, Jill has just told her boyfriend Jeff that she has taken a pregnancy test, which has come out negative.

SBC028 Hey Cutie Pie 🎧

🗨 1	Jeff:	you knOw what i'm SAYing,=
2		like could you get-
3		is it POSsible that you could still be POSi- (0.23) POSitive,
4	(0.49)	
5	Jill:	.hh
6		I thInk (0.19) there'd be a S::L:IGHT CHANCE,
7	(0.33)	
8		of it being a FAL:SE NEGative,
9	(0.43)	
10		.hh
11		bUt –
12	(0.18)	
13		I don't THINK so;
14		cause i'm PRETty LATE?
15	(0.13)	
16		and i thInk i'm LATE enOUgh,
17		.hh
18		where I would HA:VE;
19	(0.45)	
20		like (0.19) eNOUGH of;
21	(0.32)	

EXERCISE 4.2

(Continued)

22		the HORmone that;
23	(0.17)	
24		the prEgnancy tEst TESTS for?
25	(0.22)	
26		.hh
27		i thInk i would have eNOUGH of that in my Urine;
28		thAt –
29	(0.19)	
30		of ↑COURSE it would show up;
31		if i had any IN there?
32	(0.37)	
33	Jeff:	<<p> YEAH;>
34	Jill:	you KNOW?=
35		sO I-
36	(0.1)	
37		I i'm pret-
38		i tOOk that;
39		as a prEtty GOO:D;
40	(0.36)	
41		SI:GN.
42	(1.4)	
43	Jeff:	<<p> Oh my GO:D;
44		HONey;
45		HOW come you've been;
46	(0.15)	
47		KEEPing all this in[SI:DE;>
48	Jill:	[ts
49		I:: KN:OW;
50		i didn't MEAN to keep it inside-
51		i mean i i didn't [mean-
52	Jeff:	[<<p> dOn't you LOVE mE -> 🗲

4.3 Research on pitch range and pitch register in natural conversation

In the local negotiation over interactional issues, pitch register is relevant as a continuously changing prosodic feature. The two studies below show that the analysis of pitch register is often closely intertwined with consideration of participants' pitch range. Couper-Kuhlen (1996a) investigates forms of repetitions and their prosodic delivery in different pitch registers, while Klewitz and Couper-Kuhlen (1999) explore the use of pitch register in sequences containing reported speech. Drawing on the above distinction between studies that begin with a prosodic phenomenon and describe interactional practices that are achieved through it, and those that begin instead with an interactional practice and describe its prosodic design, the first study below falls partially in the first category, whereas the second follows the last pattern.

4.3.1   Elizabeth Couper-Kuhlen (1996a): The prosody of repetition: on quoting and mimicry

This study investigates the interrelation between verbal repetition and prosody in a corpus of radio phone-in programmes. Most telephone conversations in this corpus contain instances of verbal repetition, as callers are asked to guess the solution to a riddle. When callers present their candidate answers, hosts frequently repeat their turns verbatim. Couper-Kuhlen is interested in the relation between the original turn and the copy: when is the turn containing the repetition simply a quotation, when does it become mimicry, particularly with respect to prosody? Or, 'what are the limits which determine how much copying is socially acceptable in a given culture or speech community?' (p. 367).

Given the differences in speakers' pitch ranges, Couper-Kuhlen begins her analysis by showing that comparisons of pitch register must be made on a relative scale, rather than an absolute one. She presents an instance of repetition in which the male radio host repeats a turn by a female caller. By locating the respective turns within each of the participants' pitch ranges, the author shows that the radio host quotes not only the words, but also the pitch register, of the caller, and does so on a relative scale. His repetition is located in the same pitch register, according to his pitch range, as the original turn in the caller's voice; although in absolute terms his Hz values are considerably lower than the caller's.

In a second step, Couper-Kuhlen shows that repetitions on an absolute scale also exist, even in cases of gender difference, i.e. a male radio host repeating a female caller's turn. She presents several examples that show the male radio host matching exactly the high pitch register of his female callers. Interactionally, these instances differ from repetition on a relative scale: while relative repetition of pitch register is treated by participants as simply quoting a previous speaker, repetition on an absolute scale is treated as mimicry.

Finally, the study shows that this distinction not only holds for the riddle-guessing sequences, but also for other types of sequences in the radio phone-in data. However, the broader selection of sequences shows that mimicry is not only carried out through register repetition on an absolute scale. In cases where female callers speak in a perceptibly low pitch register, the male host does not repeat their exact pitch register absolutely, but relatively. This means that, in those cases, he adopts a pitch that is low in his own pitch register, rather than repeat the female low pitch, which would not be heard as low in his voice. 'Relative and absolute register matching can be viewed as different contextualization cues for the same interactional task, that of mimicry. The choice of one as opposed to the other, however, is not arbitrary, but depends on the natural voice ranges of the speakers involved' (p. 401). Couper-Kuhlen concludes that mimicking next turns contains implicit comments on previous turns, and that, in mimicking callers, radio hosts criticise and exercise social control over their female callers.

4.3.2 Gabriele Klewitz and Elizabeth Couper-Kuhlen (1999): Quote–unquote? The role of prosody in the contextualisation of reported speech sequences

In this study the authors set out to investigate how reported speech is marked in natural conversation. Starting with written text, and an example from Jane Austen's *Pride and Prejudice*, Klewitz and Couper-Kuhlen describe five aspects of reported speech-marking in written language: quotation marks are used as boundaries for reported speech; the boundaries of reported speech are clearly established; the original producer of the utterance is explicitly referred to in most cases; however, in longer sequences the original speaker may no longer be made explicit once he or she has been mentioned in the text; and reported speech by different original speakers does not receive varying typographic representation. As the authors turn to conversational speech, some of these conventions are shown to be handled differently by participants in natural conversation, and one of their main tools for doing so are changes in pitch register, loudness and rhythm. First, these changes are shown to occur in instances in which participants use a *verbum dicendi*, that is a verb that initiates the reported speech, such as 'she said' or 'they'd be like'. In a next step, examples are analysed in which the prosodic pattern is the only marker of reported speech. The authors argue therefore that prosodic marking acts in the same way as quotation marks do in written texts. They go on to show that prosodic marking of others' speech is not restricted to direct reported speech, but also occurs with indirect speech. However, participants have the option to mark reported speech or not, and the authors make the important point that, just as reported speech may be delivered without prosodic marking, participants may employ similar types of prosodic patterns for speech that does not quote others.

In an example of high pitch register in a reported speech sequence, Klewitz and Couper-Kuhlen show that unlike quotation marks in written texts, prosodic formatting does not have to cover the whole stretch of reported talk. A participant may start in high register, and thus signal that current talk is a quotation, and then ease back into medium register, even though he or she is still engaged in reported speech. Similarly, participants may 'foreshadow' an upcoming voice by delivering prequotation talk with a marked prosodic format. Finally, the authors show that different reported speakers' voices can be distinguished by participants through the use of different prosodic markings.

FURTHER READING

A roughly similar notion of pitch register has been described by Brazil et al. (1980: ch. 2), who refers to it as 'key'. Crystal (1969, pp. 143–52) refers to it as 'pitch range'. Cruttenden (1997, pp. 44–7) differentiates between 'accent range', i.e. the lowest and highest pitch level in a given pitch accent; 'key', i.e. the pitch span of a given intonation phrase; and 'register', i.e. the raising of the baseline, similar to our understanding in this book.

From the perspective of interactional linguistics, pitch register has been investigated by Couper-Kuhlen (1996a); Klewitz and Couper-Kuhlen (1999) and Local (1992).

Time: Sound and Syllable Duration

The following chapters introduce the influence of time and timing on spontaneous speech production and discuss how it can best be described and interpreted as part of natural conversation. Time affects speech in a variety of ways and across varying stretches of talk. It can become relevant through the lengthening of individual sounds or syllables, changes in the speech rate and rhythm of intonation phrases or turns, and interactionally relevant pauses. Where speech is part of social interaction, time and timing play an important role in participants' negotiations over conversational meaning. Lengthened words, fast or slow talk, breaks in rhythm or noticeable pauses are oriented to by participants as interactionally meaningful.

This chapter presents the shortest stretches of talk, that is sounds and syllables, and their duration. Time is relevant to those smaller entities of speech in that they can be lengthened or shortened. We look at excerpts from natural conversation to explore how participants manipulate the duration of sounds and syllables, and in what contexts this can be interactionally relevant. The following three chapters also introduce issues of time and timing: Chapter 6 discusses speech rate and tempo, comparing two methods for measuring how fast participants are speaking and exploring interactional contexts for changes in speech rate. Chapter 7 turns to speech rhythm, that is to the placement of stressed syllables at regular intervals of time. There we take a closer look at how conversationalists rhythmicise their talk for interactional purposes, particularly at turn transitions. Chapter 8 presents pauses in interaction. While they contribute to our perception of other matters of timing, such as speech rate and rhythm, they are also interesting in their own right as interactionally meaningful prosodic events. In particular, I discuss what constitutes a pause and how silences are made interactionally relevant by participants.

In this chapter, as in previous chapters, the most relevant contrasts are presented first. When discussing duration a distinction is made between sounds and syllables that are lengthened beyond their default duration and those that are shortened. In section 5.1 I make a further distinction between the lengthening of individual sounds and the lengthening of entire syllables, and I discuss how shortening of vowels occurs in stressed and unstressed syllables. In section 5.2

I use the example of a longer stretch of talk to show how syllable duration can be analysed in natural conversation. Section 5.3 introduces Tanaka (2004), who shows that lengthening can be one of several cues for turn finality in Japanese conversation. Section 5.4 provides suggestions for further reading.

5.1 Contrasts in sound and syllable duration

When interactional linguists speak of 'lengthening' they typically refer to either one of two practices: (i) lengthening of a single syllable, or more specifically lengthening of the vowel in a syllable – this type of lengthening is known as *syllable lengthening*; or (ii) lengthening of an individual (consonant) sound before or after the vowel – this type of lengthening is referred to as *sound lengthening*. In contrast, *shortening* is typically only applied to syllables, that is vowels in syllables.

One important distinction we have to make from the beginning is the one between long and short vowels as they occur in the dictionary pronunciation of words on the one hand – such as the short vowel in 'lid' vs the long vowel in 'lead' – and, on the other hand, the choice which participants have to shorten or lengthen vowels beyond their citation forms – such as pronouncing the word 'lead' as 'lea:::d'. The first is a linguistic distinction that is part of the phonemic repertoire of a given language; it rarely becomes interactionally relevant, as it cannot be manipulated for interactional purposes. Instances in which this distinction does become conversationally meaningful are utterances in which non-native speakers of English use short instead of long vowels, or vice versa, which may result in subsequent repair sequences. A similarly linguistic, rather than interactional, distinction is that between vowels affected by certain phonetic environments. The vowel /æ/, as in 'bag', for example, although classified as a short vowel, is pronounced slightly longer when preceding a lenis consonant such as /g/, than when it occurs before a fortis consonant, such as /k/, as in 'back'. This is once again not a participant's choice depending on the individual interactional context, but it is a phonetic rule that applies to all instances of /æ/ in the same phonetic context, and can be expected to affect the speech of most native speakers with a great degree of similarity in pronunciation.

In this book, we are concerned with the role of phonetic and prosodic practices for interaction, and therefore our focus is on instances in which participants employ lengthening and shortening as interactional resources. In order to do so, they need to have the choice to lengthen or not lengthen a sound. We are therefore not so much interested in the above distinctions between long and short vowels or the longer or shorter pronunciation of vowels in certain phonetic contexts. Instead, we focus on participants' employment of sound and syllable duration for interactional purposes.

The following two extracts show the distinction between syllable lengthening – that is lengthening of the vowel in the syllable – and sound lengthening, that is lengthening of sounds other than the vowel. Note that contrasts in the length of syllables are not only interactionally relevant in themselves as lengthening or shortening, but they are also vital contributors to our perception of a speaker's speech rate and speech rhythm. Therefore, many of the issues mentioned in this chapter remain relevant for subsequent chapters.

In Extract 5.1, Kendra describes a chest of drawers that belonged to her grandmother. She uses syllable lengthening on the word *sweet* (line 5). Figure 5.1 shows the duration of this word, compared to other words in the same intonation phrase.

Extract 5.1   SBC013 Appease the monster 🎧

```
 1 Kendra:   there's a CHEST,
 2           it's lIke a i-
 3           it's either like a CEdar,
 4           or SOMEthing;
 5           i m[ean it's SWEE::T.
 6 Ken:         [m;
 7 (0.63)
 8 Kendra:   it's a HOPE CHEST.
 9 (0.3)
10 Ken:        m;
```

We can hear that what is being lengthened here is the vowel [iː]. Rather than just speaking of 'vowel lengthening', we refer to an instance such as this as 'syllable lengthening'. The reason behind this use of terminology is the traditional phonological concept of the syllable, which places the vowel at the core of

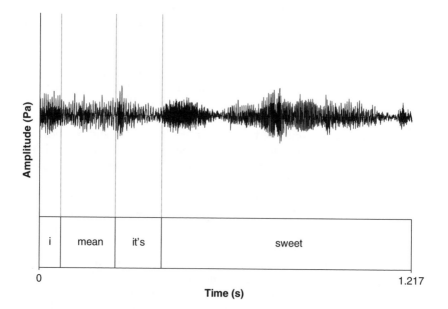

Figure 5.1   Syllable lengthening on *sweet*, line 5 in Extract 5.1

any syllabic structure; thus, when analysts speak of syllable lengthening, they typically refer to lengthening of the vowel.

Consonants can also be lengthened beyond their default duration. In Extract 5.2 below, Tom2 talks about his life in the merchant navy. At the beginning of the transcribed extract he comes to a potential point of sequence closure, summing up his previous experiences on a ship. As he begins his next narrative sequence, he lengthens the initial sound in the word *fifty* (line 5). Figure 5.2 shows the lengthening of the sound /f/.

Extract 5.2   SBC032 Handshakes all around 🎧

```
  1  Tom2:   so I SAILED on hEr for a little whIle.
  2  (0.44)
  3           uh:m -
  4  (0.73)
  5           and thEn in F:::IFty:,
  6           fOrty-NINE i guess;
  7  (0.63)
  8           [uh a guy named-
  9  Tom3:   [now let me STOP you nO:w -
```

Participants may also shorten syllables or, more precisely, vowels in syllables. In some phonetic literature, the shortening of vowels is referred to as 'clipping'. When we speak of shortening here, we refer to participants' reduction of vowel length compared to the length that would have been expectable in a given

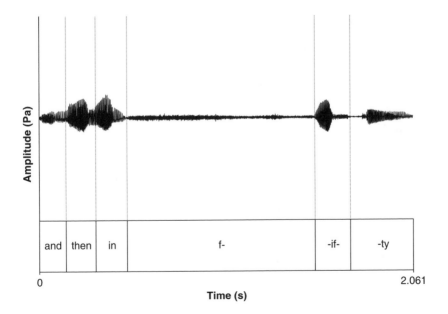

Figure 5.2   Sound lengthening on *fifty*, line 5 in Extract 5.2

phonetic context. Once again, we are only interested in noticeable shortening of vowels when it is interactionally relevant. For example, syllables are regularly shortened when they are not stressed; that is, compared to the typical length of a given syllable as pronounced in isolation, the same syllable in connected speech is likely to be considerably shorter, especially if it is not given prominence by its speaker. For example, the pronunciation of the word 'have' is considerably longer if the word is spoken in isolation, than when it occurs in a real life discourse environment, for instance in the phrase 'have you finished?'. This difference in syllable length depending on stress is an inherent aspect of English speech rhythm, as will become evident in Chapter 7. It is not as such interactionally relevant, as participants who are native speakers of English almost always shorten unstressed syllables. However, some instances of shortening are made interactionally relevant by participants. See, for example, the following extract in which Kathy is helping her boyfriend Nathan prepare for a maths test. On two occasions she can be heard to shorten words and syllables.

Extract 5.3   SBC009 Zero equals zero   🎧

```
 1  Nathan:   SO:;
 2  (0.2)
 3            would THAT one be:;
 4  (0.42)
 5            square root of one HALF,
 6  (0.52)
 7  Kathy:    mhM,
 8  (0.6)
 9  Nathan:   it WOULD,
10  (0.67)
11  Kathy:    mhM,
12  (2.7)
13            <<shortened> YEAH, >
14  (1.95)
15            but do y'ALL have to do that (0.15) uhm;
16  (0.6)
17            you hAve to li:ke;
18  (0.25)
19            HAVE it where you do <<shortened> that- >
20  (0.16)
21            there's NO –
22  (0.95)
23            Uhm;
24  (0.44)
25  Nathan:   FRACtion under the –
26  (0.25)
27  Kathy:    UNder the;
28  (0.27)
29            In the (0.1) denominator, 🙷
```

Kathy's turn *yeah* at line 13 is prematurely ended with a glottal closure, that is a complete closing of the vocal folds, which hearably blocks off the air stream. This pronunciation of *yeah* is similar to *yep*, where the air stream is blocked off by closure of the lips: in both cases, the airflow is stopped abruptly, resulting in a shorter vowel than that in a default pronunciation of *yeah*. This shortened use of *yeah* plus glottal closure is interactionally meaningful, in that it accomplishes a different conversational activity than a fully pronounced *yeah* would have done. Rather than accomplishing primarily confirmation, which would be the action performed by an unshortened *yeah*, the shortened *yeah* ending in glottal closure primarily accomplishes turn completion. Confirmation of Nathan's suggestion (lines 3–5) has already been provided by Kathy on two prior occasions (lines 7; 11). The blocking of the air stream on *yeah* is an iconic representation of the participant's signalled intention to say no more on this particular topic. This interpretation is confirmed by the pause of almost 2 seconds that follows the shortened word, and furthermore by Kathy's subsequent contrastive conjunction, *but*, which initiates a new sequential beginning in the form of a first pair part (line 15).

A further instance of shortening can be heard at the end of line 19, where Kathy aborts one turn design in favour of another. This is possibly the most frequent environment for shortened words and syllables. When participants break off a turn-in-progress, words and syllables just prior to the break off may be either cut off while they are still underway, or reach completion, being shortened considerably.

Like other prosodic features, the lengthening and shortening of syllables must be seen in relation to the immediate surroundings of those syllables. Speech rate and speech rhythm, both to be discussed in the following chapters, play an important part in how short or long individual syllables are pronounced at any given sequential location. Additional factors such as a participant's regional variety also have an impact on syllable duration. Furthermore, we must be careful with possible implications of defining lengthened or shortened sounds as deviations from a default duration: many instances of lengthened or shortened syllables occur as interactionally meaningful realizations of those syllables; that is the above pronunciation of shortened *yeah* followed by a glottal stop may be shorter than an isolated production of that word in a stressed position; however, in this particular conversational context it is as long or short as it needs to be. Therefore, our analysis of a syllable as lengthened or shortened relies on a perception of expectable speech production outside specific interactional locations, while our interpretations of any given instance of lengthening or shortening must be based on precisely those specific locations.

5.1.1 Summary

With regard to the analysis of the lengthening and shortening of individual sounds and syllables, we have to remember that:

- Syllable lengthening entails the lengthening of the vowel.
- Sound lengthening entails the lengthening of consonant sounds before or after the vowel.

- Syllable shortening entails shortening of the vowel and potentially subsequent consonant sounds.
- In English, shortening of vowel sounds co-occurs with absence of stress.
- Lengthening and shortening can only be interpreted as an interactional resource when they are made interactionally relevant by participants themselves.

5.2 Analysing sound and syllable duration

We now take a look at a longer extract from natural conversation to see how sound and syllable length is made relevant by participants. In the extract below, a group of women are discussing E. M. Forster's novel *Howard's End* in their reading group. There are 11 participants in total, not all of whom are speaking in this extract. However, the number of participant contributions and resulting overlap take a little bit of getting used to; it is therefore best to listen to this extract a number of times before continuing with the analysis below. Immediately prior to the extract represented here, one participant initiates the issue over who was king or queen of England in 1910. One candidate answer is 'Victoria's son', another one is 'Edward'. From this develops the following sequence.

Extract 5.4   SBC023 *Howard's End* 🎧

```
 1  Lori:      the One that [ABdicated?
 2  Sue:                    [YEAH;
 3  (0.75)
 4  Linda:     NO.
 5  Lori:      [THAT was LATer.
 6  Patty:     [NO;
 7  (0.43)
 8             THAT was LATer.
 9  (0.38)
10  Evelyn:    mhm;
11  Patty:     ts well at the beGINning of wOrld wAr (0.38) O:NE.
12  (0.42)
13             in the GUNS [of August.
14  Nora:                  [nineTEE:N –
15  (0.47)
16  Patty:     THEY[:: -
17  Nora:          [FOURtee:n.
18  (0.25)
19  Patty:     A::LL of the CROWNED HEADS.
20             was –
21  (0.19)
22             that was the LA:ST TIME they were A:LL toGETHer.
23             so it had A:Lready;
24             .h wAs –
```

25	(0.71)	
26		WELL over the hoRIzon into SETting.
27	(0.32)	
28	Linda:	[Mhm;
29	**Patty:**	**[by nInetee:n FOURtee:n.**
30	Lori:	[okAY;
31	Many:	[mhm;
32	Lori:	[so nineteen [TEN it [just-
33	**Patty:**	**[so in [<<f> NI:NE [tEE:n TEN;**
34		**there would DE::Finitely have BEEN;**
35	(0.22)	
36	Lori:	Un[dercUrrents;
37	**Patty:**	**[the WI:NDS;**
38		**[o:f CHA:NGE;>**
39	Linda:	[mhm;
40	**Diane:**	**[okAY:;**
41	**Patty:**	**beGINning tO:;**
42	(0.85)	
43	**Linda:**	**mhm:;**
44	**Diane:**	**but ENGland didn't really start LOSing her <<p> cO:lonies::;**
45	(0.74)	
46		DID she,
47		**until more like SECond world wA:r?>**
48	(2.5)	
49	**Evelyn:**	**[that's when [they div- diVE:STed;=**
50	Diane:	[mAYbe-
51	Linda:	[mhm;
52	**Evelyn:**	**was after (the/r) SECond wOrld [wA:r:.**
53	**Diane:**	**[okAY:,**
54	Lori:	mhm;
55	(0.5)	
56	**Diane:**	**may[be the POWer over them was becoming WEA:K,**
57	Evelyn:	[(( ))
58		mhm:,
59	Lori:	[i-
60	Diane:	[by [thIs time,
61	Lori:	[wAsn't that part of the PROBlem,
62		they HAD,
63		cause they were TRYing to;
64	(0.49)	
65		hold the COLonies together -
66		and then they Also had to dEAl with the WAR in EUrope, 💬

The first time in this extract that lengthening becomes interactionally relevant is during the short sequence between lines 11 and 19. Patty initiates a new sequence on England's history during World War One, and the beginning of this sequence contains a considerable amount of syllable lengthening.

```
11  Patty:    ts well at the beGINning of wOrld wAr (0.38) O:NE.
12  (0.42)
13            in the GUNS [of AUgust.
14  Nora:                [nineTEE::N –
15  (0.47)
16  Patty:    THEY[:: -
17  Nora:         [FOURtee:n.
18  (0.25)
19  Patty:    A::LL of the CROWNED HEADS.
```

Patty's first intonation phrase *well at the beginning of world war one* ends in the lengthened stressed syllable *one*. The pitch accent on this final syllable falls to low, although the participant has reached neither turn nor sentence completion. The lengthened falling pitch is treated by participants as a non-transition place: the pause at line 12 shows that no one else comes in to speak at this point. This is in contrast to many other instances of low-falling, lengthened pitch accents, which frequently co-occur with turn completion. However, here the lengthening is used with syntactic non-completion; partly for this reason, and partly because of the lack of subsequent co-participant uptake, this instance of lengthening is interpretable as contributing to turn holding. Furthermore, the lengthened word is preceded by a phrase-internal pause (line 11). Pausing and lengthening both are iconic signs of participants' gaining time; possibly this participant is choosing between candidate lexical items 'World War *One*' and '*Two*'. All we can say definitely is that both lengthening and pausing during an intonation phrase increase the production time taken over a turn-in-progress. A collection of such instances may reveal that typical locations for this combination are instances in which participants are engaged in word searches or similar activities.

During Patty's continuation *in the guns of august* (line 13) Nora comes in with her turn *nineteen fourteen* (lines 14 and 17). Her lengthening is of a similar kind as Patty's. She lengthens the final syllable in *nineteen*, leaves a considerable pause (line 15), and then continues with a slightly less lengthened candidate *fourteen*. Once more, lengthening and pausing co-occur in an environment of available candidates, here a variety of historic dates. Nora's turn is not treated by Patty as an interruption, nor is it designed as such. It is produced with considerably less loudness than Patty's talk, and Patty does not raise her pitch or loudness in reaction to Nora's incoming.

Patty's immediately following instance of lengthening on *they* (line 16) can be interpreted from two interactional perspectives. On the one hand it may be another instance of searching for words for an immediate turn continuation. It once again is followed by a pause. However, at this point Nora's non-competitive turn is still underway. Therefore, on the other hand, Patty can also be heard to

give Nora time to finish before she continues with her own turn. The lengthening and pause are instrumental in this practice: while not competing with
Nora, and thereby not treating her turn as an interruption, Patty's lengthening
of *they* nevertheless projects more talk to come, keeping the status as current
turn-holder while Nora is still speaking.

The final instance of lengthening in this short sequence occurs on Patty's
next word *all* (line 19), with which she regains the floor after Nora's interlude.
In contrast to *they*, Patty increases her loudness on *all*, and the combination of
loudness and lengthening establishes the floor as firmly in her hands. In contrast
to the quietly lengthened *they*, which affirmed Patty's right to the floor while
allowing Nora time to complete her aside, the loud and lengthened *all* designs
the turn as regaining exclusive speaking rights.

A brief look at the following instances of lengthening show another very
frequent and iconic use of prolonging syllables: increased emphasis.

19 Patty: A::LL of the CROWNED HEADS.
20   was –
21 (0.19)
22   that was the LA:ST TIME they were A:LL toGETHer.
23   so it had A:Lready;
24   .h wAs –
25 (0.71)
26   WELL over the hoRIzon into SETting.
27 (0.32)
28 Linda: [Mhm]
29 Patty: [by nIne]tee:n FOURtee:n.

The above instances of syllable lengthening are all down to (repeated) emphasis.
The words *all, last, all* and *already* (lines 19–23), and the words *nineteen fourteen*
(line 29), carry the primary semantic content for some of the historical issues
the group has been trying to uncover. This kind of syllable lengthening is an
iconic practice for setting words and syllables apart from surrounding speech by
sheer increase in the time allocated to them within the utterance.

The instances of lengthening immediately following the above extract can
once again be analysed as related to turn-taking:

30 Lori: [okAY;]
31 Many: [mhm;]
32 Lori: [so nineteen]   [TEN it]   [just-]
33 Patty: [so in]   [<<f> NI:NE] [tEE:n] TEN;
34   there would DE::Finitely have BEEN;
35 (0.22)
36 Lori: Un[dercUrrents;
37 Patty: [the WI:NDS;
38   [o:f CHA:NGE;>
39 Linda: [mhm;

```
40  Diane:   [okAY:;
41  Patty:   beGINning tO:;
42  (0.85)
```

As overlap increases, Patty continues to establish herself as the current and legitimate turn holder. Her repeated syllable lengthening (*ni:netee:n*) while engaged in simultaneous talk shows her to be increasing her floor time until the overlapping participant Lori has finished speaking (lines 32–33). Patty can also be heard to increase her loudness, a further sign that she is claiming the floor as legitimately hers. Her next instance of lengthening on *definitely* (line 34) can be analysed as both increased emphasis and ongoing orientation to a perceived threat of interruption. And indeed, after only a short pause (line 35), the floor is claimed again by another speaker: Lori comes in with her collaborative turn continuation *undercurrents* (line 36). Patty does not give up the floor, but continues her turn with additional syllable lengthening on *winds*, overlapping with *undercurrents*. Simultaneously with Patty's continuation *of change*, both Linda and Diane come in with response tokens *mhm* and *okay* (lines 39–40). Patty continues to lengthen her syllables on *of change*, establishing herself as primary speaker and turn holder in spite of simultaneous talk.

The last instance of lengthening in this sequence occurs on Patty's final word *to* (line 41). It is followed by a substantial pause (line 42), and the syntactic construction is never brought to completion. This location for lengthening followed by pausing is reminiscent of the word-search environment we encountered above, literally increasing the time in which to plan ahead for imminent turn continuation. However, this instance of lengthening occurs with turn completion, irrespective of the syntactically incomplete nature of Patty's turn. This use of a 'dangling' preposition followed by a pause is not uncommon (see Barth-Weingarten, 2007; Mulder and Thompson, 2008). The syllable lengthening on *to* displays the speaker's orientation to the syntactic incompleteness of her turn by giving it the same prosodic design as a turn-internal word prior to a word search. The pause shows that other participants acknowledge this turn design for a noticeable length of time, before they come in to take the floor.

Following on from Patty's syntactically incomplete turn, Diane comes in with her next turn *but England didn't really start losing her colonies* (line 44):

```
41  Patty:   beGINning tO:;
42  (0.85)
43  Linda:   mhm:;
44  Diane:   but ENGland didn't really start LOSing her <<p> cO:lonies::;
45  (0.74)
46           DID she,
47           until more like SECond world wA:r?>
48  (2.5)
```

49 Evelyn: [that's when] [they div-] diVE:STed;=
50 Diane: [mAYbe-]
51 Linda: [mhm;]
52 Evelyn: was after (the/r) SECond wOrld [wA:r:;]
53 Diane: [okAY:,]
54 Lori: mhm;
55 (0.5)
56 Diane: may[be the] POWer over them was becoming WEA:K,
57 Evelyn: [(( ))]
58   mhm:
59 Lori: [i-
60 Diane: [by thIs time,

Diane's turn contains lengthening on *co:lonies:*, both on the first syllable and on the final sound [s]. She begins her turn with default loudness, but towards the end of the intonation phrase, and noticeably on the word *colonies*, loudness is reduced considerably. This intonation phrase is treated by other participants as a non-completion point: it is followed by a pause of considerable length (line 45). The sound lengthening on the /s/, combined with the drop in loudness, seems to provide a turn design that projects more talk from the same participant. Diane's subsequent tag question *did she* (line 46) shows her to be retrospectively designing her turn as a first pair part and as eliciting confirmation. However, only after another intonation phrase ending in lengthening and a high rising pitch accent (*until more like second world war*, line 47), and a subsequent 2.5 second pause, does a next participant provide a candidate second pair part (line 49).

Evelyn's lengthening on *divested* (line 49) is once again an instance of lengthening for emphasis; this time it is combined with raised loudness, increasing the effect. Her subsequent lengthening on *war* (line 52), and Diane's elongated word *weak* (line 56), are cases of potential turn-final lengthening: when turns are designed as complete they typically end in lengthened syllables. This is related to the final lengthening commonly found at the end of intonation phrases.

We have seen in the extract above that, like many other prosodic features, lengthening plays a major role in participants' turn and overlap management. Both sound and syllable lengthening also play an important part in adding emphasis, due to the physical increase in production time. Because of its iconic display of increase in time, lengthening also contributes to all those conversational practices that are related to 'gaining time', such as turn continuation and searching for words.

5.2.1 Exercises

In the following extracts, identify the instances of sound and syllable lengthening.

EXERCISE 5.1

In the first extract, Jill has just told her boyfriend Jeff that she thought she was pregnant, but isn't.

SBC028 Hey Cutie Pie 🎧

```
 1  Jeff:    so was thAt all the DRAma?
 2  (0.22)
 3  Jill:    tch
 4           <<h> thAt was the ↑DRAma;>
 5           and thAt was the susPENSE,
 6           .hh
 7           and thAt was the reLIEF,
 8           and thAt was the ECStasy.
 9  (0.93)
10  Jeff:    <<h> REALLY?>
11  Jill:    uHU?
12  (0.46)
13  Jeff:    .hh
14           OH HONEY;
15  Jill:    <<h> ehehO - >
16  Jill:    little BUNNy;
17           is going thrOUgh the whOle wIde SPECtrum of eMOTions;
```

EXERCISE 5.2

In the following extract, Nathan's girlfriend Kathy has explained a maths task to him.

SBC009 Zero equals zero 🎧

```
 1  Nathan:  SO;
 2  (0.44)
 3           let's tAlk about this SLOWly,
 4           as i WRITE this DOWN as you're SAYing it.
 5           all RIGHT,
```

EXERCISE 5.3

This final extract is taken from the same birthday party as Extract 5.1. Kendra has received a baking set for her birthday.

SBC012 Appease the monster 🎧

```
66  1  Marci:    dOn't forget to buy yourself a COOKie sheet,=
    2            before you go to make COOKies,
    3  Wendy:    [YEAH.
    4  Kevin:    [and DON'T forget to take the TUPperware out of your
    5            Oven;
    6            before you turn it O[N;
    7  Wendy:                       [SHUSH up.
    8  (0.46)
    9  Marci:    ehehe[hehehe
   10  Kendra:       [ehehe OH YEAH;
   11            THAT TOO; 99
```

5.3   Research on syllable duration in natural conversation: Hiroko Tanaka (2004): Prosody for marking transition-relevance places in Japanese conversation: the case of turns unmarked by utterance-final objects

Although lengthening is mentioned frequently in studies on prosody in inter-action, there are few publications that focus exclusively on sound and syllable duration in natural talk. One specific interactional environment is mentioned particularly often as containing syllable lengthening: almost every study investigating turn transition contains reference to turn-final lengthening. The article presented here shows that in Japanese conversation, syllable duration is treated as relevant for turn-transition, in particular for turns that lack other language specific turn completion cues.

Hiroko Tanaka has published extensively on turn-taking in Japanese (Tanaka 1999, 2000). In her earlier work she found that the majority of turn transitions in Japanese conversation are accomplished through participants' employment of utterance-final objects, such as final suffixes, copulas and final particles. In this article she describes a minority group of turn transitions in Japanese that are characterised by an absence of such turn-final objects; these turn transitions are referred to by her as 'truncated' turns. Participants who produce truncated turns do not routinely experience interactional difficulties; that is 'truncated' turns are not treated by conversationalists as incomplete. Tanaka hypothesises that in cases where typical markers for turn-finality are missing, Japanese participants utilise other interactional practices to accomplish turn transitions. Prosody is one candidate for such interactional work, and indeed Tanaka finds that certain clusters of phonetic events are employed by participants to accomplish turn-completion in the absence of utterance-final markers. One of these phonetic practices is turn-final manipulation of syllable duration.

First, Tanaka shows one example of a word produced at the end of a truncated turn and compares its pronunciation with an instance in which the same word occurs in non-final position. She shows that the word in turn-final position is shortened and followed by a glottal stop; whereas the same word in non-final position does not receive this phonetic design. Starting with this first noticing of a potentially relevant phonetic distinction, the author examines her corpus of truncated turns. She finds five types of turn-final clusters of phonetic features, three of which are the most frequent. Type 1 and 2 both involve lengthening as one of the main contributors to the phonetic cluster that signals turn finality. In Type 1, lengthening occurs on the final syllable; in Type 2, the penultimate mora is lengthened if the final syllable consists of two moras. In addition to final lengthening on those moras, participants also increase loudness and employ pitch movements such as rising-falling pitch; however, Tanaka hypothesises that 'the most important phonetic correlate of both types is the increased duration of the pertinent mora of the final word' (p. 91). In truncated turns of Type 3, participants seem to employ the opposite prosodic effect: instead of final lengthening, the final mora is followed by a glottal stop, which does not normally occur in word-final position in Japanese, and which creates an impression of shortening. Type 4 involves an increase in speech rate towards the potential end of a turn, whereas Type 5 involves lexical repetition of final words or expressions.

After a presentation of her findings, Tanaka goes on to put them into an interactional context by discussing participants' orientation to truncated turns. Her evidence that the described prosodic patterns are interpreted and employed by participants as markers for turn-finality draws on other linguistic domains and participant behaviour. Firstly, she shows that syntactic completion points are frequently bypassed as cues for turn transition when they are not accompanied by the above prosodic features. Secondly, participants regularly start up new turns after truncated turns that end in those features. Thirdly, in cases where truncated turns ending in those prosodic features are not followed by talk by next participants, those participants that had produced the truncated turns show that their turn had indeed been designed as complete.

In her conclusion, Tanaka links her findings to an interesting distinction between Japanese on the one hand, and those varieties of English previously studied by conversation analysts on the other. In English, participants can be seen to predict the ends of turns, sometimes from quite an early stage in a turn-in-progress. Two primary cues for upcoming turn completion are final pitch accents (Schegloff, 1998; Wells and Macfarlane, 1998) and the predictability of English syntactic structure. This means that as a speaker's turn emerges, coparticipants monitor it for upcoming completion. Once turn finality is in sight, participants can be seen to get ready to speak. During the final unstressed syllables of a turn, English conversational data often display so-called 'terminal overlaps' (Jefferson, 1986); that is next participants have recognised a turn as about to come to completion, and have therefore started up slightly before the previous speaker had actually finished.

Tanaka shows that in Japanese no such projection is possible – neither in cases where participants wait for turn-final objects nor in the truncated turns described in this article. The majority of truncated turns, Types 1–3, make use of phonetic features that occur on the final syllable, leaving little time for participants to get ready for their next turn. In fact, Tanaka shows that most truncated turns are followed by short pauses. This points to a fundamental difference in turn behaviour in the two languages with respect to transition timing.

FURTHER READING

Overviews of duration in phonetics can be found in Clark and Yallop (1995, pp. 33–6), Ladefoged (2001, pp. 232–3) and Laver (1994, pp. 151–2, pp. 431–48).

In interactional linguistics syllable duration has been investigated by Ford et al. (2004), Szczepek Reed (2006, pp. 111–19, pp. 127–30) and Tanaka (2004).

Syllable duration has been studied much more extensively in phonetics and phonology than in international linguistics, mostly through experimental methods and/or using speech data gained in highly controlled conditions. Some studies with relevance for a conversation analytic approach are Bell-Berti et al. (1995), Berkovits (1984), Bolinger (1963), Cambier-Langeveld (1999), Cooper and Danly (1981) and van Lancker et al. (1988).

Time: Speech Rate

In this chapter we are concerned with how fast or slow participants are speaking, not in terms of their overall speaking habit, but during individual stretches of talk. Section 6.1 presents the main contrasts in speech rate and two basic ways of measurement: syllables per unit of time, and syllable duration. Section 6.2 shows how speech rate changes can be investigated as part of natural interaction, using the example of a single longer extract. Section 6.3 presents an example of interactional linguistic research on speech rate in conversation: Uhmann (1992) analyses speech rate changes and their role in participants' signalling of conversational relevance.

6.1 Contrasts in speech rate

Speech rate can be as much influenced by participants' actual speech *production* as by our *perception* of talk as fast or slow. That is to say, while there are physical activities of speaking that can be measured and put in relation to the time in which they were produced, different interactional contexts also have a strong influence on our perception of speech rate. In varying interactional environments we may hear the same speech rate as fast or less fast depending on expectations created by the surrounding spoken and interactional material. For example, when someone is in the process of explaining to us a piece of complex information we had not been aware of previously, we may ask them to slow down. This, however, may have nothing to do with their speaking too fast, but with our experience of receiving a large amount of information in a short stretch of time. Similarly, as learners of a foreign language we often perceive natural talk by native speakers as fast, when in reality they are probably not speaking faster than we are in our native language, but our impression is one of being overwhelmed by the amount of new input we have to process. Nevertheless, participants in naturally occurring talk do frequently change their speech rate. For example, they may slow down while in the process of closing a sequence or narrative, or they may speed up when they see themselves in danger of being interrupted.

Some speakers have a faster or slower overall rate of articulation than others, resulting in comparatively faster or slower speech rate whenever they speak fluently. Thus, in analysing speech rate we have to be careful from the outset to interpret spates of talk in their interactional context, particularly in relation to the talk produced by the same and other participants before and after the talk under analysis.

Perception of a participant as speaking fast or slow depends on a variety of factors, even when we can be sure that it is an issue of production, i.e. the speaker's own activity, rather than an issue of our perception. First of all, a speaker may produce many words or syllables in a short time, which may therefore be perceived as fast speech; vice versa, a small number of words in a comparable length of time may be perceived as slow. This type of measurement counts the number of linguistic units per unit of time (either syllables per second or segments per second). Secondly, a speaker may produce short syllables in close succession, which may also be perceived as fast speech, whereas a succession of long syllables may be perceived as slow. This form of measuring depends on duration of units, typically syllables. Lengthening and shortening, as described in Chapter 5, and pausing, as discussed in Chapter 8, can contribute to participants' speech rates, both in terms of the number of units per unit of time and in terms of unit duration. A distinction frequently made in phonetic literature is the one between *rate of articulation* and *speech rate*: the former does not take pauses into account, whereas the latter does.

The following extracts demonstrate instances of the above possibilities. While it may be intuitively easy to identify fast vs slow speech, it is not always easy to define the prosodic factor that contributes most strongly to this impression; nor is it always straightforward to locate the specific speech event from which a participant's speech rate begins to change tempo. Extract 6.1 below is an instance of a participant's employment of slow speech rate on a single turn. The recording is of a dinner table conversation between four friends, Pete, Miles and the married couple Jamie (female) and Harold. Immediately prior to the printed transcript, Miles has asked Harold about his dancing classes, to which Harold has replied that he will take more classes in the future. From this the extract below unfolds.

Extract 6.1   SBC002 Lambada 🎧

66 1 Harold: as it tUrns out as a SPOUSE.
   2   i get in FREE.
   3 Pete: oh ↑REALly.
   4 Harold: so -
   5 Jamie: to group CLASSes.
   6   YEAH.
   7 (0.78)
   8 Harold: so -

```
 9                 i should [do that;
10 Miles:                  [Oh REALly,
11 Jamie:        mhm,
12 (1.21)
13 Miles:        <<f> THAT'S why you MARried her.>
14                hehehe
15 (0.34)
16                hehehehehehe
17 Jamie:        .hh hh.
18                SOME BENefit;
19                HUH,
20                [hehe
21 Miles:        [hehehehe .hh
22 Jamie:        he .hh
23 Harold:       BETter than NOTHing,
24 (0.65)
25 Miles:        [heheheheHE:::
26 Pete:         [hehehehehehe
27 Jamie:        [OH::::;
28                <<len> i [cAnnot beL::IE::VE [you SAID tha:t;>
29 Pete:                  [hehe            [.hh hehehe
30 Jamie:        <<h> what a JERK;>
31                [<<l+p> you are;>
32 Pete:         [hehehe
33 Miles:        hehe
34 (0.51)
35 Jamie:        <<h> aren't you guys gonna stick UP for me,
36                and beat UP on him or something?>
37 Miles:        he's BIGger than I am; 💬
```

Jamie's turn *oh I cannot believe you said that* (lines 27–28) is delivered at a noticeably slower speech rate than previous talk by herself and other participants in the same immediate interactional environment. Figure 6.1 shows that Jamie's nine syllables take up 3.667 seconds; this means her speech rate is 2.45 syllables per second. Figure 6.2 shows Jamie's next turn *aren't you guys gonna stick up for me and beat up on him or something* (lines 35–36). This turn, which is delivered roughly at Jamie's default speech rate, contains 17 syllables produced in 2.67 seconds. This means her speech rate for this turn is 6.37 syllables per second, which is considerably faster than her prior turn.

In this book we measure speech rate by the method of counting syllables per second. However, in doing so we must always bear in mind the potential differences in syllable structure and their influence on speech rate and production. Syllables containing consonant clusters, such as [st] in *stick*, take more time to articulate than syllables containing single or no consonants, such as *up* and *or*. Measuring speech rate as syllables per second is therefore to be seen more as a guide to the rate of production than a clear-cut method.

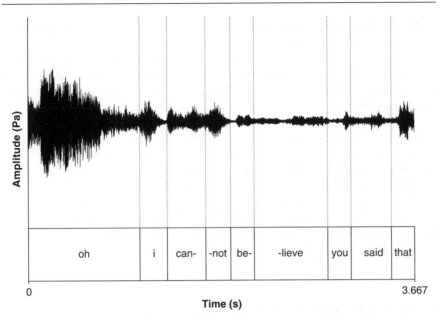

Figure 6.1   Slow speech rate, lines 27–28 in Extract 6.1

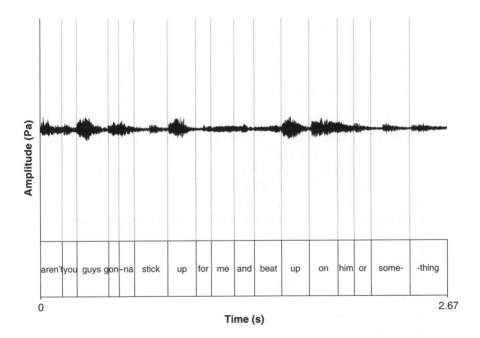

Figure 6.2   Default speech rate, lines 35–36 in Extract 6.1

A second way of measuring speech rate considers the length of individual syllables. A closer look at the reasons for our perception of Jamie's speech rate as slow reveals that her turn contains at least four instances of sound and syllable lengthening: *oh* is considerably elongated, the sound [l] in *believe* is lengthened, and so is the whole syllable *-lieve*; the final, unstressed word *that* receives lengthening too. Another factor that contributes to our perception of slow speech rate is the delivery of the unstressed syllables *i* and *–not*: while their pitch and loudness remain low, their duration is slightly longer than would be typical. This is due to those syllables receiving full vowel quality, rather than the reduced vowel quality we would normally expect for unstressed syllables.

The above example demonstrates how syllable duration contributes to the production and perception of a stretch of talk as slow. Extract 6.2 shows the influence of pauses on speech rate perception. Marci, her daughter Kendra and her daughter-in-law Wendy are talking about a mutual acquaintance, Trish. Prior to the transcribed extract they have been discussing the fact that Trish is pregnant and that she has a new hairstyle.

Extract 6.2   SBC013 Appease the monster 🎧

```
 1 Marci:    is she WORKing YET or:;
 2           STILL at HOME;
 3 (0.4)
 4 Kendra:   [I think she's still at HOME,
 5 Wendy:    [I don't think she does-
 6           she doesn't HAVE to work;
 7           DOES she,
 8 (1.03)
 9 Kendra:   she doesn't HA:VE tO unless:::;
10 (0.25)
11           you know i guess SCOTT'S making some good BU:CKS.
12 Marci:    <<breathy> YEAH but they BOUGHT like;
13           THREE CARS in a ROW.
14           SHE had that ONE;
15           and they SOLD THAT;
16           and [bought TWO OTHer:s;
17 Kendra:       [YEAH but at THAT point she was still on an;
18 (0.9)
19           IN:;
20 (0.37)
21           UnENDing:;
22 (0.81)
23           MONey;
24 (0.24)
25           STREAK.
26 (1.3)
```

27		cause of the POLicy she took out on her HUSband.
28	(0.78)	
29		<<p> EX husband.>
30		WELL -
31	Marci:	YEAH but has [thAt FINished,
32	Kendra:	[deCEASED husband.
33	Marci:	THAT hasn't FINished.
34		[HAS it,
35	Kendra:	[YEAH;
36		it FINished when she got married to TO:DD. 🙿

Kendra's turn *yeah but at that point she was still on an in unending money streak* (lines 17–25) is interspersed by pauses throughout her word search *in unending money streak*. The whole turn, containing 17 syllables, is produced in 6.93 seconds, resulting in a speech rate of 2.45 syllables per second. Although this is a very slow speech rate, our perception of Kendra's individual words is not initially as slow. The main cause for the low rate of syllables per second is the pauses in between the words, rather than the rate of articulation of the words themselves. This shows that measuring speech rate in this way does not necessarily allow us to make assumptions regarding the rate of articulation, but only the overall ratio of units of speech per unit of time. However, as the previous section on lengthening has shown, it is most helpful to interpret syllable duration as a prosodic event occurring on individual syllables. Speech rate, on the other hand, is best described as a feature of talk spanning units above the syllable. Therefore, speech rate is not measured in terms of duration in this book.

The following extract shows two clear instances of fast speech rate. In this recording, the couple Pamela and Darryl are talking about a book which deals with the concepts of death, heaven and hell. Prior to the transcribed section Pamela has mentioned her previous marriage as an example of hard times making her stronger.

Extract 6.3   SBC005 A book about death   🎧

🙾 1	Pamela:	it's like sOmetimes you go THROUGH thIng:s -
2	(0.48)	
3		and you come out the other SIDE of them;
4	(0.26)	
5		y' come out SO much BETter;
6	(0.62)	
7		.hh
8		and if i HADn't HAD that.
9		if i HADn't HAD- =
10	Darryl:	's nOt the way with FOOD;
11	(1.27)	
12	**Pamela:**	**<<all> what do you MEAN;>**

```
13  (1.19)
14  Darryl:    .hh
15             what gOEs in [ONE way;
16  Pamela:                 [ehehehehe
17  Darryl:    <<laughing> doesn't come out> hehehehe
18  Pamela:    .hh
19             KAYhe[he
20  Darryl:         [hehehe
21  Pamela:    .hh
22             comes out VERy HELLish.
23  Darryl:    .hh
24             ↑YEAH:.
25  Pamela:    VEry HELLish;
26  Darryl:    <<all> so what did that [have to do- >
27  Pamela:                            [but it's SO GOOD-
28             so good going ↑DOWN;
29             th- [(((i mean))
30  Darryl:        [what-
31  Pamela:    thEre's thEre's the OPposites again.
32  Darryl:    It's It's [ma-
33  Pamela:              [the FOOD is like;
34             [ALL uNIQUE -
35  Darryl:    [HEY;
36  Pamela:    and WON[derful and hEAvenly-
37  Darryl:           [i it's MAjor league yin and YA:NG.
38  (0.43)
39  Pamela:    tsk MAjor ↑LEAGUE.
40  (0.26)
41  Darryl:    <<all> whAt does that have to do with HEAVen and HELL in the
42             BOOK.>
43  (1.66)
44  Pamela:    WELL –
45  (0.48)
46             I'M just sort of;
47             reITerating; 99
```

The first instance of fast speech rate occurs on Pamela's turn *what do you mean* at line 12. Figure 6.3 shows this extremely contracted turn. The only word that is articulated fully is *mean*; the preceding words *what do you* are reduced to a monosyllabic *wha'*. Extreme contraction of syllables often co-occurs with frequently used or formulaic phrases. Pamela's production of *what do you mean* shows that she treats this phrase almost as a single word, rather than a string of words. The resulting speech rate for this phrase is very fast at 9.01 syllables per second, if we indeed count four syllables. An alternative approach to such an utterance would be to treat it as a single contracted entity, as in the case of *can't* for *cannot*.

A second instance of fast speech in the above extract occurs on Darryl's turn *what does that have to do with heaven and hell in the book* (lines 41–42). The 14 syllables are produced in 1.813 seconds, resulting in a speech rate of 7.72

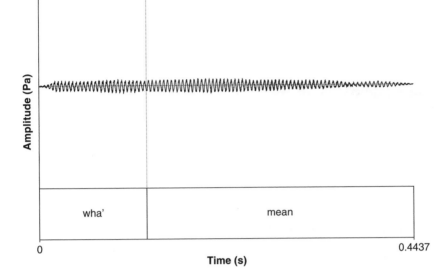

Figure 6.3   Fast speech rate: reduced syllables, line 12 in Extract 6.3

syllables per second (Figure 6.4). This is relatively fast, compared to Darryl's default speech rate in other turns, such as the one at line 10, *it's not the way with food*. In this turn, 6 syllables are produced in 1.296 seconds, resulting in a speech rate of 4.63 syllables per second (Figure 6.5). Darryl's fast turn at lines 41–42 shows an entire utterance at high speech rate, in contrast to Pamela's contracted production of a single formulaic phrase.

Pamela's pronunciation of the phrase *what do you mean* potentially opens up a dilemma similar to the one we encountered in the instances of shortened syllables at specific interactional locations (Chapter 5): if a certain pronunciation is routine in everyday speech, one could argue that an analysis of a specific occurrence should be based on that routine pronunciation, rather than on an imagined pronunciation of the phrase spoken in isolation. Thus, Pamela's speech rate on *what do you mean*, while fast when compared with out-of-context speech, is possibly default in its specific environment: because in its interactional environment her speech rate is no faster than expected. The problem with such a view is that one would have to assume the default prosodic design for any given turn – a clearly unreliable analytical starting point. In order to avoid this predicament one could decide to limit one's analysis of speech rate to instances in which speech rate itself was specifically made interactionally relevant by participants themselves. However, this is rarely the case: although prosodic features play an important interactional role, they do so almost always in combination with other linguistic and interactional features. Therefore, a compromise has to be reached. This can consist of measuring (underlying or only realised) syllables per second on the one hand, but continuously taking interactional context into consideration on the other.

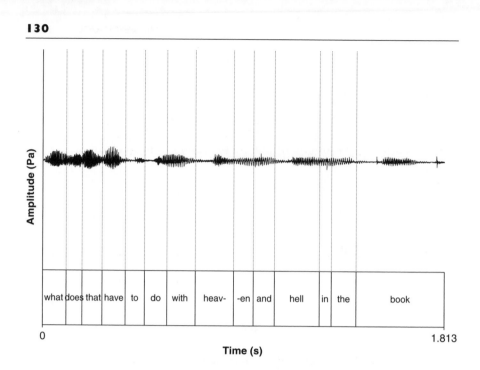

Figure 6.4   Fast speech rate, lines 41–42 in Extract 6.3

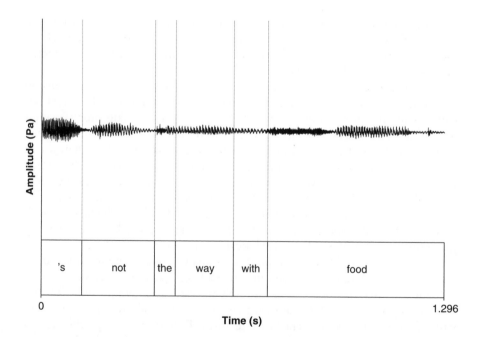

Figure 6.5   Default speech rate, line 10 in Extract 6.3

6.1.1 Summary

The most important aspects of speech rate that have been discussed in this section are:

- Speech rate is both a matter of production and perception.
- Participants speak with varying speech rates; it is therefore important to compare turns perceived as fast or slow with other turns by the same speaker.
- Speech rate can be measured by counting linguistic units per unit of time, such as syllables per second.
- Speech rate can also be measured by comparing syllable duration. In using this method careful consideration must be taken of variations in syllable structure, particularly with regard to consonant clusters.
- Pauses and lengthening play an important part in speech rate and changes in speech rate, by whichever method it is being measured.

6.2 Analysing speech rate

We now take a look at a longer excerpt from a dinner table conversation with an aim to identify and analyse instances of changes in speech rate. The extract below comes from Kendra's birthday party, including her mother Marci, her father Ken, her brother Kevin and her sister-in-law Wendy. The conversation has just turned to Kendra's birthday. At the beginning of the transcribed extract Wendy initiates a sequence concerning her present.

Extract 6.4   SBC013 Appease the monster   🎧

```
 1 Wendy:    well I have;
 2 (0.39)
 3           <<p> a FUN present.>
 4           <<all+p>i'm exCITed about it.>
 5 ((dishes))
 6 Marci:    i THOUGHT i'd [throw KENdie off the sc-
 7 Ken:                    [.hhh
 8 Marci:    OFF the TRAIL.
 9 (0.28)
10 ((dishes))
11 Wendy:    well she's IN there SO[Bbi:ng,
12 Marci:                          [SHUT your [eyeballs kEndie,
13 Wendy:                                     [i HOPE you're hAppy,
14 (0.3)
15 Kevin:    <<len> WENdy hAs;
16 (0.29)
17           TRIED her HAND;
18           for the FIRST time;
```

19		at MAKing a CLUE::.>
20	(0.48)	
21	**Ken:**	<<len> OH:;
22		a CLUE,>
23	(0.34)	
24	**Kevin:**	a [CLUE::.
25	Wendy:	[OH:;
26	Ken:	[is thIs [the kind of clUE that goes from ROOM to
27		ROOM,
28	Wendy:	[STOP it.
29		dOn't [make FUN of me.
30	Kendra:	[is it a REAL one,
31		or is it a-
32	Kevin:	it's [a r-
33	Kendra:	[is it a PERry one.
34	Kevin:	WELL;
35		[it's DEFinitely a pErry one.
36	Ken:	[((cough))
37	**Kevin:**	she [has <<all> FIT into the MOLD.>
38	Kendra:	[O:kay.
39	(0.28)	
40	Ken:	m[m
41	Kevin:	[SHE hAs;
42	(0.29)	
43		<<all> FIT in[to the GROOVE.>
44	Marci:	[ehehe
45	Wendy:	.hh
46		I don't KNOW about that.
47	(0.19)	
48		[but DON'T make FUN of me:;
49	Marci:	[you look pretty PROUD of yourself wEndy,
50	Wendy:	WE:LL -
51		i'm a LITtle proud,
52		<<all> exCEPT if you [thInk it's> ↑STUpid;
53	Kevin:	[ehhh
54	Wendy:	he
55	Kevin:	hehe 🙶

The first change in speech rate occurs during Wendy's first turn in the sequence. After her initial turn constructional unit (TCU) *well I have a fun present* (lines 1–3), she speeds up on her second TCU *I'm excited about it* (line 4).

1	Wendy:	well I have;
2	(0.39)	
3		<<p> a FUN present.>
4		<<all+p> i'm exCITed about it.>
5	((dishes))	

```
6  Marci:   i THOUGHT i'd [throw KENdie off the sc-
7  Ken:                   [.hhh
8  Marci:   OFF the TRAIL.
```

This instance of fast speech rate co-occurs with a decrease in loudness, which was begun on the previous intonation unit *a fun present*. This combination means the TCU in question is presented by its speaker as less prominent than surrounding speech: it takes up less time and is noticeably quieter. The other conversationalists in the room also seem to treat it as of little importance: roughly one second of conversational silence follows, filled only by the sound of dish-washing in the adjoining kitchen; and subsequently Marci comes in with her turn *I thought I'd throw Kendie off the sc- off the trail* (lines 6; 8), which continues a joke previous to Wendy's sequence initiation (prior to the transcribed sequence the participants engaged in a playful sequence of pretending to have forgotten about Kendra's birthday). Thus, all participants involved in this interaction can be seen to treat Wendy's fast and quiet TCU as non-prominent and not requiring a response.

The next noticeable change in speech rate occurs at line 15. As noted above, Wendy's initial attempt at sequence initiation by reference to her present for Kendra is not taken up by any of the other participants. Instead, Marci initiates a sequence concerning an earlier claim that everyone had forgotten about Kendra's birthday (lines 6 and 8). Wendy joins in with this sequence, rather than pursuing her own previous attempt (lines 11 and 13). Subsequently, Wendy's husband Kevin once again reopens a sequence concerning Wendy's present for Kendra. He does so with noticeably slower speech rate:

```
15  Kevin:   <<len> WENdy hAs;
16  (0.29)
17           TRIED her HAND;
18           for the FIRST time;
19           at MAKing a CLUE::..>
20  (0.48)
21  Ken:     <<len> OH:;
22           a CLUE,>
23  (0.34)
24  Kevin:   a CLUE::.
```

Although few of the syllables in Kevin's turn *Wendy has tried her hand for the first time at making a clue* (lines 15–19) contain lengthening, the overall speech rate can still be perceived as relatively slow. This is achieved by Kevin's division of the turn into four intonation phrases, resulting in a slower delivery. In contrast, Ken's mock repair initiation *oh a clue* (lines 21–22) and Kevin's confirmation *a clue* (line 24) are delivered with lengthening on the word *clue*, thus resulting in slow speech rate by extended duration. Interactionally, Kevin's slow speech rate on his reinitiation of the sequence makes this turn longer than could be expected, which means that it takes up a noticeable amount of time. Ken in his next turn matches Kevin's speech rate, and from this emerges a lengthy sequence involving contributions from every participant in the room. The sequence initiation produced with slow speech rate can be contrasted with Wendy's original attempt with fast speech rate and decreased loudness: the slow speech takes up considerably more conversational time and, arguably, weight, and is treated by other participants as initiating a sequence to which they choose to contribute. In contrast, the fast and quiet attempt at initiating a similar sequence is ignored by other participants.

Another change in speech rate occurs later on in the sequence with Kevin's response to Kendra's question whether Wendy's *clue* is *a Perry one*, referring presumably to a family tradition of clues in birthday cards. Kevin's affirmative reply *well it's definitely a perry one* (lines 34–35) is followed by two TCUs with fast speech rate:

```
34 Kevin:    WELL;
35           [it's DEFinitely a pErry one.
36 Ken:      [((cough))
37 Kevin:    she [has <<all> FIT into the MOLD.>
38 Kendra:       [O:kay.
39 (0.28)
40 Ken:      m[m
41 Kevin:     [SHE hAs;
42 (0.29)
43           <<all> FIT into the GROOVE.>
```

Subsequent to his initial response to Kendra's question, Kevin paraphrases his answer *it's definitely a perry one* in two very similar expressions: *she has fit into the mold* (line 37) and *she has fit into the groove* (lines 41–43). In both cases, not the entire TCU is produced with fast speech rate: only the phrases *fit into the mold* and *fit into the groove* are spoken quickly. The fast delivery of those phrases clearly sets them apart from the prosodic production of previous talk. We could argue that the fast speech rate in this case designs the phrases as for-mulaic, similar to Pamela's phrase *what do you mean* in Extract 6.3: as formulaic language is based on frequent repetition of a fixed or ready-made phrase, the prosodic delivery of such phrases is expectably faster than if they were delivered as non-formulaic. We can, however, imagine Kevin producing both TCUs with a more default speech rate; this would change the status of the phrases *fit into the mold/groove* from being used formulaically or 'as one word' to being used flexibly, as words strung together on the fly for this individual purpose. Kevin's fast speech rate is the primary reason we hear the two phrases as formulaic and 'routine', rather than idiosyncratic and 'new'.

A final instance of speech rate change occurs at line 52. In reply to Marci's teasing comment *you look pretty proud of yourself wendy* (line 49), Wendy replies with a turn that contains a short succession of fast syllables:

```
49 Marci:    you look pretty PROUD of yourself wEndy,
50 Wendy:    WE:LL -
51           i'm a LITtle proud,
52           <<all> exCEPT if you thInk it's> ↑STUpid;
```

In Wendy's turn *well i'm a little proud except if you think it's stupid*, the speech rate changes from lengthening on *well*, to default speech rate on *i'm a little proud*, to fast speech rate on *except if you think it's*, and returning to a more default production on *stupid*. The fast delivery of the beginning of this second TCU once again reduces the prominence of the words produced in this way, this time foregrounding what comes after. Wendy's prosody brings out the contrast between the playful accusation of being *proud* and her own fear of being *stupid*. Speeding up on the words leading up to the most significant word, *stupid*, increases its prominence, with additional emphasis being achieved by a high pitch accent.

6.2.1 Exercises

Identify changes in speech rate in the following extracts.

EXERCISE 6.1

In the first extract, the conversationalists are discussing living outside New York.

SBC051 New Yorkers Anonymous 🎧

```
 1 Sean:   well FRAN –
 2         I'VE been lOOking –
 3 (0.29)
 4         REALly;
 5         for a year or TWO;=
 6         at different PLACes to LIVE.=
 7         i went bAck to EUr:ope –
 8 (0.7)
 9 Fran:   mhm,
10 Sean:   <<p> to lOndon and PARis –
11 (1.66)
12         i've been in SUN vAlley -
13         TUCsO:n -
14         i've been-
15         and mOnTANa;
16         SEA:Ttle;
17         i LIKED seattle a LOT.
18 Fran:   m[hm,
19 Sean:    [but i couldn't LIVE there;
20 (1.31)
21         and –
22 (0.51)
23         OUTside of new yOrk;
```

EXERCISE 6.1

(Continued)

24		and i COULDn't go back to live in new yOrk again;=
25		it's been-
26	(0.3)	
27		i'm Over it;
28	(0.33)	
29	Fran:	[mhm,
30	Sean:	[thIs is the best PLACE;
31		i've FOUND; 🙂

EXERCISE 6.2

In the following extract, the young couple Jill and Jeff are discussing the availability of the morning-after pill.

SBC028 Hey Cutie Pie 🎧

1	Jill:	well it's NOT –
2	(0.35)	
3		aVAILable here in the united stAtes;
4		it's only in FRANCE,
5	(0.58)	
6	Jeff:	ENGland,
7	(0.2)	
8	Jill:	and –
9	(0.24)	
10		YEAH;
11		and S:WE:de::n - 🙂

6.3   Research on speech rate in natural conversation: Susanne Uhmann (1992): Contextualising relevance: on some forms and functions of speech rate changes in everyday conversation

In this article Uhmann sets out to investigate speech rate as a 'contextualization cue'. *Contextualisation* is a concept developed in Cook-Gumperz and Gumperz (1976) and Gumperz (1982, 1992), according to which participants use strategies in conversation to create contexts for their talk which aid in its interpretation. Such strategies are referred to as *contextualisation cues*, with prosody being a prime example. In her introduction, Uhmann sets the scene for her article by proposing a change of perspective on speech rate, both in terms of its interpretation as a contextualisation cue, rather than a paralinguistic feature of speech dependent on mood and emotions, and in terms of approaching speech rate from the perspective of perception, rather than production. This latter point is discussed in a section on the perception of speech rate. Uhmann introduces issues and problems surrounding the measurement of speech rate, such as the varying possibilities in counting sounds, words, syllables or accented syllables per unit of time. She then shows convincingly that both the counting of *syllables* per unit of time, and the counting of *accented* syllables per unit of time, have an impact on our perception of speech as fast or slow. The number of syllables per unit of time she refers to as DENSITY I; the number of accented syllables per unit of time is referred to as DENSITY II. The combination of these two measurement techniques allows for a variety of combinations in addition to an unmarked number of both types of syllables: a high/low number of syllables per unit of time, combined with a high/low number of accents. Some of these combinations are later shown to be used for contextualising purposes by participants. However, before analysing speech rate in interaction, Uhmann discusses analysts' treatment of pauses as related to speech rate perception and introduces the distinction between rate of articulation and speech rate. In the former, pauses are not taken into account, whereas in the latter they are. Furthermore, Uhmann identifies the intonation phrase as her basic unit of analysis, arguing that changes in speech rate are best investigated over a relatively small linguistic unit.

In the central section of the article, Uhmann investigates the contextualising role of speech rate in German conversations. She identifies five main functions. The first one is onomatopoeia. Uhmann's example shows a speaker using high speech rate (both in terms of DENSITY I and DENSITY II) on an intonation phrase in which she describes a fast and ineffective doctor's treatment, with the high speech rate contextualising the treatment itself as fast. The second function is self-repair. Uhmann shows that high speech rate is used for intonation phrases, or parts of intonation phrases, which contain self-repair. A third contextualising function of speech rate is signalling parenthesis and side comments. Here, the perception of fast speech rate is created by a combination of high DENSITY I (i.e. a high number of syllables per second) and low DENSITY II (i.e. a low number of accents per second). A fourth function is the contextualisation of afterthoughts and summaries used as turn- or topic-closing strategies. As in the previous case, these instances are characterised by a combination of high DENSITY I and low DENSITY II. The fifth function is as a device for structuring information, specifically regarding relevance. Uhmann defines a turn as more relevant 'if it contains a contribution to the ongoing topic that is not already known to the recipient' (p. 326). In her data, intonation phrases containing talk of low relevance are produced with fast speech rate, once again a combination of high DENSITY I and low DENSITY II. Talk of high relevance is delivered with slow speech rate, with low DENSITY I, but high DENSITY II.

In her summary, Uhmann subsumes all functions of high DENSITY I and low DENSITY II under the term 'low relevance' and suggests that speech rate changes can generally be interpreted as related to degrees of relevance.

FURTHER READING

Speech rate has been described as a prosodic feature by Crystal (1969, pp. 152–6). In interactional linguistics, Barden (1991) and Uhman (1989) have investigated speech rate in German conversation. Szczepek Reed (2006, pp. 50–2) describes matching of speech rate among participants.

In phonetics and phonology the distinction is made between 'rate of articulation' and 'speech rate', see Laver (1994, pp. 539–46). Most work in this area has been done in experimental research or laboratory elicited speech data; among the works that are interesting for analysts of naturally occurring talk are Miller et al. (1984), Pfitzinger (1999), Roach (1998), Scollon (1981), Tauroza and Allison (1990) and Trouvain and Grice (1999).

Time: Speech Rhythm 7

As we have seen, time impacts on conversation in more ways than one. Individual speech events can be lengthened or shortened, and longer stretches of talk can be faster or slower. A third way in which talk is structured temporally is speech rhythm, that is the organisation of speech into regular intervals of time. In this chapter, the notion of speech rhythm is introduced, in particular the rhythmic organisation of English conversation. Section 7.1 also presents different methods for measuring rhythm. Section 7.2 goes on to look at how speech rhythm can be investigated in spontaneous talk and provides exercises from everyday interaction. Section 7.3 presents research on speech rhythm: Susanne Uhmann (1996) investigates beat clashes in natural German conversation, and Elizabeth Couper-Kuhlen (1993) shows that speech rhythm plays an important role for turn-taking in English talk-in-interaction.

7.1 Contrasts in speech rhythm

Many aspects of our physical existence, such as our heartbeat, breathing and walking, are rhythmically organised. It is not surprising, therefore, that we also speak rhythmically. Speech rhythm is a feature of most languages; however, the way in which it is realised may vary from language to language. In standard varieties of English, speech rhythm is accomplished such that speakers place stressed syllables at roughly regular intervals of time. As listeners we perceive this as creating a rhythmic pattern, with every stressed syllable representing a rhythmic beat. Take, for example, the phrase

How was your trip to Belgium?

In this phrase we may want to stress the syllables *how, trip* and *Bel-*:

How was your trip to Belgium?

If a native speaker of English spoke this phrase fluently, the stressed syllables would fall on rhythmic beats. This would mean that the temporal distance between *how* and *trip* would be the same as that between *trip* and *Bel-*. We must mention, however, that this kind of speech rhythm only applies to stretches of fluent talk; there are a number of conversational events that may break the rhythm, such as hesitations or some self-repairs, although these may at times also be organised rhythmically.

The kind of rhythmic structure described in the above example has an effect on the duration of the syllables involved in any given stretch of speech: while the temporal intervals are of roughly the same length, the number of syllables in each interval may nevertheless vary. In the above instance, for example, there are three syllables in the first rhythmic interval (*how was your*) and two in the second and third ones (*trip to / Belgium*). Once the first interval has been established there is an expectation that the next interval will be of similar length. As a result, there is more time to articulate the words *trip to* than there is for the words *how was your*. Hence the syllables in the second interval are likely to be slightly longer than the three syllables in the first interval *how was your*. Generally, as the number of syllables per interval varies, the speech rate necessary for the production of those syllables varies too. The greater the number of syllables per interval, the faster their articulation; and vice versa, the fewer syllables per interval, the slower the speech rate. Thus, those syllables in more 'crowded' intervals are on average shorter than those in intervals with fewer syllables.

Stress-timing and syllable-timing

This difference in syllable duration is the main feature by which languages of the world are described with regard to speech rhythm. Research in phonetics has a long tradition of classifying languages as either *stress-timed* or *syllable-timed*. English is a stress-timed language: stressed syllables are perceived as occurring at regular intervals of time, and syllable duration therefore varies. Other examples of stress-timed languages are German, Russian and Arabic. In syllable-timed languages, on the other hand, syllables seem to be of more equal duration, and each syllable seems to represent a rhythmic beat of its own. Examples of syllable-timed languages are French, Spanish and Mandarin Chinese. The variety of English spoken in Singapore has also been shown to have a tendency towards syllable-timing.

While many researchers have found the categories of stress- and syllable-timing to be valid ways of describing the languages of the world, no language can be classified as entirely one or the other. Therefore, phoneticians have come to think of the two categories as the two ends of a broad spectrum, along which individual languages are situated. Therefore, rather than calling British English a stress-timed language, it is more accurate to call it a language with *a tendency towards stress-timing*. Similarly, French is best described as a language with *a tendency towards syllable-timing*.

It has been claimed above that as listeners we perceive the roughly regular placement of stressed syllables in English as rhythmic. However, if we were to set up a metronome alongside a fluent English speaker, he or she would soon be 'off beat'. This is because, even more so than speech rate, speech rhythm is very much a perceptive category. We perceive speech as rhythmic even if the physical placement of articulatory events does not occur at precisely regular time intervals. The perception of speech rhythm is nevertheless a conversational reality: as we will see in later sections, rhythm plays a major role for turn-taking and potential next speakers seem to monitor the ongoing rhythmic structure of emerging turns.

Speech rhythm in conversation

When we say that speech is organised rhythmically we must define more precisely the domains of speech that follow this pattern. Listening to naturally occurring talk we soon notice that spates of regular rhythm do not last for very long; this is the case even if we apply a perceptive, rather than an instrumental, determination of rhythm. In fact, most rhythmical patterns break down after a maximum of two or three intonation phrases, with the vast majority of rhythmic patterns lasting only three or four beats. Thus we can say that the domain of speech rhythm is the intonation phrase, rather than the turn or the sequence. See, for example, Extract 7.1, in which Doris describes her encounter with a local politician.

Extract 7.1   SBC011 This retirement bit   🎧

> 1 Doris: sO when hE Opened UP on tha:t.
> 2   **and SHE followed THROUGH;**
> 3   **and tOld about her HUSband.**
> 4 (0.93)
> 5   you KNOW,
> 6 (0.8)
> 7 ((door))
> 8   **nOt necessArily that shE would apPROVE of it,**
> 9 (0.67)
> 10   **but at lEAst she wAsn't ↑DISapprOving.**
> 11 (0.29)
> 12 Angela: yeah.
> 13 (0.15)
> 14 Doris: of it. 🙿

Listening to the recording of this extract we can hear that individual stretches of talk are clearly rhythmic. For example, the two intonation phrases at lines 2 and 3 *and she followed through and told about her husband* have a rhythmic structure. However, subsequently the speaker leaves a lengthy silence, followed by a phrase too short to be rhythmically structured (*you know*), as it only contains one stressed syllable, and thus only one rhythmic beat. This is followed by another lengthy pause (lines 6–7). On Doris's next intonation phrase we can once again perceive a rhythmic pattern, *not necessarily that she would approve of it* (line 8); and even more prominently the following intonation phrase *but at least she wasn't disapproving* (line 10) contains stressed syllables at regular intervals.

However, while the two phrases are rhythmically structured in themselves, the second phrase does not continue the rhythm of the first phrase. Once again, an intervening pause breaks up the rhythmic pattern.

Highly regular speech rhythm occurs primarily in fluent spates of talk and within the boundaries of individual intonation phrases. This does not mean that long stretches of speech or even whole conversational sequences cannot be structured according to a certain regularity of occurrences through time. However, the longer we set the domain for speech rhythm, the more allowances we must make for our perception of intervals as being of roughly similar length. In this book, we focus on speech rhythm that can be perceived aurally and measured instrumentally, while always leaving a certain leeway for variability in human perception and speech production. Below we will see that conversational participants themselves orient to highly regular patterns and also to the breaking of these patterns. We therefore take their precision in rhythmic perception as our guide in assuming that a relatively high degree of regularity must be perceivable if we are to classify a stretch of talk as rhythmic.

Before moving on to ways of representing speech rhythm, we must establish what a rhythmic pattern minimally consists of. It has been postulated that in order to speak of a rhythmic pattern, there needs to be a minimum of three rhythmic beats: two are needed to establish the first interval and a third one to produce an equally long second interval. However, listening to spoken language brings up many instances in which a succession of only two regularly placed stressed syllables can be perceived as a rhythmic pattern. This is the case because the length of one interval is all listeners need to hear in order to expect another interval of the same length. This second interval does not necessarily need to be followed by a third beat, as long as it is filled by unstressed syllables or even non-linguistic activities. Therefore I argue here that in order to speak of a rhythmic pattern we need a minimum of two regularly placed stressed syllables or two rhythmic intervals.

When it comes to measuring and representing speech rhythm, there are a number of methods for analysts to use, some very simple, some extremely sophisticated. The following section introduces those methods most frequently used in various phonological traditions.

7.1.1 Measuring speech rhythm aurally

Some of the most groundbreaking work on conversational speech rhythm in English has been done by researchers who simply used their aural skills in defining rhythmic regularity while listening to recordings of natural speech data. For example, they may tap or click while listening, and in doing so locate the rhythmic beats in an ongoing spate of talk. While this method is clearly prone to criticism from an experimental perspective, it takes seriously participants' *in situ* experience of talk and applies it directly to the analysis. Like participants themselves, these researchers rely on their perception of speech as rhythmic, rather than on a superimposed instrumental analysis.

The drawback of this method is the large scope for interpretative freedom in hearing speech as rhythmic. Mere aural analysis is likely to result in the interpretation of many more stretches of talk as rhythmic than an instrumental method would. This is the case because our perceptive interpretation will go a long way to find rhythmic structure, even in cases where actual temporal intervals vary widely. Furthermore, analysts using this approach have to remain entirely focused on the data themselves; as soon as we repeat back to ourselves what we believe we have heard, we are in danger of recreating a more rhythmic pattern than is present in the original. Researchers who have employed this method in the past like to point out that they are not interested in isochronous rhythm, that is precise temporal regularity as measured by instruments, but in rhythm as a perceptive category, that is regularity as perceived by listeners, such as analysts and conversational participants.

7.1.2   Measuring speech rhythm using rhythm indices

A very different approach to speech rhythm is adopted by many experimental researchers. Early instrumental analyses showed that isochronous rhythm, that is perfect equality of time intervals, does not exist in speech, even in the most stress-timed of languages. However, the way in which languages vary in terms of syllable duration, some showing almost equal syllable length, others great variability, seemed to point towards a categorical difference amongst languages. Therefore, phonologists in the experimental field have isolated two main aspects of speech production that help them describe the rhythmic features of a language: syllable structure, which may influence the regularity with which speakers place syllables at regular intervals of time; and vowel length, which shows whether syllable duration tends towards equality or variability in a given language.

In terms of syllable structure, it has been proposed that particularly consonant clusters at the beginning of a syllable may have an effect on the precision with which syllables are placed on the next rhythmic beat. For example, in the phrase

Emi̱ly's o̱lder bro̱ther

the first stressed syllable begins directly on the vowel (*Emi̱ly*), and so does the second one (*o̱lder*); however, the third stressed syllable starts with the consonant cluster *br-* before reaching the vowel (*bro̱ther*). In these cases, research has revealed that when speakers orient to a stress-timed speech rhythm, what is being placed on the next rhythmic beat is not the syllable onset, i.e. the initial consonant(s), but the vowel. Thus, rather than claiming that in stress-timed rhythm speakers place stressed syllables at regular intervals, it is more correct to say that they place the *vowels in stressed syllables* at regular intervals. From this finding derives the practice of measuring speech rhythm from vowel onset, rather than syllable onset.

When it comes to determining whether a language tends towards stress- or syllable-timing, it is helpful to measure the overall variability in syllable duration. As we saw above, syllable-timed languages tend towards equal syllable length, whereas syllable duration in stress-timed languages varies. Following the above point that consonants and consonant clusters can distract from the rhythmically relevant length of a syllable because of the time it takes to artic-ulate them, experimental researchers found that rather than measuring whole syllables to see whether they were of variable or equal length, a much more reli-able way was to measure only the length of the vowel. Languages with an overall tendency towards equal vowel length are classified as tending towards syllable-timing; those with great variety in vowel duration are classified as tending towards stress-timing.

The latter issue of measuring the rhythmic characteristics of a language by comparing vowel length has been explored via the use of a variety of *rhythmic indices*. They typically represent the mean difference in duration between succes-sive pairs of vowels in the utterances analysed. The higher the variability index for a given language, the greater the difference in vowel duration, and thus the stronger the tendency towards stress-timed speech rhythm.

This experimental approach is very useful for the overall classification of lan-guages along the stress-timed–syllable-timed spectrum. The utterances used for analysis are typically instances of read aloud speech, recorded in experimental settings. Therefore, this method does not tell us much about speech rhythm in spontaneous talk, or the role of speech rhythm for individual conversa-tional activities. The very aim of reaching a mean result is in contrast to the necessity of conversation analysis to investigate individual instances of rhythmic talk. Instead, this method focuses on the overall picture of an entire language and allows researchers to make meaningful statements about its phonological structure and rhythmic classification.

7.1.3 Measuring speech rhythm using speech analysis software

In this book I use a way of analysing speech rhythm that combines the advan-tages of both of the above approaches, while hopefully avoiding some of their shortcomings. For the analysis of naturally occurring conversation, an investiga-tive method that takes seriously the experience of participants *in situ* is most appropriate. However, simply tapping along to what we perceive as rhythmic may result in a high degree of subjective interpretation. I therefore suggest iso-lating instances of speech rhythm via an initial aural analysis, followed by a more detailed investigation of specific instances using speech analysis software. This approach allows us to show specific rhythmic intervals as sections in a wave form.

From the experimental approach I take the finding that speakers seem to ori-ent to vowel onsets, rather than syllable onsets, in their production of speech rhythm. However, as the examples below show very clearly, this is not a pattern that can be generalised for all instances of conversational speech: while a certain propensity to orient to vowel onsets can generally be observed, some stretches of talk can be clearly heard as rhythmic, but an analysis from the vowel onset does not show any rhythmic pattern. In many of those cases, a closer investiga-tion shows that participants are at times placing consonant onsets on rhythmic beats. I therefore use a default representation of rhythmic intervals from vowel onsets in stressed syllables, with a continuous awareness that participants may be orienting to the consonantal beginnings, instead. Such awareness is particularly helpful when a stretch of talk can clearly be heard as rhythmic, but the analysis does not show a rhythmic pattern. In such cases, it can help to change the representation from vowel to consonantal onset in order to represent the rhythmic delivery. Regarding the measurement of rhythmic beats from the vowel onset, an analysis of natural data also shows that exceptions have to be made for certain types of consonants: nasals, that is the sounds /m/ and /n/; and approximants, that is the sounds /w/, /r/, /j/ and /l/, are often oriented to by speakers as the beginning of a rhythmic beat, possibly because they contain a high degree of voicing. Furthermore, in instances where these sounds occur before a vowel, the change from consonant to vowel is extremely gradual, so that deciding on a location for the vowel onset would to a degree be a random decision.

Representing individual instances of speech rhythm in wave forms remains as close as possible to the recorded data, while showing the reality of regular rhythmic patterns through instrumental evidence. Take, for example, Extract 7.1. Doris's phrase *but at least she wasn't disapproving* can clearly be heard as rhythmic. Figure 7.1 shows a presentation of this phrase in a wave form with an underlying text tier. The vertical unbroken lines in the text tier below the wave form show the onsets of the stressed syllables. In the case of *least* and *was-*, syllables were measured from their consonant onset, as both begin with approximants. In the case of *dis-*, the measurement starts from the vowel. The last stressed syllable, *-prov-*, is measured from the approximant /r/. The vertical pecked lines across the wave form show the first interval; for the rest of the figure, regular intervals of the same length have been automatically superimposed on the wave form. Thus, in the text tier we can see how the pecked lines representing the regular time intervals and the unbroken lines representing

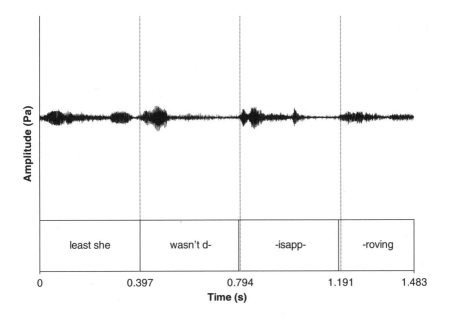

Figure 7.1   Speech rhythm, line 10 in Extract 7.1

actual speech boundaries relate to each other: were they to overlap completely, speech rhythm would be isochronous; were they to be far apart, there would be little evidence of regular rhythm. The phrase represented in Figure 7.1 is an instance of highly regular speech rhythm.

This method of representing speech rhythm is most suited to the analysis of short spates of talk; long extracts would be difficult to represent in this manner. However, this coincides with our general finding that instances of highly regular speech rhythm rarely last for much longer than one or two intonation phrases. In fact, the most rhythmic utterances are typically very short. While researchers using the aural approach have transcribed long passages of talk as rhythmic, the data used for this book suggest that clear rhythmic structure is rarely maintained for such long periods.

While the above method allows for the representation of small rhythmic irregularities, it prevents us from forcing our perception of rhythm onto a spate of talk. However, this method is not very good at representing those instances of talk that sound undeniably rhythmic, but simply do not show regular placement of vowel and syllable onsets. Those instances remind us that speech rhythm is a complex prosodic parameter, depending on a variety of factors, both in terms of perception and production. For example, it may well be that in reality participants sometimes orient to vowel onsets and at other times to consonantal syllable onsets. Similarly, our own perception may at times follow vowels, at other times syllable-initial consonants in perceiving a rhythmic pattern. The most powerful evidence that speech rhythmic patterns exist, even if instrumental analysis cannot always represent it well, is orientation to those patterns by coparticipants during emerging talk. Section 7.2, shows such instances.

7.1.4 Summary

The most important things to bear in mind with relation to speech rhythm are:

- In standard varieties of English, and during fluent talk, speakers place stressed syllables at roughly regular intervals of time.
- The regular placement of stressed syllables on rhythmic beats is called stress-timing.
- The regular placement of stressed syllables on rhythmic beats means that syllable duration varies.
- Other languages and varieties, such as French and Singapore English, have a tendency towards less variation in terms of syllable duration.
- Equal syllable duration is referred to as syllable-timing.
- Languages of the world are situated on a continuum between the two extremes of stress- and syllable-timing.
- Speech rhythm in English can be measured aurally by tapping, or instrumentally by using rhythmic indices or speech analysis software.
- Speech rhythm is very much a perceptive category. The human ear perceives speech patterns as rhythmic, even if the intervals between stressed syllables are not always of precisely the same duration.

- Highly regular speech rhythm typically occurs only over stretches of two or three intonation phrases. Therefore, the intonation phrase is the primary domain of speech rhythm.

7.2 Analysing speech rhythm

We now take a closer look at a longer excerpt from natural talk, to see how we can best analyse speech rhythm in conversation. Hearing speech rhythm is not always easy and spates of talk frequently contain varying degrees of rhythmicity. It is therefore important that we learn to listen out for rhythmic patterns as real acoustic events, rather than hearing what we expect to hear, while at the same time making allowances for the perceptive nature of rhythm. The following excerpt comes from a medical consultation in which dietician Kristen advises patient Paige on managing her diabetes. At the beginning of the transcribed section the two are in the process of putting together a calorie table for Paige's daily meals.

Extract 7.2   SBC041 X units of insulin 🎧

1	Kristen:	kay so thAt gives us a twEnty EIght;=
2		**tO: distrIbute throughOUt the rEst of the DAY:.**
3	(0.9)	
4		A:nd -
5		hh. Uh:m -
6	(0.3)	
7		**mAking a decIsion of HOW to dO tha:t;**
8	(0.15)	
9		rEA:lly invO:lves: (0.15) your INsulins.=
10		NOW –
11	(0.12)	
12		in the MORning;
13	(0.69)	
14		you've got a GOOD aMOUNT;
15		**of rEgular INsulin that you tAke?**
16	Paige:	[Mhm -
17	Kristen:	[so I would want to put a LITtle bit higher percEntage –
18	(0.61)	
19		for your SNA:CK there?
20		[like -
21	Paige:	[Mhm,
22	**Kristen:**	**I would say;**
23		**MAYbe even:;**
24	**(0.31)**	
25		**TEN percent hEre?**
26	**(1.05)**	

27		**Uh:m –**
28	(0.28)	
29	Paige:	tch see i hA:te that SNA::CK;
30		having to EAT SNA:CKS.
31	(0.47)	
32		**I just dOn't have TI:ME.**
33	**(0.81)**	
34		**y' KNOW,**
35	(0.21)	
36	Kristen:	the ONly (0.38) TROUble with thA:t Is;
37	(0.23)	
38		A:t BREAKfas:t;
39	(0.26)	
40		YOU:;
41	(0.28)	
42		**JUST WON'T HA:VE;**
43	(0.5)	
44		your Insulins THE:RE for yOU: -
45	(0.54)	
46		**to EAT –**
47	**(0.18)**	
48		**the B:IG CARbo BREAKfast.=**
49		**T:YPica[lly.**
50	Paige:	[m: -
51	(0.21)	
52	Kristen:	unLE:SS:;
53	(0.13)	
54		you (0.21) RUN ↑HI:GH.
55	(0.3)	
56		After BREAKfast.
57		and then it COMES DO:WN –
58	(0.48)	
59		when the Insulins fInally DO get working.
60	(0.13)	
61	Paige:	[mhm -
62	Kristen:	[but THEN you're running HIGH.
63	(0.15)	
64	Paige:	[mhm -
65	Kristen:	[and thAt's-
66	(0.65)	
67		you know thAt's [the only way to proTECT yourself is;=
68	Paige:	[RI:GHT -
69	Kristen:	YEAH;=
70		**you eat a BUNCH of CARbo;=**
71		**you take a BUNCH of Insulin;**
72	**(0.22)**	
73	**Paige:**	**RI:GH[T -**

```
74  Kristen:        [you RUN HIGH for an hOUr and a hAlf;
75  (0.36)
76                  and then all of a sUdden it comes S::KYrocketing
77                  [DOWN;
78  Paige:          [Mhm –
79  (0.29)
80  Kristen:   when All the INsulins get on [BOARD.
81  Paige:                                  [Mhm -
82  Kristen:   S:O: -
83             Uh:m –
84  (1.03)
85  Paige:     RI:GH[T -
86  Kristen:        [Anyway; 🙶
```

The first instance of very regular speech rhythm occurs in Kirsten's first turn:

```
1  Kristen:   kay so thAt gives us a twEnty EIght;
2             tO: distrIbute throughOUT the rEst of the DAY:.
```

Particularly the second intonation phrase is produced with great regularity. We can hear that the speaker leaves minimal micropauses after each rhythmic beat in order to be able to place the next stressed syllable on the next projected beat. For example, after *distribute* the final [t] is held in an unreleased articulatory position for 0.9 seconds; similarly, the final [t] in *throughout* is held for 0.12 seconds. When we measure and display in a wave form the rhythmic pattern of this phrase (Figure 7.2) we can see that in her placing of stressed syllables on regular time intervals, the speaker orients to the first syllable of *throughout* as the onset of a rhythmic beat. According to its dictionary citation form, this word has only secondary stress on the first syllable, with primary stress on the second. Therefore one may be surprised to find the placement of the first, rather than the second, syllable on the rhythmic beat. However, words such as *throughout*, which contain two syllables, both of which carry lexical stress – one primary, one secondary – can undergo stress shift, with the first, rather than the second, syllable receiving the main stress. However, the case here is slightly more complex: while the first syllable in this particular instance is not stressed in terms of loudness or duration, it is treated as if it were stressed by being placed on a rhythmic beat. In addition to the secondary lexical stress pattern, there is a second explanation for the rhythmic placement of the first syllable. While the word *throughout* consists of two syllables phonologically, the boundary between the two syllables contains no consonant. Thus, the speaker has to move from one vowel /u:/ to the next one /au/ in a single articulatory adjustment. Such syllabic boundaries have a tendency to be more blurred than those containing a consonant, resulting potentially in an almost monosyllabic pronunciation. This effect can be heard clearly when listening to the recording.

The most important point here is that the analysis takes seriously our aural perception of a stretch of talk as rhythmic. In a clear case such as this one, where a whole intonation phrase can be heard to be produced with a regular stress

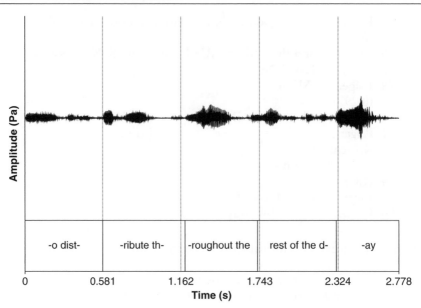

Figure 7.2 *To distribute throughout the rest of the day*, line 2 in Extract 7.2

pattern, we have to test our analysis to find the phrase-internal places to which participants are orienting as rhythmic beats. Such an analysis can at times lead to a deeper understanding of what counts as a prominent place in structure for participants themselves.

Kristen's continuing turn shows more spates of rhythmic talk, interspersed with less rhythmic intervals:

```
 4 Kristen:   A:nd -
 5            hh. Uh:m -
 6 (0.3)
 7            mAking a decIsion of HOW to dO tha:t;
 8 (0.15)
 9            rEA:lly invO:lves: (0.15) your INsulins.=
10            NOW –
11 (0.12)
12            in the MORning;
13 (0.69)
14            yOU've got a GOOD aMOUNT;
15            of rEgular INsulin that you tAke?
```

In this short stretch of speech we can see the turn emerging phrase by phrase. Line 7, *making a decision of how to do that*, is hearably rhythmic. However, Kristen's subsequent continuation *really involves your insulins* (line 9), although grammatically integrated into the prior intonation phrase, does not continue its rhythm and is not itself rhythmically structured. Rather, the word-by-word emergence of this phrase, prosodically apparent by sound and syllable lengthening on *rea:lly* and *invo:lves:*, prevents a coherent rhythmic pattern. Immediately latched on is the beginning of the next syntactic construction: *your insulins now* has a faster speech rate than the surrounding material and is followed by more unrhythmic talk: *in the morning / you've got a good amount* (lines 11–14). These phrases show that talk by native speakers of a stress-timed language is not automatically rhythmic and that rhythmic speech production requires participants to speak with a certain degree of fluency. It is only by the end of this TCU, the phrase *of regular insulin that you take* (line 15), that Kristen again orients to a roughly regular pattern. This is consistent with many other instances in the data where participants seem to increase the rhythmicity of their talk towards the end of potential turns or TCUs. We will see later that this tendency is used by participants to rhythmically integrate their next turns into prior turns by previous speakers.

As we have seen above, a rhythmic pattern can be broken by a participant leaving only a short pause, either internally or externally to an intonation phrase. However, pauses do not necessarily mean that a rhythm cannot be continued. The next instance of rhythmic talk shows that rhythm can be carried across pauses, possibly even across missed beats:

```
22  Kristen:   I would say;
23             MAYbe even:;
24  (0.31)
25             TEN percent hEre?
26  (1.05)
27             Uh:m –
28  (0.28)
29  Paige:     tch see i hA:te that SNA::CK; h.
```

Kristen's turn *i would say maybe even* (lines 22–23) is a clearly rhythmic pattern, as can be seen in Figure 7.3. This initial turn beginning is followed by a noticeable pause of 0.31 seconds. The next stressed syllable *ten* is not placed on the next projected rhythmic beat (see Figure 7.3). However, the following stressed syllable *here* appears to be 'back on track': the wave form shows it to be overlapping with a fourth rhythmic beat, according to the pattern set up by the phrase *i would say maybe even*. Yet, a note of caution is in order here: while this interpretation looks convincing in the wave form, it might well be a coincidence. Listening to the sound file, the rhythmic pattern is not one that can be identified easily.

Subsequently, the speaker establishes a second rhythmic pattern from her phrase *ten percent here* (line 25, Figure 7.4). This phrase is once again followed by a pause, then by *uhm* (line 27). Looking at the wave form (Figure 7.4) we can see that *uhm* is placed on a rhythmic beat and that the intervening pause contains a *silent beat*, that is, a beat which receives no vocalisation. This silent beat is, however, oriented to as a beat by the participant herself, who places the following stressed syllable on the next beat, continuing the established pattern.

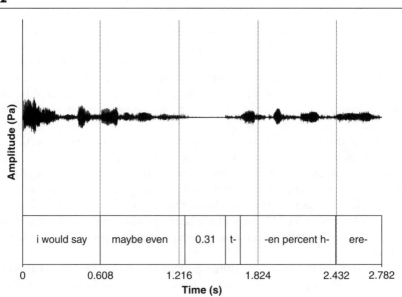

Figure 7.3 *I would say maybe even ten percent here*, lines 22–25 in Extract 7.2

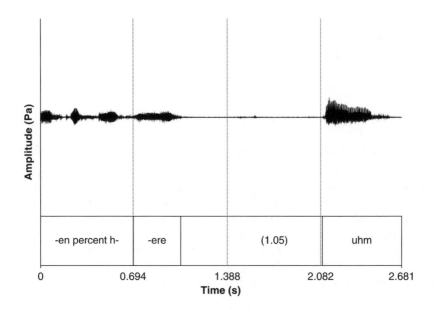

Figure 7.4 *Ten percent here uhm*, lines 25–27 in Extract 7.2

Paige's TCU *i just don't have time* (line 32) is the next intonation phrase to be structured very rhythmically:

```
29  Paige:    tch see i hA:te that SNA::CK; h.
30            having to EAT SNA:CKS.
31  (0.47)
32            I just dOn't have TI:ME.
33  (0.81)
34            y' KNOW,
```

Once again, there is a clearly perceivable regularity in the placement of the stressed syllables *I*, *don't* and *time*. However, the rhythmic pattern only comes out clearly on the wave form if we measure the third beat *time* from the consonant, rather than the vowel onset. Figure 7.5 shows that the rhythmic beat overlaps precisely with the onset of the [t]. The figure also shows that the final word *time* stretches across almost two beats.

Once again, this rhythmic pattern continues beyond a single intonation phrase and across a lengthy pause (line 33). The word *time* itself is lengthened to cover almost two rhythmic intervals and is followed by another silent beat, before the next intonation phrase *you know* begins precisely on the seventh beat in this pattern (Figure 7.6). As was the case in line 2 above, where the word *throughout* was placed on a rhythmic beat starting on an unstressed first syllable, here the phrase *you know* is positioned in a similar manner: the first syllable *you* coincides with the rhythmic beat. This first syllable is strongly contracted to a mere /j/, transcribed above as *y' know*, which points to the participant's treatment

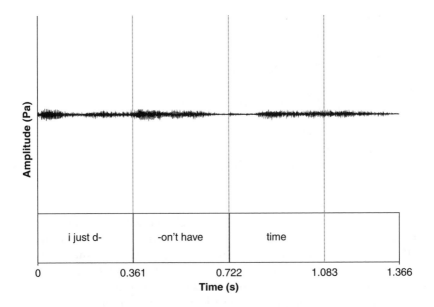

Figure 7.5 *I just don't have time*, line 32 in Extract 7.2

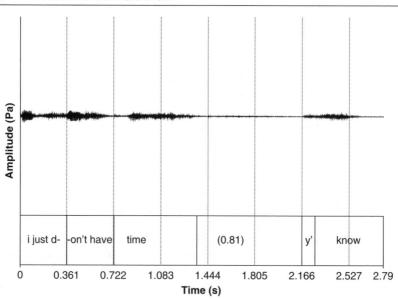

Figure 7.6 *I just don't have time y' know*, lines 32–34 in Extract 7.2

of this phrase as a single entity, rather than as two words. In this single entity, the initial approximant [j] is placed at the beginning of the rhythmic beat.

In the subsequent turn by Kristen we encounter a rare instance of rhythm where each syllable is stressed, resulting in one beat per syllable (*just won't have*, line 42):

```
40  Kristen:   YOU:;
41  (0.28)
42             JUST WON'T HA:VE;
43  (0.5)
44             your Insulins THE:RE for yOU:;
45  (0.54)
46             to EAT –
47  (0.18)
48             the B:IG CARbo BREAKfast.=
49             T:YPically.
```

The practice of placing prominence on each individual syllable creates an increased measure of emphasis on this turn; section 7.3.1 shows Uhmann's (1996) analysis of this phenomenon as a 'beat clash'. Similarly, Kristen's way of packaging her phrase *the big carbo breakfast typically* (Figure 7.7) makes it rhythmically distinct from the surrounding material. Once again, every word receives strong prominence in this phrase, resulting in noticeable emphasis.

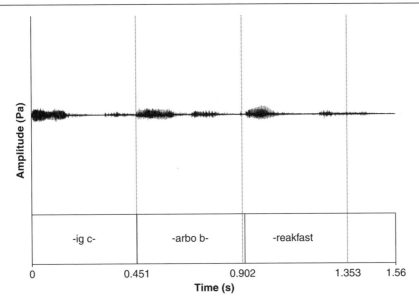

Figure 7.7 *Big carbo breakfast*, line 48 in Extract 7.2

Towards the end of the extract, two instances of speech rhythm can be shown to have an impact on turn-taking. At lines 70–71 Kristen sets up a rhythmic pattern on her phrases *you eat a bunch of carbo you take a bunch of insulin*. Following the rhythmic pattern set up by these four beats Paige comes in with her response token *right* (line 73) on the next projected rhythmic beat (Figure 7.8).

69	Kristen:	YEAH;=
70		you eat a BUNCH of CARbo;=
71		you take a BUNCH of Insulin;
72	(0.22)	
73	Paige:	RI:GH[T -
74	Kristen:	[you RUN HIGH for an hOUr and a hAlf;
75	(0.36)	
76		**and then all of a sUdden it comes S::KYrocketing**
77		**[DOWN;**
78	**Paige:**	**[Mhm –**

Such orientation by an incoming participant to a rhythmic pattern set up by a first speaker shows the interactional reality of participants' use of rhythm. Note the intervening pause between the two turns (line 72): this pause is necessary for Paige to continue the rhythmic pattern-in-progress; it is therefore not a noticeable pause or a sign of hesitation on Paige's part. On the contrary, it is part of her turn design to come in on time and in rhythm with Kristen. Figure 7.9 shows a similar instance. This time, Paige's continuer *mhm* (line 77) overlaps precisely with Kristen's third beat *down* (line 76). This shows once again

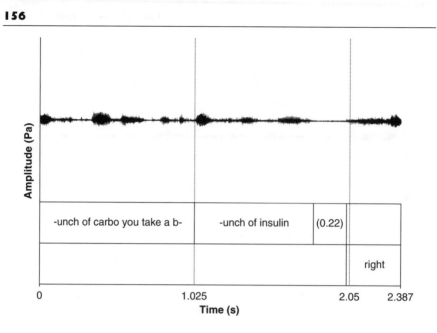

Figure 7.8   *Bunch of carbo, you take a bunch of insulin; right,* **lines 70–73 in Extract 7.2**

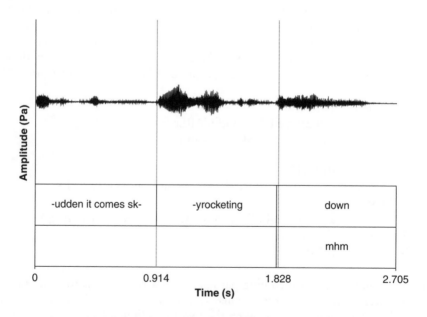

Figure 7.9   *Skyrocketing down; mhm,* **lines 76–77 in Extract 7.2**

how next speakers can at times continue previous participants' speech rhythmic patterns in their onset of next turns.

This kind of rhythmic collaboration highlights a potential role played by speech rhythm for turn-taking. In their accomplishment of smooth transitions from one speaker to the next, participants seem to orient to a continuation of a previously established rhythmic pattern by placing their first stressed syllable on the projected next beat. This topic will be explored in more detail in our overview of Elizabeth Couper-Kuhlen's work on speech rhythm (section 7.3.2).

7.2.1 Exercises

Identify those intonation phrases that are produced with clear rhythmic patterns.

EXERCISE 7.1

In the first extract, Lynne talks about her course in blacksmithing.

SBC001 Actual blacksmithing 🎧

```
 1  Lynne:   tsk uh Oh and it's rEAlly TIRing though.
 2  (0.61)
 3           .hh and it-
 4  (0.11)
 5           you KNOW like;
 6  (0.47)
 7           YOU get stu-
 8           I:'ve (0.33) only dOne like.
 9           .hh
10  (1.36)
11           <<h> WELL –
12           hh.
13  (0.92)
14           at the END of the yEAr;>=
15           now sEE i tOOk the sEcond hAlf of the COURSE;
16  (0.79)
17           A:nd –
18  (0.91)
19           <<len> rIght NOW:;
20           i've PROBably: Only SHO:D abOUt;
21           FIVE HORSES ->
```

EXERCISE 7.2

In the following extract, Lajuan talks about his upbringing.

SBC044 He knows 🎧

1	Lajuan:	i lIstened to my sIster when my nEphew;
2	(0.3)	
3		started COLlege how she was sAYing;
4		.hh
5		SHE filled out All of his applicAtions for where he was gOing: and;
6		.hh
7		SHE did all of these THINGS;=
8		when he had to apply for a SCHOLarship or whatEver;
9		.hh
10		SHE filled out Everything and I'm lI:ke;
11		hh. I did it bY mySE:LF;
12	(0.34)	
13		.hh
14		you READ the fOrm;
15	(0.14)	
16		And you fIll it OUT.
17	(0.41)	
18	Cam:	[m;
19	Lajuan:	[NO one dId it for ME:;
20	(0.51)	
21		.hh you knOw and I was vEry (0.47) mUch –
22	(0.39)	
23		whatEver i NEEDed;
24	(0.53)	
25		.hh
26		i I gOt my mOney from my FA:ther,
27	(0.12)	
28		he paid for SCHOO:L,
29	(0.47)	
30		.hh
31		but –
32	(0.13)	
33		I <<all> did everything on my OWN.>

7.3 Research on speech rhythm in natural conversation

This section presents two important pieces of research in the area of rhythm in natural conversation. Uhmann (1996) shows that rhythmic beat clashes are regularly used by participants in naturally occurring German assessment sequences. Couper-Kuhlen (1993) demonstrates that participants in sponta-neous English talk employ speech rhythm as a resource for turn-taking by continuing previously established rhythmic patterns in their next turns.

7.3.1 Susanne Uhmann (1996): On rhythm in everyday German conversation: beat clashes in assessment utterances

In this article, Susanne Uhmann investigates rhythmic implications for German assessment sequences. After introducing the structure of assessment sequences in English and German, she goes on to give a brief introduction to metrical phonology and its perspective on rhythm. Speech rhythm from a metrical per-spective is closely related to prominence relations between the syllables of any given utterance. According to Selkirk's (1984, p. 52) principle of rhythmic alter-ation, rhythmic patterns in speech by default consist of the alteration between strong and weak syllables, thus avoiding successions of stressed syllables. How-ever, such successions cannot always be avoided, and when they occur, they are referred to as *beat clashes*. Uhmann then begins her analysis of speech rhythm in assessment sequences in naturally occurring German conversations. She shows that in spontaneous talk beat clashes are not accidental occurrences, but are in fact employed by participants for specific interactional goals. In Uhmann's instances of beat clashes, syllables that would otherwise not receive promi-nence are produced with extra emphasis. For example, in one instance the word *entsetzlich* (dreadful), which would normally only receive stress on the second syllable *–setz–*, receives the same degree of prominence on all syllables: *ENT-SETZ-LICH*. The author shows that participants use this practice to emphasise assessment terms: *ENT-SETZ-LICH*, pronounced with a beat-clashing stress pattern, is used by participants to express a concept of 'much more awful' than *entSETZlich*, produced with its default prominence on only one syllable.

Subsequent to these general observations, Uhmann proceeds to show that beat clashes occur only in certain sequential contexts. While assessments as such regularly occur at four different interactional locations, i.e. as firsts or seconds in assessment pairs and as firsts or seconds in news deliveries or story tellings, beat clashes only occur regularly as part of narratives or informings, but not in assessments pairs. Uhmann shows that beat clashes are at times employed by par-ticipants to design assessments as sarcastic, by providing means for exaggeration, or as emotionally charged. The author then goes on to ask why beat clashes can-not be found in assessment pairs, either as first or second assessments. She argues that first assessments containing a beat clash would not allow a next participant to upgrade his or her next assessment any further, although it is often interac-tionally appropriate to do so. A first assessment done with a beat clash leaves nothing to add for a next speaker. The lack of beat clashes in second assessments is explained by their potential role as initiating expanding talk. Uhmann argues that such a strong assessment may not be the preferred choice for a sequence closing. Providing additional prominence to assessment utterances, beat clashes are shown to be used regularly only with certain conversational activities, such as showing appreciation and affect.

7.3.2   Elizabeth Couper-Kuhlen (1993, pp. 115–62): Analysing speech rhythm at turn transitions

Elizabeth Couper-Kuhlen's book *English Speech Rhythm: Form and Function in Everyday Verbal Interaction* introduces rhythm as an important aspect of conversational English prosody. After chapters on isochrony, rhythm as a perceptual category, and metrical representations of rhythm, the fourth chapter turns to speech rhythm in naturally occurring interaction and shows that it plays an integral part for turn transitions in English.

The author starts by reviewing conversation analytic literature which states that the majority of turn transitions in English contain no noticeable gap and no overlap. However, the norm is a short but unnoticeable pause between two turns. Without such a pause, turn transitions are referred to as *latched*, a non-default practice highlighted in most transcription notations. Couper-Kuhlen goes on to introduce the concepts of overlap and pause in relation to turn-taking. Conversation analysts have shown in the past that some turn transitions do involve short stretches of simultaneous talk, referred to as *transitional overlap*. These short periods of two participants speaking at the same time are interpreted as resulting from second speakers' predictions that a turn currently in progress is about to be brought to completion; they are typically analysed as distinct from interruptions, that is illegitimate talk by non-turn holders at points of non-completion.

On the other hand, some turn transitions involve short gaps, or pauses, the duration of which can cause interpretative problems for analysts. Pauses of a certain duration may be noticeable in one context, but not in another. The shortest of gaps may have interactional ramifications in one case, but remain entirely unnoticed in the next. Thus, Couper-Kuhlen highlights two unresolved issues of conversational timing: why is latching not considered the norm for turn transition, if by default participants orient to the no gap/no overlap rule? And why are pauses of similar length meaningful in some contexts, but not in others?

Couper-Kuhlen shows that it is the rhythmic structure of talk that accounts for both these issues, by demonstrating that English turn-taking is rhythmically organised. In what she calls 'a rhythm based metric for turn-taking', she demonstrates that the unmarked case for turn transitions in English is for a next speaker to start up on the next rhythmic beat, as projected by the previously speaking participant, thus maintaining the prior speaker's rhythmic pattern. In order to do so, next speakers have to place their first stressed syllable on the next rhythmic beat. This has strong implications for the role of both pauses and overlap. If a next turn contains unstressed syllables preceding the first strong syllable, it may be necessary for a next participant to start up in overlap with a participant who is in the process of completing a turn, particularly if the turn being completed ends in unstressed syllables. If, however, neither the turn being completed, nor the next turn, contain any unstressed syllables at their end and beginning, respectively, that is if the first turn ends in a stressed syllable and the next turn begins with one, there may well be a gap between the two. This gap is made necessary by the rhythmic pattern in progress. An earlier onset by the next speaker would be too early and thus off-beat.

With these distinctions in mind, turn transitions can be classified as by default *rhythmically integrated*. Next turns may also be *non-integrated*; however, this is the non-default option. Gaps resulting from rhythmic integration may not be noticeable to analysts and typically do not have interactional ramifications, irrespective of their length. However, pauses resulting from a late onset by a next speaker may be noticeable, even if they are very short, because they are part of a non-default turn transition.

In her book, Couper-Kuhlen presents empirical evidence for the rhythmic structuring of turn transitions and the resulting analytical treatment of pauses, overlap and latching. Her chapter provides seminal evidence that any individual aspect of talk, in this case pausing and overlap, must be described and interpreted as part of its immediate interactional context.

FURTHER READING

Rhythm is described as an aspect of prosody in Collins and Mees (2008, pp. 123–32), Cruttenden (1997, pp. 20–2), Crystal (1969, pp. 161–5), Couper-Kuhlen (1986, pp. 51–62) and Laver (1994, pp. 523–33).

In interactional linguistics, two seminal publications are Auer et al. (1999) and Couper-Kuhlen (1993). Further studies of rhythm in naturally occurring conversation include Auer (1990), Auer and Couper-Kuhlen (1994), Couper-Kuhlen (1991, 1992) Couper-Kuhlen and Auer (1991), Cowley (1994), Erickson (1992), Erickson and Shultz (1982), Szczepek Reed (2009, 2010b) and Uhmann (1996).

Among the works discussing the isochrony of speech rhythm are Cutler (1980), Darwin and Donovan (1980), Faure et al. (1980), Hoequist (1983), Jassem et al. (1994), Kohler (1991) and Lehiste (1977).

Among the studies discussing the distinction between stress timing and syllable timing are Benton et al. (2007), Cauldwell (1996), Cummings and Port (1998), Dauer (1983), Dellwo et al. (2007), Laver (1994, pp. 527–32), Marks (1999), Miller (1984) and Roach (1982).

The rhythm indices mentioned in section 7.1.2 are described in Barry et al. (2003), Grabe and Low (2002), Low (2006), Low et al. (2000) and Ramus et al. (1999).

Time: Pauses

Although pauses are by definition instances of absence of speech, they are considered a prosodic phenomenon because of their contribution to the overall nature of talk as temporally organised and situated in time. During interaction, they are made relevant not only when they contribute to prosodic parameters, such as speech rate and rhythm, but also when they become interactional events in their own right. In section 8.1, pauses are introduced as interactionally meaningful phenomena, and a number of important distinctions between different kinds of pauses are presented. In section 8.2, an example is provided of how pauses can be investigated as part of natural talk. Section 8.3 presents two pieces of research on pauses in natural conversation: Local and Kelly (1986) show that participants treat holding pauses as signalling turn continuation, and released pauses as doing turn-yielding. Szczepek Reed (2009) shows that pauses in a specific sequential position define the sequential status of post-pause turns as either first or second pair parts.

8.1 Contrasts through pauses

As we have seen in Chapter 7 on speech rhythm, the fact that participants refrain from speaking does not necessarily have noticeable implications for interaction. Speakers may, for example, remain silent for short periods of time in order to place their first/next stressed syllable on a projected rhythmic beat, either during their own turn or when beginning a new turn following a previous speaker. Conversationalists may also not speak because they are physically unable to do so at a certain point in time, for example because they are about to sneeze, are yawning or have food in their mouth; in all these instances they may well be orienting to the fact that it is their turn to speak, for example through certain types of gestures and direction of gaze. However, in terms of speech production, they are technically 'pausing'. Furthermore, participants who do not currently hold the turn often remain silent for considerable lengths of time. This could also be described as 'pausing'; however, in terms of the rules of conversational turn-taking this is default behaviour. For an analysis of conversation, none of the above instances of silence are what we would consider interactionally relevant pauses; that is they are not treated by participants as absences of otherwise expectable conversational actions. We thus have to be careful to distinguish between pauses that are interactionally meaningful and those that are not. In this book, I therefore define pauses as *noticeable absences of talk*.

One way to differentiate types of pauses is by their sequential location. Put simply, pauses may occur within a single participant's turn or in-between turns by different speakers. However, this distinction between intra-turn and inter-turn pauses is in many instances an analyst's, rather than a participant's: if a speaker pauses at the end of a potential turn, no other participant comes in to speak, and the same participant therefore starts up again, the pause is a turn-internal pause. However, it is only so in retrospect, and as a result of the emerging interactional pattern. If another participant does come in to speak after the pause, and the previously speaking participant does not continue, the same pause is then turn-external. Thus, an interpretation of pauses as internal to turns on the one hand, and in-between turns on the other, is helpful only when it takes the emergent nature of conversation into consideration.

A related question is that concerning which participant a pause 'belongs to'. Once again this is mostly an analytical issue, as with participants *in situ*, pauses emerge with the interaction at hand. If a pause is located at a non-completion point, and a participant's turn is clearly still underway, that silence can under certain circumstances be attributed to that speaker. However, even in such cases there are several possible explanations for pauses; for example, a current speaker may be eliciting a minimal response token which is not being provided by coparticipants. Furthermore, it is not always appropriate to speak of pausing as something participants *do*, which implies a deliberate activity. In many cases, pauses are very much a result of participants' positioning of other interactional events, such as speech, and in the case of face-to-face interaction, gestures, gaze, body posture, etc. In other cases, pauses may indeed be themselves employed as such events.

All the issues mentioned above have an implication for the transcription of pauses in this book. Unless they occur internally to an intonation phrase, as in Extract 8.1, pauses are allocated (a) their own line in the transcript and (b) a position in line with speaker identification, i.e. further to the left of the transcript, rather than in line with the transcribed talk. If we transcribed pauses in line with the transcription of talk, this would imply that we understand them to 'belong to' the participant whose speech is being transcribed up to the pause. A transcription of pauses in line with speaker IDs treats them as interactional events potentially unrelated to any individual participant.

Transcription of the length of pauses also deserves mention here, as different practices are currently in use amongst discourse and conversation analysts. Some transcribers differentiate simply between two kinds of pauses: micropauses, which are perceived by the analyst as being relatively short, and macropauses, which are perceived as relatively long. Transcripts following this principle typically contain two different symbols, such as (.) for micropauses and (-) for macropauses. Other researchers use a symbol such as (.) or # for short pauses of up to 0.2 seconds, while giving exact measurements of any longer silences. This book has adopted the practice of measuring every pause, by creating wave forms of every transcribed extract, and measuring the exact length of any absence of talk. This method allows the analyst to present relatively accurately what lengths of pauses occur in any given interaction. However, it does not allow analysts to indicate in the transcript whether they judge a given pause to be particularly noticeable or whether they perceive the pause as long or short. It is therefore necessary in reading the transcripts to take note of the transcribed length of pauses and of participants' treatment of them. For example, in the following extract in which a couple discuss life after death, the first line contains a very short pause of 0.11 seconds and another one of considerable length at one second. While the first is a typical micropause, the second would be perceived by most analysts as a macropause.

Extract 8.1   SBC007 A book about death 🎧

66 1 Pamela: people who **(0.11)** HAD **(1.0)** TECHnically died;
   2   and thEn had been reVIVED;
   3 (0.3)
   4   **.hh**
   5 (0.4)
   6   SAW –
   7 (0.18)
   8   RELatives COMing for them –
   9 (0.29)
10 Darryl: ts i've READ THAT,
11 (0.64)
12 Pamela: .hh
13   ↑cOUrse ↑THAT may be what hAppen:s: –
14 (0.23)
15   PRIor to the bIgʰ –
16 (1.81)
17   the BIG NOTHing. 99

At lines 3–5 Pamela pauses before she continues with her turn. The overall time during which she refrains from speaking is 0.82 seconds. However, she can be heard to breathe in during this time, which has resulted in the transcription above. An instance such as this raises at least two issues: one concerning our definition of pauses and a second one concerning the observability of conversational activities. Regarding the first issue, the transcription treats breathing as a potentially interactional event (see also line 12). While not every in- or out-breath is necessarily oriented to by participants as relevant, there are many instances where this is the case. Furthermore, in-breaths are often placed on rhythmic beats, thus serving the function of continuing an established rhythmic pattern. It is therefore suggested here that breathing be transcribed, rather than treated as a variation of pausing. However, this opens up the second issue: not all breaths can be heard on a recording, and, more broadly, not all relevant actions, be they related to speech or other physical activities, can be observed in a given analysis. This is the case whether we are working with audio or video recordings; as analysts we can never see, or be aware of, every aspect of an ongoing interaction in the way that participants themselves can. This is particularly relevant to the analysis of pauses: what may seem like a pause to us, i.e. a time interval during which a participant is refraining from speech, may in fact contain activities we as analysts simply are not aware of. For example, a participant may be raising his or her eyes to the ceiling or stroking another participant's arm. Thus, analyses of pauses must always contain a final element of caution, and interpretations of them as interactionally relevant should show that participants in the conversation orient to a pause as a noticeable absence.

At line 9, a 0.29 second pause occurs between Pamela's turn completion (line 8) and Darryl's next turn onset (line 10). This pause is a product of cross-speaker speech rhythm (see Chapter 7). Figure 8.1 shows Pamela's pattern on *RELatives COMing for them*. After a silent beat, Darryl's first stressed syllable *read* overlaps with the next projected rhythmic beat, if we measure the second interval *coming for them* from the consonant onset.

Pauses following potential turn completions always bring up the issue of speaker selection, that is the question whether participants are negotiating over who speaks next. A pause after a potentially completed turn may show that potential next speakers are not volunteering to speak, or at least are hesitating to do so. Pauses at such locations are often also interpreted as evidence for turn completion from current speakers, in that they show that these participants are not continuing their previous turn. However, the above extract shows that any naïve equation of pauses with reluctance to speak misses the many

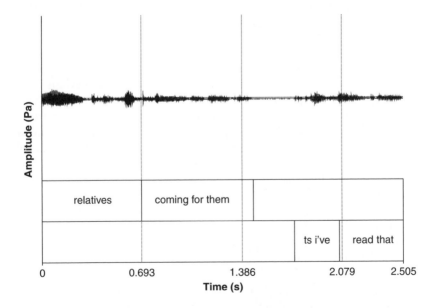

Figure 8.1   Pauses, lines 8–10 in Extract 8.1

other sequential reasons there may be for silence after a completed turn. In this case, the pause is a result of rhythmic integration of the next turn into the previous one.

The 0.64 seconds pause at line 11 is not related to rhythmic integration of the subsequent turn and can be explored for the above-mentioned relation between pauses and turn-taking. Initially, a pause at a potential transition relevance place (TRP) brings up two very simple facts: the first participant is not continuing and no other participant is self-selecting to speak next. While those observations seem rather obvious, they can be interpreted as showing currently speaking participants' treatment of a specific interactional location as a potential TRP and showing potential next speakers' refraining from taking the floor at a TRP. However, this case is not so clear-cut. Pauses can also show that potential next speakers do not treat a previous speaker's utterance as a potentially complete turn, at least not immediately. The turn preceding the pause at line 11, Darryl's turn *i've read that*, ends in a rise-to-mid, which is not a pitch accent that is frequently used in turn completions. Furthermore, in the more global context of this conversation, Darryl's utterance is a comparatively short turn from a participant who before and after this sequence has got much more to say on the topic discussed. The pause at line 11 may therefore show that Pamela is giving Darryl time to continue, thus not treating his turn as complete.

The pause at line 14 follows Pamela's new sequential beginning *course that may be what happens* (line 13). With this intonation phrase she shows that she is presenting a new local beginning by placing a high pitch accent on the first two words *course that*. At the end of this intonation phrase, the final syllable of the word *happens* contains noticeable sound lengthening on the final /n/ and /s/. As we have seen in previous chapters on syllable lengthening and speech rate, pauses often co-occur with lengthening. The final lengthening in this case, coinciding with level pitch and an incomplete syntactic construction, strongly projects more talk to come from Pamela, and thus the subsequent pause can be interpreted as internal to her ongoing turn. Similarly, the pause at line 16 follows a projection of more talk from Pamela. The final sound of the previous intonation phase (line 15), the [g] in *big*, is audibly released with additional aspiration, which can be interpreted as the equivalent to lengthening on a stop consonant. This, in combination with the incomplete syntactic construction and the level pitch accent, creates a clear projection of turn continuation. The remarkably long pause of 1.81 seconds shows the strength of this projection: neither Pamela nor Darryl treat the prepause turn as aborted.

In addition to the pauses that occur at the boundaries between turns and intonation phrases the above extract also contains pauses that are located within an intonation phrase. At line 1 Pamela halts her speech flow for one second in between two stressed syllables belonging to the same intonation phrase. It is clear from listening to the recording that she is designing her talk as projecting continuation, not only of her turn – this is clear from the grammatical structure of the sentence involved – but also of her intonation phrase. This hearing is attributable to the way in which the pause is produced at the level of articulation.

In terms of articulation, pauses can be either *held* or *released*. These terms refer to the state of the vocal folds. In the case of a held pause, the vocal folds are in the state of a glottal stop, that is they are closed, but not vibrating. This is the kind of vocal setting we experience, for example, when we are about to begin a cough. Held pauses frequently occur when participants are in the middle of a turn, and they are often treated as a strong sign that a speaker has not finished (Local and Kelly, 1986; for a summary of their article, see section 8.3.1). In contrast, released pauses are those for which the vocal folds are in a relaxed state, that is wide open and not vibrating. Released pauses are more often instances of no articulatory activity, in contrast to the articulatory effort required for held pauses.

The pause at line 1, above, is a held pause: not only is it characterised by a closure of the vocal folds, but we can also hear that at the end of the word *had* the tip of the tongue is not released from its position near the alveolar ridge, that is behind the upper teeth. Instead, the tip of the tongue is held in this position for the entire length of the pause, until the onset of the next word *technically*, which requires a similar tongue position.

Another instance of a held pause is the following extract from the same conversation. The second pause at line 5 is marked by Pamela's glottal closure, which gives a strong physical projection of more talk.

Extract 8.2   SBC005 A book about death

```
1 Darryl:   <<all> whAt does that have to do with HEAVen and HELL in the
2           BOOK.>
3 (1.66)
4 Pamela:   WELL –
5 (0.48)
6           I'M just sort of;
7           reITerating;
```

A final distinction we have to address in relation to pauses is the notion of 'filled' vs 'unfilled' pauses. Research on conversation frequently mentions filled pauses, a term which refers to non-lexical vocalisations such as *uh, ehm, hm*, etc. See, for example, the following extract in which Tom2 is in the process of closing one part of a narrative sequence and opening another one.

Extract 8.3   SBC032 Handshakes all around

```
1 Tom2:   so I SAILED on hEr for a little whIle.
2 (0.44)
3         uh:m -
4 (0.73)
5         and thEn in F:::IFty:,
```

6   fOrty-NINE i guess;
7 (0.63)
8   [uh a guy named-
9 Tom3:   [now let me STOP you nO:w - 🎗

In-between the closing of the first narrative sequence at line 1 and the initiation of the next narrative sequence at line 5 we observe a silence (line 2), followed by a lengthened *uhm* (line 3), followed by another silence (line 4). This instance of *uhm* is what has traditionally been referred to as a filled pause. The underlying reasoning for this interpretation is that utterances such as this one do nothing more than fill an otherwise empty sequential position with prolonged articulations of reduced vowels, such as /ə/, and nasals, such as /m/, which do not in themselves carry linguistic, that is lexical, meaning. We could say that according to this perspective, filled pauses are looked upon as *absences of linguistic events*, in contrast to our previously established notion of pauses as *absences of talk*. As *uh, ehm*, etc. are not 'words' in the sense that they would appear in a dictionary, a perspective on them as 'filled pauses' treats them as negligible utterances that do nothing more than replace silence.

This view of *uh*, and other vocalisations like it, is no longer compatible with what we now know about the interactional status of these utterances. They have long been shown to do interactional work in their own right. For example, the lengthened *uhm* in the above extract is oriented to by participants as a turn holding device, projecting more talk from the same speaker: in spite of the substantial pause of 0.73 seconds following Tom2's *uhm* other participants do not come in to speak. Instead, Tom2 himself continues. *uhm* in this instance is thus employed by Tom2, and oriented to by the other participants, as projecting more talk to come, and thus as interactionally meaningful.

8.2 Analysing pauses

In this section we take an in-depth look at an extended conversational sequence, analysing the pauses that occur. We specifically focus on the connection between pauses and dispreferred next turns, as this is a wide-ranging area in which pauses have been shown to be particularly relevant. The notion of *preferred* and *dispreferred* turns is typically applied to second pair parts. For example, acceptances of invitations are generally preferred, whereas refusals are typically dispreferred. It is important to note that in this usage the term 'preference' does not refer to participants' personal opinions or attitudes, but to the way in which participants display their treatment of other speakers' turns as default or non-default, or unmarked and marked. Dispreferred turns are typically non-default and linguistically marked, whereas preferred turns show no extraordinary features. Typical contributors to interactional markedness are pauses and other forms of delay.

The extract below is taken from a telephone conversation between Andrew and his sister Darlene. Immediately prior to the transcribed section Andrew has been speaking to his sister Brenda, who then hands over to Darlene. His interaction with Darlene does not start with a greeting, but with a light-hearted exchange between the three participants. The transcript below shows the immediately following interaction.

Extract 8.4   SBC052 Oh you need a breadbox   🎧

1	Andrew:	<<f+h> well MERry CHRISTmas;>
2	Darlene:	MERry [CHRISTmas;
3	Andrew:	[.hh
4		<<f+h> so what YOU been dOing;>
5	**(0.36)**	
6	Darlene:	OH:,
7		RUNning from phOne to phone - =
8		ANswering it;=
9		when Every time you HUNG ↑U:P;
10	**(0.41)**	
11	Andrew:	WHAT,
12	**(0.75)**	
13	Darlene:	dIdn't you CA:LL -
14		have to dIal about FOUR or fIve tImes,
15	**(0.87)**	
16	Andrew:	I sta-
17	**(0.32)**	
18		in u- NO one uh: Ever picked it ↑UP -
19		it rA:ng it'd ring TEN TIMES -
20		and then QUIT.
21	**(0.85)**	
22	Darlene:	OH.
23		SEE –
24	**(0.42)**	
25		sOmething was WRO:NG -
26		<<all> you nEEd to call the tElephone company then> because I –
27	**(0.73)**	
28		EIther ME or ans- uh JENN answered it about fIve tImes.
29	Andrew:	yOU DID?
30	Darlene:	YEAH.
31		the [phOne-
32	Andrew:	[cause WE literally started;
33		the MINute darLENE sa-
34		<<l> UH;
35		NOT darlEne;>
36		jaNINE said;
37		.hh
38		CALL at ONE ↑THIRty.
39	**(0.15)**	
40		o[KAY,
41	Darlene:	[YEAH,
42	Andrew:	.hh::

```
43              A:::nd -
44              abOU:t Every TENTH TI:ME;
45              we'd get pA:st the BUSy ↑CIRcuit thing.
46 Darlene:    YEAH,
47 (0.73)
48 Andrew:     but we got through ↑NOW.
49              whAt's the ↑DIFference.
50 (1.01)
51 Darlene:    [the BUSy CIRcuit tIme -
52 Andrew:     [si-
53 Darlene:    and thEn did you get a BUSy signal hEre sometimes?
54 (0.25)
55 Andrew:     SOMEtImes, 🎧
```

This first noticeable pause occurs at line 5 in the transcript, following Andrew's question *so what you been doing* (line 4).

```
4               <<f+h> so what YOU been dOing.>
5 (0.36)
6 Darlene:     OH:,
7               RUNning from phOne to phone - =
8               ANswering it;=
9               when Every time you HUNG U:P;
```

Telephone opening sequences typically begin with an initial series of adjacency pairs. The ringing of the phone and its answering constitute a summons–answer pair; typically, this is followed by an exchange of greetings (Schegloff, 1986). Following these, participants then frequently initiate pairs of *howareyou*-s. In the telephone conversation above, the summons–answer sequence is replaced by the telephone receiver being handed over from Brenda to Darlene; and the greeting sequence is missing. Thus, the opening interaction between the two participants is their mutual wishes of *merry christmas* (lines 1–2), which compare to a greeting sequence in their adjacency pair structure. Andrew's next turn picks up the default opening pattern with a token of the *howareyou* type (*so what you been doing*, line 4).

The pause that follows this turn occurs at a sequential location at which a next participant, Darlene, has clearly been selected to speak – the pause has to be interpreted in the light of this specific location. Looking ahead to the turn following the pause we see that when Darlene does produce a next turn it contains a complaint: she has been *running from phone to phone answering it when every time* (Andrew) *hung up* (lines 7–9). Complaints are potentially face-threatening activities, as they typically contain criticism of coparticipants, and therefore they are not preferred second pair parts in routine telephone opening sequences. The pause at line 5 can thus be interpreted as relating to the dispreferred nature of the upcoming turn. Next turns that do not follow routine conversational expectations are often temporally deferred; therefore, breaks in speech rhythm and overall conversational flow may often herald upcoming trouble.

Similarly, the following pauses display participants' awareness of interactional problems:

```
 6 Darlene:   OH:,
 7            RUNning from phOne to phone - =
 8            ANswering it;=
 9            when Every time you HUNG ↑U:P;
10 (0.41)
11 Andrew:    WHAT?
12 (0.75)
13 Darlene:   dIdn't you CA:LL-
14            have to dIal about FOUR or fIve tImes?
15 (0.87)
16 Andrew:    I sta-
17 (0.32)
18            in u- NO one uh- Ever picked it ↑UP -
```

Andrew's turn *what* (line 11) is a repair initiation in response to Darlene's complaint. Repair initiations by participants other than the producer of the trouble source are also dispreferred next actions; they are frequently delayed, as potential next speakers give current turn holders the chance to resolve the problem themselves. The pause at line 10 is such a delay of a next turn repair initiation. The repair initiating turn *what* is followed by another silence (line 12), this time a rather lengthy one. A similar pattern can be observed here: as Darlene's complaint clearly identified Andrew as the culprit for the telephone problems, this pause could be seen as her allowing him to resolve the accusation without the necessity for her to expand on the complaint. With no talk from Andrew forthcoming, Darlene resorts to repair herself (lines 13–14). Andrew's next turn is once again delayed (line 15) – another dispreferred pause at a sequential location where he has clearly been allocated the next turn. Following this pause Andrew begins, but aborts an intonation phrase; the subsequent pause is a held one, that is we can hear glottal closure until the onset of the next word *in* (line 18); the beginning parts of the next intonation phrase are similarly held and hesitant. This articulatory delay iconically displays Andrew as 'speechless': he is hearably without words, following his sister's complaint.

From the latter parts of the intonation phrase at line 18 Andrew gathers fluency and subsequently produces a candidate response. This response is in turn followed by another silence:

```
19 Andrew:    it rA:ng it'd ring TEN TIMES -
20            and then QUIT.
21 (0.85)
22 Darlene:   OH;
23            SEE –
24 (0.42)
```

```
25          sOmething was WRO:NG -
26          <<all> you nEEd to call the tElephone company then> because I –
27 (0.73)
28          EIther ME or ans- uh JENN answered it about fIve tImes.
```

Andrew's turn *it'd ring ten times and then quit* (lines 19–20) contains the explanation for his behaviour, which was previously the topic of Darlene's complaint. Her reply *oh* (line 22) shows her to be treating Andrew's turn as genuine news, and in this function *oh* is typically preceded by a pause, as it is here (line 21). Darlene's continuing turn contains two pauses after clear projection of more talk to come: *see* (line 23) is a turn preface, while *because I* (line 26) stops in the middle of a syntactic construction and ends in a level pitch accent. Thus, these pauses are designed as internal to Darlene's emerging turn, delaying a fluent delivery. While there may be a cognitive reason for this delay, conversationally Darlene orients to the 'hold up' created by the pauses by delivering parts of the intervening speech material very quickly. Her phrase *you need to call the telephone company then* (line 26) is produced with high speech rate, which in temporal terms seems to be 'making up' for the time lost while pausing. Such speeding up following a turn internal pause is very frequent and shows participants to be claiming the floor space during the silence retrospectively as theirs.

The next pause in this extract is related to participants' negotiation over turn completion:

```
36 Andrew:   jaNINE said;
37           .hh
38           CALL at ONE ↑THIRty.
39 (0.15)
40           o[KAY,
41 Darlene:   [YEAH,
42 Andrew:   .hh::
43           A:::nd -
```

At line 38, Andrew's turn design can be heard as complete, at least intonationally. He places a high pitch step-up on his final accent *thirty*, followed by a fall-to-low. The following pause of 0.15 seconds may be considered too short to be interactionally relevant; however, it is made relevant by both participants: Andrew's *okay* (line 40) shows his treatment of his previous turn as requiring recompletion, this time explicitly eliciting a reply from Darlene; while Darlene's reply *yeah* displays her acknowledgement that the onus is on her to take the floor, if only temporarily. Andrew's following lengthened in-breath and production of *and* (lines 42–43) show him to take considerable time over his turn continuation, thus potentially orienting to his previous turn design as closed and as handing over to Darlene as potential next speaker.

The final two pauses in our transcript show further instances in which next participants do not seem to provide the type of talk their coparticipants are attempting to elicit from them:

```
43  Andrew:    A:::nd -
44             abOU:t Every TENTH TI:ME;
45             we'd get pA:st the BUSy ↑CIRcuit thing.
46  Darlene:   YEAH,
47  (0.73)
48  Andrew:    but we got through ↑NOW.
49             whAt's the ↑DIFference.
50  (1.01)
51  Darlene:   [the BUSy CIRcuit tIme -
52  Andrew:    [si-
53  Darlene:   and thEn did you get a BUSy signal hEre sometimes?
```

Andrew's turn contains more lengthening (lines 43–44) and once more ends in a high pitch step-up, followed by a final fall-to-low, a clear design of turn completion. Once again, Darlene replies only with a single response token (*yeah*, line 46). Another pause shows Andrew to be orienting again to the possibility of continued talk from Darlene, and Darlene to refrain from such talk (line 47). Andrew's subsequent intonation phrases both end in the same pitch pattern, the second phrase containing a first pair part (*what's the difference*), which now clearly allocates the floor to Darlene (lines 48–49). The following pause of over one second shows another delay, which once again projects a dispreferred next action: when Darlene does come in to speak, it is not with a reply to Andrew's question; instead, it is with an initiation of a new first pair part of her own, which fails to provide both a second pair part, and an answer.

8.2.1 Exercises

Try to identify the pauses in the following excerpts. If you have access to a speech analysis tool, try to measure their exact duration.

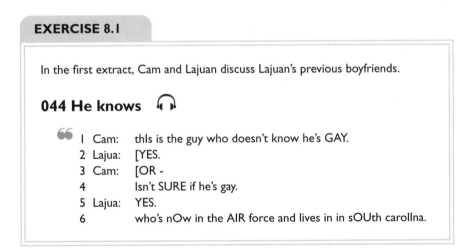

EXERCISE 8.1

In the first extract, Cam and Lajuan discuss Lajuan's previous boyfriends.

044 He knows 🎧

```
  1  Cam:     thIs is the guy who doesn't know he's GAY.
  2  Lajua:   [YES.
  3  Cam:     [OR -
  4           Isn't SURE if he's gay.
  5  Lajua:   YES.
  6           who's nOw in the AIR force and lives in in sOUth carolIna.
```

EXERCISE 8.1

(Continued)

7		SO.
8	Cam:	<<p> WAIT a second.
9		I thought this w- guy t- was was MARried.>
10	Lajua:	RON.
11	Cam:	RON.
12		he's MARried RIGHT?
13	Lajua:	thAt's DARren. 🙶🙶

EXERCISE 8.2

In the following extract, Cindy tells her sister-in-law the reason why she picked a certain kind of Christmas card for her.

SBC052 Oh you need a breadbox 🎧

🙶 1	Cindy:	did uh ↑(Andy) <<all> mention anything about> the uh CARDS,
2		that we got for CHRISTmas,
3	Darle:	UH uh;
4	Cindy:	<<all> CHRISTmas cards,>
5		.hh
6		Oh WHY don't i let hIm tell you because - =
7		it was SOMEthing wE rEAlly got strUck by it because it's uh;
8		whAt is the <<p> POet?
9		or SOMEthing?
10		that DID the VERSE,
11		.hh
12		that your MOM really liked?
13		whAt was [it?>
14	Darle:	[OH:[:: uh:m -
15	Andre:	[<<background> hElen stElner rIce;>
16	Cindy:	YEAH.
17		what's uh-
18		[wait a se-
19	Andre:	[HELen,
20	Cindy:	.hh
21		HELen [stElner RICE or some[thing;
22	Darle:	[(HEL-)
23		[HELen KELLer RICE.
24	Cindy:	or SOMEthing like that.=

EXERCISE 8.2

> **(Continued)**
>
> | 25 | but ANnyway hE was All exclted so we - |
> |---|---|
> | 26 | KINDa made sUre that we - |
> | 27 | sEnt them all to YOU guys; 🙶 |

8.3 Research on pauses in natural conversation

This section presents two pieces of research on pauses in spontaneous interaction. Local and Kelly (1986) show the distinction between pauses that achieve turn-holding and those that 'trail off'. Szczepek Reed (2009) investigates adjacency pairs in broadcast telephone calls and finds that pauses may play a major role in the design of a next turn as responding or as initiating a new sequence.

8.3.1 John Local and John Kelly (1986): Projection and 'silences': notes on phonetic and conversational structure

In this article, Local and Kelly are concerned with different types of projection of next actions during naturally occurring talk. In the first part of their paper they show how certain articulatory practices, such as a specific articulation of *well*, project very specific next actions, such as reported speech. They then turn to silences. Firstly, they show that instances of silences are not necessarily instances of phonetic inactivity: certain pauses may be achieved through glottal closure, that is they may only be released at the beginning of post-silence talk. Secondly, the authors turn their attention to a corpus of conjunctionals such as *well, but, so* and *uh*, followed by pauses. In some cases, the conjunctionals + pause are followed by turn transitions, in others, by talk from the same speaker. Local and Kelly show that the difference can be attributed to participants' orientation to pauses as either 'holding' or 'trailing off'. Holding pauses involve the glottal closure described above, whereas trail-off silences involve no glottal stop, but audible out-breathing.

Following this first finding, the authors show that participants systematically orient to holding and trail-off silences, respectively. Firstly, there seems to be clear evidence that in the majority of cases potential next speakers do not take the floor if a currently speaking participant produces a holding silence. However, if next participants do come in in spite of a holding silence, they either drop out after no more than one syllable or their simultaneous talk is of the kind that can be done in overlap, such as agreement tokens and other non-competitive talk.

Secondly, trail-off silences are typically followed by turn transitions. In instances of trail-off silences where the same participants continue talking, Local and Kelly show that those participants are in fact orienting to the pause as belonging to their coparticipants. Trail-off pauses that are followed by same-speaker talk are instances in which those speaking participants show their orientation to a noticeable absence of response from potential next speakers.

8.3.2 Beatrice Szczepek Reed (2009): Prosodic orientation: a practice for sequence organization in broadcast telephone openings

At the centre of the phenomenon described in this article is the first noticing of the potential for a pause in a certain sequential location. While studying telephone openings in radio phone-in programmes I noticed that some opening sequences contained a pause after the first turn by the host, in which he or she greets the caller and initiates the interaction; while others seemed to contain no pause, that is the first turn by the host was immediately followed by a next turn by the caller. This distinction occurred even in cases where the verbal design of the opening sequences was the same. For example, in two instances in which the host's turn ended in a greeting token, and the caller's first turn on the air started in a greeting token, one instance contained a pause between the two turns, the other one did not.

After making sure there were no technical reasons for this kind of delay, I took a closer look at the turn-by-turn development in those sequences. I found a clear distinction between those that contained a pause and those that did not: most of the opening sequences where the host's introductory turn was followed by a pause before the caller's first turn on the air were sequences in which the caller started a new sequence. Even in cases where the caller's choice of words could have been read in the transcript as a second pair part, if it was preceded by a pause, it typically was also prosodically designed as initiating a new sequence. Cases where there was no pause between the two turns were instances in which the caller's turn was designed as a reply to the host's introduction, typically as part of an adjacency pair.

Consider, for example, Extracts 1.3 and 1.4. In the first extract, the two turns form an adjacency pair, with the caller's greeting clearly designed as a return greeting to the host's. In the second case, the host's introduction ends in a greeting token and the caller's first turn starts with a greeting token. However, sequentially, the caller's turn is clearly not designed as a second greeting to the host's greeting, but is offering a new first greeting. It is then treated as such by the host, who produces a second greeting.

Extract 1.3   Brainteaser: Nigel2 🎧

```
  1 Dave:     next is NIgel HIBbits;
  2           who lives in PRESTwich.
  3           <<h> ↑HI `NI:GE,>
  4 Nigel:    <<h> ↑HI `DA:VE,>
  5 Dave:     <<all> how ARE ya.>
```

6   (0.25)
7   Nigel: .hh
8   nOt too BAD,
9   Dave: GOOD to speak to you agAIn, 🙾

Extract 1.4   Brainteaser: Ann   🎧

🙾 1   Dave: a:nd we have ANN,
2   who lives in GORton.
3   (0.23)
4   who's FIRST.=
5   and then of COURSE,
6   .h
7   After our two callers we do have RAchel back again.
8   .h
9   ANN.
10   HI.
11   (0.26)
12   Ann: <<breathy> HELL:^O:.>
13   Dave: <<breathy> HELL:^O:.>
14   <<h> how ARE you Ann,>
15   (0.25)
16   Ann: I'm FINE,
17   THANKS,
18   Dave: GOOD.
19   WELcome to piccadilly rAdio. 🙾

Although pauses, and the absence of pauses, were the cues that brought this phenomenon to my attention initially, a closer inspection of the data showed that participants employed a wider range of prosodic features to accomplish the distinction between callers' first turns as replying or initiating. In fact, it was not individual participants' use of any individual prosodic feature, but participants' collaborative orientation to each others' prosodic designs that allowed them to distinguish their turns' sequential status in this way. As Extracts 1.3 and 1.4 show, those turns that are designed as replies to previous turns repeat the prosodic features of those first turns; whereas turns that initiate a new sequence do not. In Extract 1.4, Ann's turn *hello* (line 12), which initiates a new adjacency pair, is designed as markedly different from Dave's turn *hi* (line 10); whereas Dave's subsequent return greeting *hello* (line 13) repeats Ann's breathy voice quality, strongly rising-falling pitch contour and lengthening on the /l/. In Extract 1.3, caller Nigel repeats host Dave's high pitch register, pitch step-up on the first syllable, falling-rising intonation contour and vowel lengthening, thus designing his turn as a reply to Dave's turn.

Eventually, I found that it was this practice of *prosodic orientation* (Szczepek Reed, 2006) that was the main interactional device callers used to design their first turns on the air as replies to the host or as new beginnings. While the presence or absence of pauses was highly relevant, it turned out not to be the defining factor, but had to be seen in the wider context of participants' use of prosody.

FURTHER READING

Pauses are described as a prosodic phenomenon in Cruttenden (1997, pp. 30–2), Crystal (1969, pp. 166–72), ten Have (2007, pp. 101–3) and Laver (1994, pp. 535–9).

Pauses have been studied as part of naturally occurring talk in Goodwin (1980), Jefferson (1989), Local and Kelly (1986), Miura (1993), Schegloff (2007, pp. 19–21), Szczepek Reed (2009), Tannen and Saville-Troike (1985), and Wennerstrom and Siegel (2003).

Loudness

This chapter is concerned with loudness, particularly loudness across more than a single syllable. We have seen in Chapter 3 on intonation that a combination of increased loudness, duration and pitch results in the perception of a syllable as stressed. Therefore loudness constantly varies during speech, depending on whether a speaker is producing stressed or unstressed syllables. Furthermore, loudness varies throughout the course of an intonation phrase, as the final syllables are typically softer than those at the beginning. However, loudness is also employed by participants for interactional goals and across longer stretches of talk. Section 9.1 presents the main contrasts in terms of loudness; section 9.2 demonstrates an analysis of loudness in an extended extract of naturally occurring conversation and contains a number of exercises. Section 9.3 presents two instances of conversation analytic research on loudness in interaction. French and Local's (1983; 1986) work on interruptions shows that in cases of turns that are begun while other turn-holders are still speaking, participants make a distinction between those incomings that are louder than the ongoing turn and those that are louder and higher. Those interruptions that are only louder seem to signal that incoming speakers consider themselves to be legitimately taking a turn that should be theirs. Those interruptions that are louder and higher in pitch are treated as illegitimate interruptions. Auer and Rönfeldt's (2004) study of aphasic speech shows that a speech behaviour previously classified as symptomatic of the aphasic impairment can also be analysed as a conversational strategy. Aphasics are shown to employ a decrease and subsequent increase in loudness across intonation phrase boundaries to bridge word-retrieval problems and potential turn competition.

9.1 Contrasts in loudness

The term 'loudness' is used here to describe our perception of the *overall vocal intensity*, or force, with which speech is produced. Speaking intensity depends on the pressure of the air stream during sound production and thus on the respiratory effort and capacity of an individual speaker. Intensity is measured in decibels (dB), with 0 dB being the weakest perceptible sound signal. An average conversation is typically conducted at around 60 dB, whereas whispering occurs at around 30 dB. However, the relation between decibels and our perception of loudness is not straightforward: roughly, an increase in 10 dB translates to a perception of a sound as twice as loud. Thus, ordinary conversational speech is perceived roughly eight times as loud as a whisper.

However, our perception of speech as loud or soft is also highly dependent on other factors. One is the sociolinguistic background of the speakers involved. For example, many non-native speakers of British English coming into conversation with native speakers from 'middle-class' backgrounds notice the soft speaking volume. Therefore, a certain degree of loudness may be perceived as louder than average in a conversation amongst middle-class speakers of British English than, for example, amongst native speakers of German of a similar social background. Furthermore, men typically speak more loudly than women, which can in part be explained by their greater lung capacity, but is probably more convincingly attributed to social conventions. Another factor influencing our perception of speech as loud or soft is the social environment in which a given utterance is made. The same loudness may be perceived as normal in a formal institutional setting where only two participants are conversing, but as soft in a playful family interaction involving several participants.

Finally, interactional factors play a role. Some conversational actions or sequential locations are routinely accomplished more loudly than others; thus, our interpretation of loudness must take into consideration whether a participant is, for example, engaged in a greeting sequence or a sequential aside. A degree of caution is required with regard to analysing and measuring loudness contrasts, both between participants and within single participants' talk. As naturally occurring talk is rarely recorded in a laboratory environment, where speakers would receive individual microphones, variations in loudness can often be due to speakers' varying distances from the microphone, rather than to changes in their speech production. Loudness is generally agreed to be a difficult prosodic parameter to analyse, both because of these technical implications and also because of the challenges in separating its perception from a perception of other features, mainly pitch. The clearest examples of loudness changes co-occur with changes in pitch, and most of our examples below show this overlap.

Measuring loudness instrumentally can be done relatively easily through the use of speech analysis software. In the first instance, sound production can be presented as a wave form, which shows oscillations caused by air pressure during speech. As stressed syllables are produced with greater loudness than unstressed ones, stressed syllables can be seen in the wave form as increases in air pressure. Consider, for example, the analysis of the phrase *you have to take this class* in Figure 9.1, taken from Extract 9.1. The final stress on *class* is clearly visible as the most prominent in the wave form. The same point made in Chapter 2 regarding the length of a sample for instrumental analysis

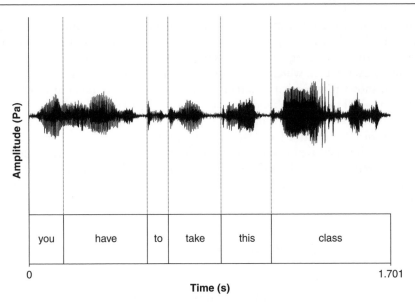

Figure 9.1   Wave form of line 8, Extract 9.1

applies here: if we are interested in detailed changes in loudness across a short spate of talk, it is advisable to analyse extracts that are of a relatively short duration.

Extract 9.1   SBC001 Actual blacksmithing 🎧

```
 1  Lynne:   dOwn thEre um it's MANdatory –
 2           you have to-
 3           to GRADuate,
 4           you KNOW,
 5           wEll to get the deGREE,
 6           you KNOW,
 7           .hh
 8           you HAVE to tAke this ↑CLASS.
 9           .hh
10           and you can ONly ta-
11           if you WANT to you can only take it for EIGHT WEEKS;
```

While it is always helpful to analyse specific stretches of talk instrumentally, our initial analysis of loudness should be an aural and impressionistic one. However, when it comes to identifying changes in loudness in conversational data, one of the most important issues is listeners' tendency to perceive high pitch as louder, even if intensity has not actually increased; vice versa, we perceive a low pitched sound of the same intensity as softer than a higher pitched sound of the same intensity. As this is a perceptual reality, we have to be mindful of its implications when we interpret changes in loudness that co-occur with changes in pitch. The following example, in which a participant uses a falsetto pitch register of around 800 Hz, shows that participants themselves also may make no clear distinction between raised pitch and raised loudness. The extract is taken from a conversation between two friends. Alina is in the process of giving an account of a recent meeting with her relative Jan. Her impersonation of Jan's voice is delivered with a considerable increase in loudness; however, it is most characteristically defined by its extremely high pitched falsetto voice quality. Nevertheless, when Alina later refers to her vocal delivery, she mentions its 'volume', but not its extreme pitch.

Extract 9.2   SBC006 Cuz   🎧

```
66 1 Alina:    NO::;
   2            <<acc> JAN talked the whole time;=
   3            <<falsetto+extra high+all> in a voice like THIS -
   4 (0.44)
   5            <<higher falsetto> HI:: ((alina)) -
   6            i'm so HAPpy to see YOU::;>>
   7            <<laughing> and we're going - >
   8 (0.4)
   9            .hh
  10            <<h> GO::D;
  11 (0.34)
  12            turn the VOLume <<laughing> dOwn;>
  13 (0.18)
  14            .hh
  15            lEt me OUTa HE:RE;> 99
```

Alina's pitch for the speech delivered in falsetto averages around 800 Hz, as can be seen in the frequency analysis in Figure 9.2. It is obvious that this frequency is extreme; this is the only instance of 800 Hz in the entire corpus used for this book. Figure 9.3 shows that Alina's change into falsetto voice is also accompanied by an increase in loudness, and, when she subsequently comments on Jan's voice as portrayed by her, she refers to this aspect, rather than the extreme pitch: *God turn the volume down* (lines 10–12). This is evidence from a participant's own perspective that our perception of overall pitch and overall loudness are closely connected, such that a reference to loudness be used as referring to pitch and loudness combined.

While perceiving high pitch as louder and low pitch as softer is a normal aspect of human perception, there is also a conversational relation between the two features of pitch and loudness. In natural talk, high pitch and increased loudness frequently occur together and, similarly, we often find that low pitch

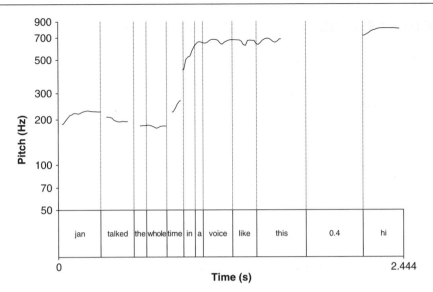

Figure 9.2   Pitch changes in lines 2–5, Extract 9.2

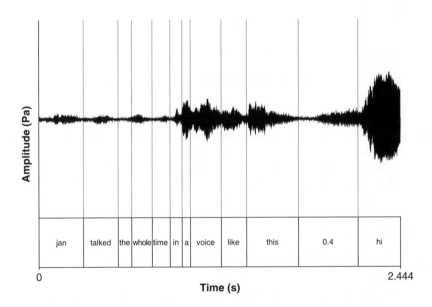

Figure 9.3   Loudness changes in lines 2–5, Extract 9.2

co-occurs with a soft speaking volume. This shows that the correlation holds not only for speech perception, but also for speech production: participants themselves frequently employ loudness and pitch in combination. For a typical example of combined raised pitch register and loudness, consider the following extract from a family birthday party.

Extract 9.3   SBC013 Appease the monster 🎧

```
  1  Marci:     THIS stuff is G:OOD.=
  2             it's like SPARKling:;
  3             GRAPE JUICE -
  4  (0.45)
  5             COCKtAll,
  6             or SOMEthing:,
  7             you KNOW –
  8  (0.13)
  9             remEmber that whi[te-
 10  Wendy:                       [<<h+f> they Only make that> with nUtrasweet
 11             though;
 12             do-
 13             DON'T they;
 14  (0.24)
 15             they don't mAke (0.44) REGular –
 16  (0.42)
 17  Marci:     a REGular grape?=
 18             I don't KNOW;
 19  (0.55)
 20  Wendy:     Every time i've LOOKED at bot- that bOttled WAter;
 21  (0.14)
 22             or the SPARKling WAter;
 23             [it's All with-
 24  Marci:     [but they don't make THIS kind at ↑A:LL anymore.
```

At lines 10–11 Wendy interrupts Marci at a non-completion point, that is Marci had not shown any signs of turn closure prior to Wendy's turn onset. Wendy's interruption is characterised by a combination of high pitch and increased loudness. This combined prosodic design accompanies the first half of Wendy's first intonation phrase, after which she returns to her default pitch and loudness (see Figures 9.4 and 9.5). This instance shows that increases in pitch and loudness may be employed for short stretches of talk at a time. A combined use of the two features also frequently occurs on single syllables; we have already mentioned the combination of increased loudness, pitch and duration for linguistic stress. However, words and syllables may also be emphasised beyond their expectable degree of prominence, and in such extreme cases, pitch and loudness also frequently work together. An example is Marci's prosodic design of the word *all* at line 24, which is made particularly prominent by a combination of marked loudness, increase in pitch and lengthening (see Figures 9.6 and 9.7).

At the other end of the spectrum, decreases in loudness often co-occur with low pitch. In the following extract, Stephanie tells her mother about a college that used to organise sit-ins, before it became more conservative. Figures 9.8 and 9.9 show the low pitch register and decreased loudness on the phrase *the sit ins*, compared to higher pitch register and loudness on surrounding speech.

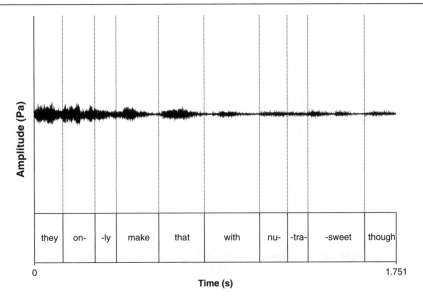

Figure 9.4   Local increase in loudness in lines 10–11, Extract 9.3

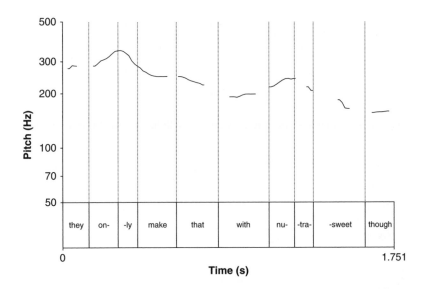

Figure 9.5   Local increase in pitch register in lines 10–11, Extract 9.3

Extract 9.4   SBC035 Hold my breath

1 Stephanie: <<h> THEY HA:D;
2 (0.76)
3   YEARS agO;
4 (0.12)

5   THEY HA:D;>
6   **<<l+p> the SIT I:NS - >**
7 (0.12)
8   EVErything you know;
9 (0.24)
10   REal LIBeral;
11 (0.17)
12   NOW they're going to conSERvative; 99

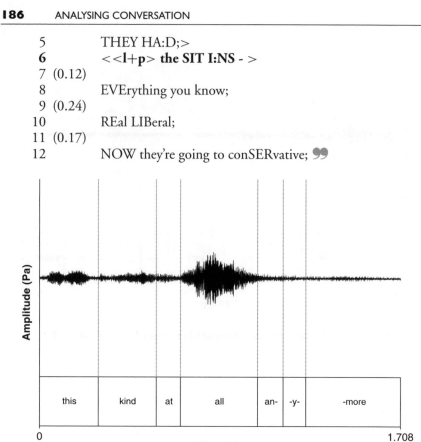

Figure 9.6 Increase in loudness on one syllable in line 24, Extract 9.3

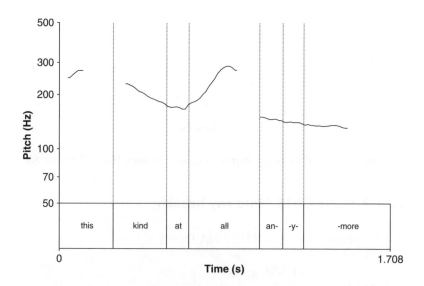

Figure 9.7 Increase in pitch on one syllable in line 24, Extract 9.3

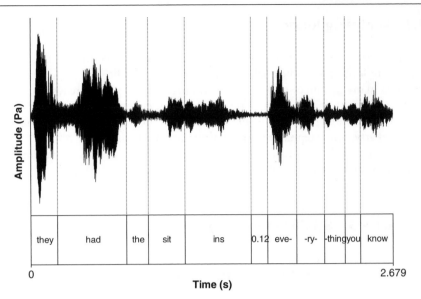

Figure 9.8   Decrease in loudness in lines 5–8, Extract 9.4

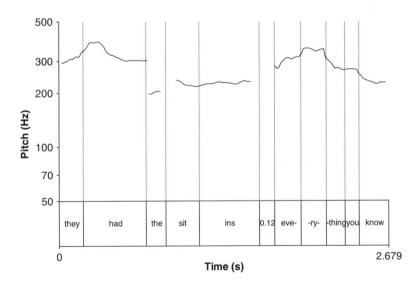

Figure 9.9   Decrease in pitch register in lines 5–8, Extract 9.4

This combination of pitch and loudness is particularly common in certain inter-actional environments. As we will see in section 9.3.1, French and Local (1986) show that one such environment is that of turn competitive incomings, as shown in Extract 9.3, line 10. However, at times loudness alone is also employed and oriented to by participants as an interactionally relevant prosodic factor, as the next section demonstrates.

9.2 Analysing loudness

In this section an extended conversational sequence is investigated to see how changes in loudness can be analysed as part of natural talk. The sequence below contains many instances of overlap, so in order to prepare an analysis it is necessary to listen to it a number of times. However, changes in loudness are most frequent, and most relevant, in the vicinity of turn competition. Stephanie, her mother Patty, and Stephanie's friend Erika are discussing SAT results. Immediately prior to this sequence, Patty has suggested special classes that improve students' results, which Stephanie dismisses as *learning tricks* (line 2).

Extract 9.5   SBC035 Hold my breath 🎧

```
 1  Stephanie:   YEAH:;
 2               but thAt's jUst by learning TRICKS.=
 3               i KNOW what the trIcks are.=
 4               that's ALL you need to KNOW.
 5  Erika:       TEACH them to [me.
 6  Stephanie:                 [<<f> the Only [way you can-
 7  Patty:                                    [<<f+h> but whAt you HAVE to
 8               remEm[ber I:s that-
 9  Stephanie:        [<<f+h> the Only way you can SCORE high> <<dim> is if you
10               READ a lot.>
11               [THAT'S ALL.
12  Patty:       [<<f+h> what you HAVE to re[MEMber is;>
13  Stephanie:                               [you CAN'T study;
14  Patty:       <<f> that the SAT is nOt a whole mEAsure of WHO you A[RE.>=
15  Stephanie:                                                         [<<h+f>
16               ↑OH i [↑KNOW;>
17  Patty:             [<<f> it dOEsn't measure your creaTIVity,>
18               [<<dim> it does[n't ((measure [you)) so;>
19  Stephanie:   [↑MOM;
20                             [i KNOW;
21                                      [MOM;
22               i'm not SAYing that;
23               but i DO need to have a better SAT score;
24               <<p> for appli↑CAtions.>
25  (0.46)
26               so i WANT to bring it ↑U:P.
27  (0.24)
28  Patty:       what'd you sAY your SCORE was?
29  (0.16)
30  Stephanie:   TEN SEVenty.
31  (2.32)
32  Erika:       I'd [be happy to get seven HUNdred.
33  Patty:          [well you'd ONly taken it ONCE so;
34  (0.5)
35  Stephanie:   <<breathy> YEAH::;>
36  (0.3)
37  Patty:       i thInk CLAIRE [took hers [a cOUple times;>
38  Stephanie:                  [WHAT,
```

39	Erika:	[i said I'd be happy to get seven HUNdred.
40	(0.36)	
41	Stephanie:	I- i mEAn-
42		YEAH;
43		pEOple in my SCHOOL;
44		when I told them my SCORE were like;
45		OH;
46		YOU won't need to take it again,
47		but THEN like;
48		**my frIEnds who have like <<f> THIRTEEN F:IFty on their S[AT[s>**
49	Erika:	[WHO'S
50		THAT;
51	Patty:	[but
52		((stephanie;))
53	Gail:	[yeah but I mean you can you CAN'T comPARE yourself;
54	**Patty:**	**[<<f> you CANnot comPARE yourself;**
55		**you are unIQUE[ly ↑YOU;>**
56	Stephanie:	[MARK,
57	**Patty:**	**[<<f> you CAN'T [↑DO that;>**
58	Stephanie:	[JOHN,
59	Erika:	[GLEN,
60	**Stephanie:**	**<<ff> GLEN got s::::- >**
61		**<<f> WHAT;**
62	**(0.28)**	
63		**GLEN got F:IFTEEN S:EVenty> [or something like that;**
64	**Patty:**	**[(((Stephanie))**
65		**<<f> you CANnot com- >**
66	**Stephanie:**	**<<f> I was like you make me SICK.>**
67	**Patty:**	**((Stephanie))**
68	**Erika:**	**[(((but dOn't you be like GLEN I:s.))**
69	**Patty:**	**[<<f> you CAN'T comPARE your[self.>**
70	Stephanie:	[I know;
71		glEn has to like
72	(0.16)	
73		[get DATES through the comPUTer.
74	**Erika:**	**[<<f+h> hOw do you think I: feel> when i get around [glE:n.**
75	**Patty:**	**[<<f+h> when you**
76		**LEARN that you cAn't compAre;>**
77		**you'll REALly be grown Up.**
78	**Patty:**	**you are uNIQUE[ly YOU.**
79	**Stephanie:**	**[<<h+f> NO:;**
80		**i m[EAn - >**
81	**Patty:**	**[you are <<f> NOT like [anybody ELSE.>**
82	**Stephanie:**	**[<<h+f> I-**
83		**( )**
84		**[MOM;>**
85	**Patty:**	**[<<f> you have [to acCEPT that.>**
86	**Stephanie:**	**[<<f> the REAson i'm SAYing> that i need to bring**
87		**them Up;**
88		**and the fact that Other people have higher SCORES;**
89	**(0.41)**	
90		**Is that;**
91		**i DO need to bring them up from ten SEVenty;**
92		**if i want to have a better CHANCE;**
93		**at getting into COLleges.** 🙶

The first instance of a change in loudness occurs at line 6. Stephanie comes in to speak during the final part of Erika's prior turn and is immediately interrupted by her mother Patty:

```
 5  Erika:      TEACH them to [me.
 6  Stephanie:                 [<<f> the Only [way you can-
 7  Patty:                                 [<<f+h> but whAt you HAVE to
 8              remEm[ber I:s that-
 9  Stephanie:       [<<f+h> the Only way you can SCORE high> <<dim> is if you
10              READ a lot.>
11              [THAT'S ALL.
12  Patty:      [<<f+h> what you HAVE to re[MEMber is;>
13  Stephanie:                              [you CAN'T study;
14  Patty:      <<f> that the SAT is nOt a whole mEAsure of WHO you A[RE.>=
15  Stephanie:                                                       [<<h+f>
16              ↑OH i [↑KNOW;>
17  Patty:            [<<f> it dOEsn't measure your creaTIVity,>
18              [<<dim> it does[n't ((measure [you)) so;>
19  Stephanie:  [↑MOM;
20                             [i KNOW;
21                                       [MOM;
22              i'm not SAYing that;
23              but i DO need to have a better SAT score;
24              <<p> for appli↑CAtions.>
```

Stephanie's incoming turn at line 6 is slightly early and overlaps with the last word *me* of Erika's turn. This type of overlap is a case of turn transitional overlap, that is it occurs in the vicinity of a transition relevance place. Instances of turn transitional overlap are not typically treated or designed as illegitimate in terms of turn-taking and Stephanie's increase in overall loudness is unlikely to be influenced by it. However, as soon as she has started to speak, her mother comes in with a turn of her own. It is therefore possible that Stephanie has detected signs of imminent turn onset in her mother's facial or gestural expressions and is designing her turn as if already in competition with her mother's. Research by French and Local (1986), summarised below, shows that an increase in loudness is used by participants to show themselves to be legitimate current turn-holders, whereas illegitimate interruptions are designed with an increase in both loudness and overall pitch register. Stephanie's prosodic behaviour seems to pre-empt a scenario of being interrupted, as she designs herself as the legitimate turn-holder even when there is not yet any hearable sign of turn competition.

Both Patty's and Stephanie's next turns (lines 7–9) display the prosodic design for competitive interaction: both use an increase in loudness, combined with an increase in pitch register. Patty aborts her turn as she finds herself in direct competition with Stephanie. As soon as Stephanie's turn is in the clear, her prosody drops back to unmarked pitch and loudness.

Immediately after Stephanie's turn constructional unit (TCU) ending at line 10, Patty recycles her previously aborted turn, once again with the prosodic design of an illegitimate interruption, that is high loudness and pitch register (line 12). Stephanie continues at her unmarked loudness and pitch register, a practice by which she shows herself to be a legitimate current turn-holder who does not take up the fight for the floor (lines 11 and 13). As her turn is brought to completion, Patty's pitch register returns to a default level, while her loudness remains raised (line 14). This post-overlap use of increased loudness shows Patty to be employing loudness as an emphasis marker, underlining the point she is making to her daughter.

Stephanie's next turn *oh I know* (lines 15–16) is also delivered with increased loudness and increased pitch register. As it occurs in complete overlap with Patty, we can once again interpret it as a turn designed for floor competition. Patty's talk remains at a level of increased loudness while Stephanie interrupts her (lines 16–17); in overlap with Stephanie's next high pitched interruption, which is a direct plea for her attention (*mom*, line 19), Patty's loudness decreases gradually as her turn gradually fades out (line 18).

Patty's decrease in loudness across her two intonation phrases *it doesn't measure your creativity / it doesn't measure you so* (lines 17–18) also shows another sequential use of loudness changes, first identified by Goldberg (1978). She showed that a gradual decrease in loudness is the default practice for designing next talk by the same participant as a 'within-sequence affiliate' (p. 207) to prior talk. That is participants routinely gradually lower their loudness in the course of a continuing sequence. A new sequential beginning, on the other hand, is typically accompanied by an upward shift in loudness. The latter finding corresponds with Couper-Kulen's (2004) evidence that new beginnings are accomplished with an increase in pitch and loudness. This sequential role of loudness can be seen in Patty's successive phrases: her second intonation phrase is clearly produced with softer volume than her first phrase, while on a thematic level it continues her list of non-attributes of the SAT scores.

Stephanie's turn (lines 19–24), once in the clear, returns to a default pitch and loudness level, diminishing gradually and ending in a soft intonation phrase (*for applications*, line 24). Soft loudness on final turn elements such as this one display participants' confidence that no other speaker will interrupt them, as this is the turn location most prone to overlap, even if it is not turn competitive. Thus, Stephanie's decrease in loudness after prolonged prior turn competition shows her to display herself as a current turn-holder who has 'nothing to fear' from participants at this moment in time.

The next instance of noticeable loudness increase occurs on Stephanie's telling of her friends' SAT scores:

47 Stephanie: but THEN like;
48   my frIEnds who have like <<f> THIRTEEN F:IFty on their SATs>

A local increase in loudness over an individual item such as this one (*thirteen fifty on their SATs*) shows prominence due to contrast, in this case a score of *thirteen fifty* by one of Stephanie's friends over her own of *ten seventy*. Participants' employment of loudness increase for emphasis is an iconic use of prosody, by which an increase in physical breath force is used to communicate an increase in interactional prominence. During the ensuing sequence, more changes in loudness occur, mainly in relation to turn competition and emphasis:

```
48  Stephanie:   my frIEnds who have like <<f> THIRTEEN F:IFty on their S[AT[s>
49  Erika:                                                              [WHO'S
50               THAT;
51  Patty:                                                                [but
52               ((stephanie;))
53  Gail:        [yeah but I mean you can you CAN'T comPARE yourself;
54  Patty:       [<<f> you CANnot comPARE yourself;
55               you are uNIQUE[ly ↑YOU;>
56  Stephanie:              [MARK,
57  Patty:       [<<f> you CAN'T [↑DO that;>
58  Stephanie:   [JOHN,
59  Erika:                    [GLEN,
60  Stephanie:   <<ff> GLEN got s::::- >
61               <<f> WHAT;
62  (0.28)
63               GLEN got F:IFTEEN S:EVenty> [or something like that;
64  Patty:                                  [(((Stephanie))
65               <<f> you CANnot com- >
66  Stephanie:   <<f> I was like you make me SICK.>
67  Patty:       ((Stephanie))
68  Erika:       [(((but dOn't you be like GLEN I:s.))
69  Patty:       [<<f> you CAN'T comPARE yourself.>
```

Interestingly, in this sequence only one participant designs her turns as floor competitive: Patty's TCUs *you cannot compare yourself you are uniquely you* (lines 54–55) and *you can't do that* (line 57) are noticeably loud; however, the recipient of these turns, Stephanie, does not raise her volume. In fact, she does not even design her talk as in interaction with Patty, but continues interacting with Erika. Stephanie provides a reply to Erika's previous question *who's that* (lines 49–50) in her turn *Mark John* (lines 56, 58), which overlaps entirely with Patty's louder talk without acknowledging it. When she does raise her loudness for her turn *Glen got s- what Glen got fifteen seventy* (lines 60–63), this is once again a marker of increased emphasis, rather than a sign of turn competition with her mother.

In the final sequence of this extract, loudness is raised both by Patty and Stephanie, as they are in turn competition with each other. Initially, Erika secures the floor by raising her loudness and her overall pitch register when she starts up simultaneously with Stephanie after a brief pause in the middle of Stephanie's emerging turn (lines 72–74):

```
70  Stephanie:   I know;
71               glEn has to like
72  (0.16)
73               [get DATES through the comPUter.
74  Erika:       [<<f+h> hOw do you think I: feel> when i get around [glE:n.
75  Patty:                                                           [<<f+h> when you
76               LEARN that you cAn't compAre;>
```

77		you'll REALly be grown Up.
78	Patty:	you are uNIQUE[ly YOU.
79	Stephanie:	[<<h+f> NO:;
80		i m[EAn - >
81	Patty:	[you are <<f> NOT like [anybody ELSE.>
82	Stephanie:	[<<h+f> I-
83		( )
84		[MOM;>
85	Patty:	[<<f> you have [to acCEPT that.>
86	Stephanie:	[<<f> the REAson i'm SAYing> that i need to bring
87		them Up;
88		and the fact that Other people have higher SCORES;

Once Erika's turn is in the clear, her loudness and pitch register return to her neutral level. The same practice is employed by Patty in her immediately following turn: subsequent to Erika's illegitimate interruption, Patty interrupts Erika, using the same prosodic design, that is increased loudness and high pitch register; and similarly she returns to her usual prosodic delivery once her speech is not in overlap with anyone else's (lines 75–77).

Stephanie's use of pitch and loudness at lines 79–80 and 82–84 once again confirms the relevance of these prosodic features for turn competition. Coming in to speak at a non- transition relevance place (TRP), she uses high pitch and loudness; however, both turns are aborted while Patty, who increases her loudness in reaction to Stephanie's interruptions, positions herself as the current turn-holder.

9.2.1 Exercises

Identify changes in loudness in the following extract. Try to distinguish between instances of gradual changes in loudness, such as a participant's voices *becoming* louder or softer throughout an utterance, and sudden changes in loudness.

EXERCISE 9.1

In the first extract, Richard tells his brother Fred about his new job as a car salesman.

SBC047 On the lot 🎧

1	Richard:	it's LONEly coming home after pUtting in t- twelve hours on the
2		LOT - = and wOrking All DAY and -
3		yOU know wOrking all EVEning - =
4		and then you don't have anybody to come home and SHARE it
5		with.

EXERCISE 9.1

(Continued)

```
 6  (0.32)
 7  Fred:      YEAH;
 8  (0.54)
 9             .hh
10             a- are y-
11             are yOU WORKing twelve hours?
12  (0.23)
13             you're go[nna be-
14  Richard:            [YEAH,
15  (0.13)
16  Fred:      you're [gonna be DOing that?
17  Richard:          [YEAH,
18  (0.23)
19  Fred:      [NINE to NINE?
20  Richard:   [DEFinitely;
21             NINE to NINE.
22             WELL I m-
23             IF I wA:nt. 99
```

EXERCISE 9.2

In the following extract, three elderly friends have just finished a discussion about growing basil.

SBC011 This retirement bit 🎧

```
 1  Doris:    is your CIGarette OUt -
 2  (0.31)
 3            EverybOdy's -
 4  (0.22)
 5  Angela:   yEAh.=
 6            it's OUT.
 7  (1.95)
 8  Doris:    you smOked it dOwn into the (0.18) CORK.=
 9            DIDn't you.
10  (1.1)
11  Angela:   PARdon?
12  (0.41)
13  Doris:    .hh
14            you SMOKED it DOWN Into the CORK.
15  (0.54)
```

EXERCISE 9.2

(Continued)

16	Angela:	.hh
17		WELL;
18		YEAH;
19		YOU don't LIKE that;
20		DO you but;
21	(0.38)	
22	Doris:	NO it CHOKES me to DEATH.
23	(0.2)	
24	Angela:	it's-
25	Doris:	ehehe
26	(0.3)	
27	Angela:	It's THE:RE;=
28		might as well SMOKE it;
29	(0.28)	
30	Doris:	OH:;
31	(0.36)	
32	Angela:	hehe
33	(1.4)	
34	Doris:	.hh
35		NO GOOD.
36	(0.33)	
37	Angela:	NO GOOD. 99

9.3 Research on loudness in natural conversation

While high pitch and raised loudness co-occur in many sequential contexts, there are instances in which the distinction between raised loudness on the one hand, and a combination of raised loudness and raised pitch register on the other, are interactionally relevant. French and Local (1986) show that for illegitimate interruptions, that is instances in which next participants initiate turns while other turn-holders are still speaking, participants orient to interrupting turns that are higher *and* louder differently than to those that are only louder. Their study therefore provides evidence for the fact that conversational participants distinguish between different clusters of prosodic features.

Auer and Rönfeldt (2004) investigate the speech of a man with aphasia. They find that his 'prolixity', that is his tendency to speak at great length and with increased loudness, a speech behaviour traditionally classified as a symptom of aphasic impairment, is much better understood as a strategy for covering up word-finding problems and potential interruption. Their study is a fascinating example of how aspects of talk, when studied from the perspective of participants themselves, can be understood as participants' resources for the accomplishment of conversational goals, rather than only as cognitive functions or, as in this case, malfunctions.

9.3.1   Peter French and John Local (1986): Prosodic features and the management of interruptions

In this paper, Peter French and John Local investigate instances of conversational interruptions and participants' orientation to certain combinations of prosodic features in the context of interruptions. After an introductory section on their methodology, the authors differentiate between two types of interruptions, turn-competitive and non-competitive, and define only the first type as their object of study. That is they are interested in interruptions 'in which one speaker comes in clearly prior to the completion of another's turn and can be heard as directly competing with the other for possession of the turn' (p. 159). The authors show in a selection of data extracts that the mere positioning of interruptive speech at a non-completion point does not make that speech turn-competitive, nor does its thematic relation to prior speech per se define it as competitive or non-competitive. The main feature of turn-competitive interruptions is their prosodic design as higher and louder than talk by current turn-holders, and higher and louder than the interrupter's previous speech.

The authors provide four pieces of evidence for this claim. First of all, the prosodic design of <h+f> is only sustained as long as the overlapping talk continues. It is dropped as soon as the interrupted participant stops talking. The second piece of evidence is the most relevant in terms of loudness: whereas participants who are being overlapped by non-competitive talk continue their turns with default pitch register and loudness, those who are being illegitimately interrupted raise their loudness and decrease their speech rate. The third piece of evidence again relates to a comparison between competitive and non-competitive talk. Participants who are being overlapped by non-high, non-loud speech can be seen to give their interrupters time to complete their turn, before resuming their own talk, rather than competing for the floor by raising their speaking volume. The fourth piece of evidence for participants' orientation to <h+f> as turn-competitive is turn-holders' prosodic design after hesitations. If turn-competitive talk has started during a hesitation which was clearly not designed as a turn completion, original turn-holders resume their talk by raising only their volume but not their pitch. This shows again that one way of designing talk as legitimately turn-holding is to increase loudness but not pitch.

9.3.2   Peter Auer and Barbara Rönfeldt (2004): Prolixity as adaptation: prosody and turn-taking in German conversation with a fluent aphasic

Auer and Rönfeldt begin by introducing their area of study: prosodic features of fluent aphasic speech, in particular a symptom known as 'prolixity'. In lay terms, prolixity refers to an excessive use of words in speech or writing. However, in the diagnosis of aphasia, it describes patients' incapability to control outpourings of speech. The patient analysed by the authors is diagnosed as having poorly developed control over his verbal output. In this diagnosis, the patient's perceived continuous claim to the floor is attributed to the cortical brain injury causing the aphasia.

The first transcribed data extract from a conversation between the aphasic patient and an interviewer shows clearly that the patient himself is aware of his prolixity. He refers to it as 'waffling' in the face of word-searching problems: continuing talk allows him to search for words while not losing the floor to other speakers. The patient himself expresses regret at having to use such strategies when 'proper' speech should be more 'precise'. This is the first strong evidence that the problem is not (only) located in the brain, but is employed as a conscious strategy for managing talk.

Following on from this point the authors move on to investigate a possible link between turn-taking and the patient's word-finding problems. They find a prosodic pattern at the heart of the phenomenon: reduction in loudness at the end of one intonation phrase, followed by a sudden increase in loudness at the beginning of the next one. The authors call this pattern *diminuendo & forte restart*.

After introductory remarks concerning loudness as a prosodic feature of conversation, and the use of loudness in unimpaired talk, the authors go on to investigate the diminuendo&forte restart pattern as a strategy in aphasic speech. Their main finding concerns the sequential location of the pattern within the narrative structure of the patient's turns. Loudness is reduced in places where the most relevant information is expected, even though no turn-transition is in preparation. Neither of these practices follow default conversational patterns. The moment of diminuendo overlaps precisely with a moment where vital information is not accessible to the patient, ending in unsuccessful word-searches and leaving the turn-in-progress syntactically and semantically incomplete. Thus, the intonation phrase is designed prosodically as ending, through the use of the decline in loudness; however, syntactically and semantically, it is incomplete, with the most vital piece of information missing from it. These intonation phrases are followed by a sudden increase in loudness on subsequent talk. The intonation phrases immediately following the diminuendo typically continue the overall narrative, either with grammatically dependent subclauses or with new subtopics. This practice enables the participant to make the problematic word-searches 'disappear' acoustically, while quickly moving on to a continuation of the narrative and turn-in-progress.

What is described by doctors and other coparticipants of the patient as uncontrolled outpouring of speech is revealed as a conversational strategy, similar to floor-holding devices such as the 'rush-through' (Schegloff, 1998) at potential turn endings in the face of turn competition. By concealing the word-retrieval problem, the patient saves face and remains in control of floor distribution.

FURTHER READING

Acoustic aspects of loudness are part of acoustic phonetics; see, for example, Clark and Yallop (1995, pp. 222–36), Fry (1979), Johnson (2003), Ladefoged (1962/1996), Lieberman and Blumstein (1988) and Stevens (2000).

Loudness as a prosodic feature is discussed in Cruttenden (1997, p. 2–3), Crystal (1969, pp. 156–61) and Laver (1994, pp. 500–8).

Work in interactional linguistics relating to loudness includes Auer and Rönfeldt (2004), French and Local (1986), Goldberg (1978), Jefferson (1983), Local and Walker (2004) and Szczepek Reed (2006, pp. 46–50, 57–60, 119–23).

Voice Quality

The term voice quality describes a speaker's vocal configurations beyond those for individual sounds, pitch and loudness, although all three may be affected by certain vocal settings. Some of the more frequently encountered voice qualities are breathy voice, whisper, creaky voice and falsetto. Individual voice qualities are often referred to as articulatory *settings*, a term which implies a rather long-term physiological state, in contrast to more short-term modifications made for the articulation of individual sounds. This is indeed the perspective that has traditionally been adopted for the study of voice quality. John Laver, who has written the most in-depth account of voice quality to date, defines it as 'the long-term average configuration of the vocal organs. This configuration constitutes the setting underlying the more momentary segmental articulations' (Laver, 1980/2009, p. 13). From this point of view, voice quality is what gives an individual speaker his or her unique vocal identity. However, in this chapter we will see that voice quality can also be employed on a short-term basis for the accomplishment of specific conversational actions.

Most approaches to the study of language do not consider voice quality a part of linguistics proper. As it is typically perceived as speakers' overall vocal setting, that is as a 'quasi-permanent' aspect of their speech (Abercrombie, 1967, p. 91), voice quality is not considered contrastive for the signalling of linguistic meaning, at least not in English.[1] It does not, for example, contribute to English grammatical structure in the way that stress and pitch have been shown to do. However, there are several reasons why it makes sense to include voice quality in an investigation of English talk-in-interaction. Firstly, certain vocal settings, such as nasality, are considered a voice quality when they accompany longer stretches of speech; however, when they contribute to the manner of articulation of certain sounds, as in the case of [m] or [n], they are considered linguistically relevant. Therefore, a purely temporal distinction is made between the same voice quality, occurring over the course of a single segment, and a longer utterance. This distinction is the one we have described in our introductory chapter as the one between 'segmental' and 'suprasegmental' aspects of speech, with the term *segmental* referring to aspects relating to individual sounds, or *segments*; and the term *suprasegmental* referring to stretches of speech longer than an individual segment. The line between these two domains is not always clear-cut. For example, while protruding lips create the articulatory setting known as *labial protrusion*, the pronunciation of the word 'soon' would involve the same lip rounding, not only on the vowel /u:/, but already on the first consonant /s/, in anticipation of the rounded vowel. This process, known as *assimilation*, or *coarticulation*, means that the same articulatory activity is spread over more than one segment. Thus, articulatory settings are clearly relevant to stretches of speech of varying length.

Secondly, voice quality deserves a place in any approach to linguistics that takes language seriously as a resource for social action. As we will see in the following sections, vocal settings are not necessarily always 'quasi-permanent' features of individual speakers, although of course they can be. Voice quality can also accompany speech for the duration of a single word, utterance, turn, or conversational sequence. When it does, we can often observe it to play an interactional role. Therefore a distinction must be made between an individual speaker's *habitual voice quality* and his or her *temporarily contrastive voice quality*. The former may involve a vocal setting that remains in place for the duration of an entire conversation, for a certain social environment, for the time of a certain physical condition or for a speaker's entire life. Like overall voice range and pitch range, voice quality is part of a broader construction of sociolinguistic identity which locates an individual as of a certain age, gender, health condition or ethnic background, and simultaneously defines his or her speech as unique.

Speakers use voice quality contrastively and temporarily in identifiable interactional environments, where they change into particular vocal settings, at specific sequential locations, and can be seen to employ those settings with observable interactional impact. In those instances, voice quality becomes interactionally relevant and can be analysed for its role in the construction of meaning in locally emerging conversation. Thus, in this book voice quality is considered a conversationally relevant prosodic feature in cases where it is employed by participants as *interactionally contrastive*. It is therefore treated as a suprasegmental feature of talk that can be analysed alongside other prosodic features such as pitch, loudness and time, if it is clearly employed by participants in the same way, that is as a resource for constructing and interpreting interactional meaning.

Section 10.1 introduces different vocal settings and describes in detail those that are most frequently made interactionally relevant: creaky voice, falsetto and breathy voice. Section 10.2 demonstrates how those voice qualities can be investigated as part of natural talk. The section also provides extracts that will allow readers to practice their analytical skills in identifying different vocal settings. Section 10.3 presents research on voice quality in conversation. Ogden (2004) shows how in Finnish conversation combinations of various voice qualities contribute to turn completion and turn yielding, respectively. Szczepek Reed (2006) shows how conversational participants match previous speakers' voice qualities in certain interactional contexts.

10.1 Contrasts in voice quality

When articulation is achieved with what we would consider default settings for a non-impaired speaker, this is called *modal voice quality* or *neutral setting*. In describing modifications in a speaker's voice quality, we can make a basic phonetic distinction between two articulatory places where the vocal organs are modified: inside the larynx, that is modifications in the type of vibration of the vocal folds, and outside the larynx, that is modifications affecting the shape of the vocal tract. All of the settings described in greater detail below are of the first type. We therefore begin by briefly introducing the second type of settings, as they may be shown to be interactionally relevant by future research. Our descriptions follow for the most part John Laver's book *The Phonetic Description of Voice Quality* (1980/2009).

Vocal settings that affect the shape of the vocal tract are referred to as *supralaryngeal settings*. They can be divided into three basic types: those that lengthen or shorten the vocal tract (*longitudinal settings*); those that widen or narrow it (*latitudinal settings*); and those that affect nasality (*velopharyngeal settings*). There are two ways by which the vocal tract can be lengthened or shortened: by raising or lowering the larynx, and by protruding or retracting the lips. Position of the larynx is most prominently relevant for different styles of singing: traditionally classical opera singers use a lowered larynx, while some popular singing styles require a raised larynx. During speech, the position of the larynx can also have clearly identifiable effects on overall voice quality. Speaking with a raised larynx is usually part of an overall tense voice production, which may result in a slightly higher overall pitch range. In contrast, lowering the larynx often has the effect of lowering overall fundamental frequency. Lowered larynx voice is associated with some varieties of English, such as Received Pronunciation. Trained news readers can often be heard to speak with a lowered larynx, which gives their voice a dark and authoritative quality. However, most speakers whose native variety does not involve lowering the larynx have to learn the muscular processes involved in manipulating the position of the larynx through vocal training.

At the other end of the vocal tract, a small degree of length can be added by protruding the lips. As in the case of lowering the larynx, *labial protrusion* also slightly lowers overall fundamental frequency. In contrast, the vocal tract can be minimally shortened by retracting and raising the lower lip (*labiodentalized voice*), although this has little effect on audible voice production.

Articulatory settings that widen or narrow the vocal tract are settings brought about by the lips (*labial settings*), the tongue (*lingual settings*), the faucal pillars (*faucal settings*), the pharynx (*pharyngeal settings*) and the jaw (*mandibular settings*). The lips can expand or constrict the space between them, either horizontally or vertically, in addition to the above mentioned option of protruding or retracting. This leads to a large number of theoretically possible options (such as horizontal expansion plus vertical constriction plus labial protrusion; or horizontal expansion plus vertical expansion without protrusion), only very few of which are used regularly. For interactional purposes the most relevant voice quality in terms of latitudinal lip settings is the so-called 'smiley voice', which is sometimes mentioned in conversation analytic literature. However, closer examination of instances of actual smiley voice may reveal that it is not only the lip configuration that contributes to our perception of a speaker's voice production as smiley, but also other vocal cues typically associated with laughing.

The tongue can be manipulated for different settings at various places, such as the tip and blade of the tongue, the body of the tongue or the root of the tongue. In all these cases, articulatory settings are produced by changes from the neutral tongue position. The result is usually a slight change in vowel quality, since tongue shape is most centrally involved in the process of articulating vowels. The greatest impact on voice quality is made by moving the body of the tongue forwards and upwards, a vocal setting referred to as *palatalized voice*, which is the basis of some speakers' version of 'baby-talk' (Laver, 1980/2009, p. 47; Pike, 1947, p. 66).

Constrictions of the vocal tract caused by the faucal muscles and the muscles of the pharynx wall are typically aspects of an overall tense voice, which has been described in the past as being of a 'metallic' quality. The position of the jaw influences speech production mostly in terms of the degree of closure: standard varieties of British English are often described as employing a lower jaw that remains raised. This vocal setting has a considerable effect on voice quality, and may in the future emerge as one being employed by participants for interactional purposes. Similarly, nasality is a distinctly recognizable articulatory setting. Put very simply, nasal voice quality is the result of the voice resonating in the nose, instead of, or as well as, in the mouth. This is routinely the case for nasal consonants, such as [m] and [n], but it can also be added to otherwise non-nasal vowel sounds.

The contrasts in voice quality that have proven so far to be most interactionally relevant are creaky voice, falsetto voice and breathy voice. All three are settings that are affected by changes in *phonation*, that is vocal fold vibration, and are therefore referred to as *phonatory settings*.

10.1.1   Creaky voice

Creaky voice is sometimes also referred to as *vocal/glottal fry*. This vocal setting is typically accompanied by extremely low fundamental frequency, which is why we often find it at the end of an intonational declination line, and thus at the end of intonation phrases, TCUs and turns. Its effect is one of individual pulses, famously compared to the sound of a stick being run along railings (Catford, cited in Laver, 1994, p. 195). The extract below from a family birthday party contains an instance of creaky voice quality. The transcript starts with a sequence initiated by Marci.

Extract 10.1   SBC013 Appease the monster 🎧

    1 Marci: <<h> whY do these CA:NS:;
    2   get so WARPED.
    3   Only the-

```
 4  (0.1)
 5              Only the> SAM'S clUb cAns get so wArped.
 6  (1.02)
 7  Wendy:     I [think you should [write-
 8  Ken:          [cause they're-
 9  Kendra:                             [cAUse they're  [CHEAP CA:NS;
10  Wendy:                                              [just-
11  Kendra:    [that's WHY;
12  Wendy:     [write a LETter to 'em;=
13             and com<<creaky> PLAIN mArci.> 99
```

Wendy's turn *i think you should write- just write a letter to 'em and complain Marci* (lines 7, 10, 12–13) ends in creaky voice on the final three syllables – *plain Marci*. In terms of the overall pitch contour of this turn, we can hear that Wendy's pitch accent on *letter to 'em* (line 12) ends in a fall-to-mid; however, it is located rather low in her pitch range. In order to bring the declination line down to a fall-to-low, she has to drop below this level. As she does so, her voice enters a creaky setting. Compare this turn to Marci's turn ending *only the sam's club cans get so warped* at line 5. Here, too, a turn is ended with a fall-to-low; however, Marci does so while remaining in her neutral articulatory setting.

As creaky voice typically involves very low pitch, it can be found most frequently in sequential environments in which low frequencies are common. Such environments include turn endings, as was already pointed out by Laver (1980/2009, p. 126): 'in English … speakers of Received Pronunciation often use creak or creaky voice, simultaneously with a low falling intonation, as a signal of completion of their turn as speaker, yielding the floor to the listener'. Conversation analytic research has produced similar findings, such as Ogden (2004), whose work on creaky voice in Finnish conversations is summarized in section 10.3.1.

As I mentioned above, it is also possible for participants to speak with an articulatory setting for much longer. In the case of creaky voice, it is unlikely that a speaker would be able to sustain this setting for a whole conversation, as it is difficult to maintain on higher pitch accents. However, some speakers do use creaky voice as their default setting to which they return frequently and for long stretches of talk. Speakers of American English varieties have often been linked anecdotally to this practice. See, for example, the speaker in the following extract. Michael uses a creaky voice setting for the majority of his speech; however, when he employs higher pitch accents, his voice changes to a more neutral setting.

Extract 10.2   SBC017 Wonderful abstract notions 🎧

```
66  1  Michael:  <<creaky> but there's ONE techNOLogy that's uh:m;
    2  (0.19)
    3            gonna overtake THA:T and that's;
    4  (0.17)
```

```
 5              d: n A research.
 6 (0.12)
 7              WHICH is: -
 8              LIKE –
 9 (0.11)
10              a TOtal SCAM at THIS point STILL it's;
11              they're just like (0.18) bomBARDing;
12              .hh
13 (0.75)
14              ORganisms with radiAtion to see what comes UP.
15 (0.31)
16              .hh
17              you KNOW;
18              we have vEry little conTROL over it;
19              but once we> ↑DO;
20 (0.58)
21              .hh
22              we'll be able to prOgrA:m –
23              <<creaky> biOlogy as WELL.>
24 (0.83)
25 Jim:         well THA:T'S pretty <<creaky> frIghtening cOncept.>
26 Michael:     it IS <<creaky> frIghtening but- >
27 (0.3)
28 Jim:         we [cAn't even <<creaky> control our FREEways.>
29 Michael:        [<<creaky> UH:M - > 🙶
```

In this extract, Michael speaks in creaky voice almost continuously. At line 19, however, he employs a rising-falling pitch accent on the word *do*, for which he briefly changes to a more neutral setting. Following this, his voice gradually returns to a creaky voice (line 23). Similarly, his slightly higher pitched words *it is* (line 26) are produced in a neutral setting, before he returns to creaky voice. Coparticipant Jim also uses predominantly creaky voice quality. In both speakers, we can hear that the creaky quality of their voices is a matter of degree, being most prominent on very low pitched talk.

Figure 10.1 shows Michael's speech before the rising-falling pitch accent *do* as located relatively low, between 54 and 85 Hz, whereas his rising pitch reaches 140 Hz at its highest point.

Another phonatory setting, *harsh voice*, is similar to creaky voice in that it also gives the auditory impression of a series of taps. However, harsh voice does not involve the same low fundamental frequency and is rarely continued for longer periods of time. Our corpus contains no example of harsh voice, but is often anecdotally mentioned as co-occurring with extreme displays of anger.

10.1.2 Falsetto

Falsetto voice quality is often associated with singing; however, it also plays a role in conversational speech. Its most prominent characteristic is its fundamental

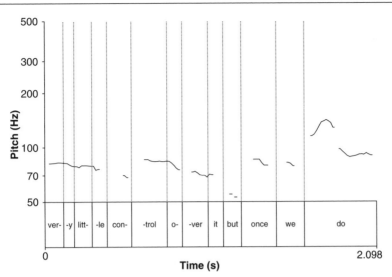

Figure 10.1   Creaky voice, lines 18–19 in Extract 10.2

frequency, which is typically considerably higher than in a neutral setting. In falsetto voice, the vocal folds are stretched extremely thin, especially at the edges. It can be slightly breathy, a result of a very small opening in the glottis. However, in our example below this is not the case, as participant Alina uses a loud falsetto setting as she imitates another speaker.

Extract 10.3   SBC006 Cuz 🎧

1 Alina: NO::;
2   <<acc> JAN talked the whole time;=
3   <<falsetto+extra high+all> in a voice like THIS -
4 (0.44)
5   <<higher falsetto> HI:: ((alina)) -
6   i'm so HAPpy to see YOU::;>>
7   <<laughing> and we're going - >
8 (0.4)
9   .hh
10   <<h> GO::D;
11 (0.34)
12   turn the VOLume <<laughing> dOwn;>
13 (0.18)
14   .hh
15   lEt me OUTa HE:RE;>

At the beginning of this extract we can hear Alina speaking in a neutral setting; her change into falsetto occurs at line 3, where she initially reaches a top

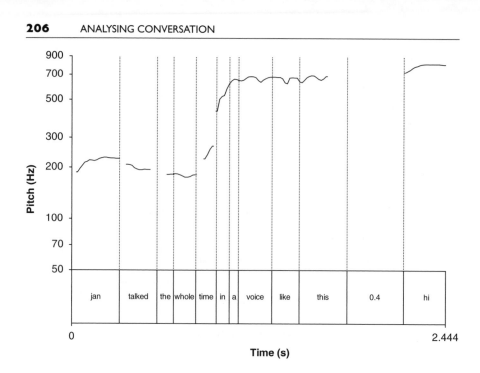

Figure 10.2 Falsetto voice, lines 2–5 in Extract 10.3

fundamental frequency of 694 Hz. In her subsequent intonation phrases (lines 5–6) she moves further up to an extremely high top frequency of 812 Hz. Figure 10.2 shows a pitch curve of the step-up from the neutral to the falsetto setting; the analysis window has been extended to 900 Hz in order to accommodate the very high pitch.

This change in voice quality accompanies an instance of *voicing*, that is the participant's adoption of another speaker's voice. A typical environment for voicing is direct reported speech; however, as we can see in this extract, change of prosodic features may occur before the onset of the actual quoted turn (see Chapter 4.3.2 for Klewitz and Couper-Kuhlen's (1999) investigation of prosody and voicing). In the above example, Alina's change into falsetto voice begins with her phrase *in a voice like this* (line 3), i.e. before she begins her imitation of the other voice (lines 5–6).

Alina's use of falsetto voice quality is not only an instance of voicing another speaker's talk. Her indexical phrase *in a voice like this* refers directly to the voice being used for its production; this means that the referent of the word *this* is not one that has been referred to verbally or is being pointed to in the physical world outside talk. Instead, we could argue that *this* refers to itself, the falsetto voice as a phonetic event. Interestingly, Alina later refers to the main prosodic feature of this voice as *volume* (line 12), instead of pitch, even though the increase in pitch is much more extreme than that in loudness.

10.1.3 Breathy voice

Breathy voice is caused by excessive air escaping through the vocal folds, which remain slightly open during speech production. Breathiness is a gradual phenomenon, since, of course, all speech is accompanied by some airflow and some sounds also involve *aspiration* as part of their articulation, most prominently the sound /h/, but also audibly released pronunciations of /tʰ/, /kʰ/ or /pʰ/. Speaking with a breathy vocal setting always results in a reduction in loudness, as a certain amount of breath force is not used for voice support, but is allowed to escape as audible air.

In the extract below, Pamela tells her husband Darryl how she and their daughter discussed the existence of Santa Claus earlier in the day.

Extract 10.4   SBC005 A book about death   🎧

66 1 Pamela: she said but some aDULTS: talk about sAnta claus,=
    2   <<h> i said thAt's becAUse: they WANT to> believe in sAnta
    3   <<breathy> claus.>
    4   .hh
    5   <<breathy> and that's what i TOLD her.=
    6   i said ↑I want to believe in sAnta claus?
    7 (0.82)
    8   in fact sOmetImes i DO believe in santa> <<whisper> claus.>
    9 (2.42)
    10   <<breathy> and that-
    11   that really [SATisfied her;>
    12 Darryl: [.hh
    13   [yeah but whAt-
    14 Pamela: [but i thought it was VEry pragMATic of her to
    15   ASK about that in JUNE. 99

Pamela's talk at lines 2–3 ends in breathy voice on *claus*, before she continues in an overall breathy setting. As in the case of creaky voice, breathy turn endings can in part be explained by the overall decline in muscular effort as turns and intonation phrases are brought to a close. Relaxing vocal fold vibration allows in the extra air, which leads to breathy voice. However, as Pamela's turn continues, breathy voice remains the dominant vocal setting (lines 5–11). Later on, she returns to a more neutral setting (line 14), which shows that she does not normally employ breathiness as her default voice quality. Therefore it must have interactional relevance at this particular sequential location.

Once again, the change in voice quality occurs in the vicinity of direct reported speech. However, once again the different vocal setting does not overlap precisely with the onset and closure of the reported speech. It begins at lines 5–6, *and that's what I told her I said*, one intonation phrase before the beginning of the quotation, continues during the actual voicing, *i want to believe in santa claus in fact sometimes i do believe in santa claus* (lines 6–8), and then continues further *and that that really satisfied her* (lines 10–11). Nevertheless, the breathy voice quality clearly separates a spate of talk from other talk by the same participant. Continuing after a potential turn completion point (lines 3–4), the intonation phrase *and that's what I told her* (line 5) initiates a move away from Pamela's telling of her conversation with her daughter, towards her own perspective on the existence of Santa Claus (lines 6–8). After another transition relevance place (lines 8–9) the talk is brought back to the daughter and this section of Pamela's turn is closed (lines 10–11). When she starts up again, her voice quality has returned to a neutral setting (line 14).

A type of phonatory setting closely related to breathy voice is whisper. In Extract 10.4, Pamela changes from breathy voice into whisper at the end of her phrase *in fact sometimes i do believe in santa claus* (line 8). In this instance, the whispered final word is an expectable result of a continuing decrease in muscular effort throughout the intonation phrase. Anecdotally we also know that whispering can communicate a sense of intimacy or the attempt not to be overheard. Future research may show other interactional uses for this setting.

10.2 Analysing voice quality

This section takes a closer look at how creaky voice, falsetto and breathy voice can be analysed as part of natural conversation. The interaction below involves Joanne and her partner Ken, and their visitor Lenore. Talk immediately prior to the transcribed section has been about Nicaragua; Joanne initiates the following sequence with her turn at line 1, *I'd rather go to Mexico though*.

Extract 10.5   SBC015 Deadly diseases 🎧

```
 1  Joanne:   I'd ra[ther go to MEXico though –
 2  Ken:           [I-
 3  (0.49)
 4  Joanne:   hh.
 5            hehehe[he
 6  Lenore:         [not QUITE the sAme;
 7  Ken:      .hh
 8            I'd kind of like to  <<creaky> go to guateMAla but:ʰ;>
 9  Joanne:   i thInk MEXico's like the <<len> PLA:CE: -
10            to GO: - >
11            becAUse it's got EVErything.
12            .hh
13            it's got HIStory: -
14            it's [got big CITies -
15  Ken:           [<<creaky+p> YEAH it's got-
16            [it's got disEA[Ses that i keep>  <<laughing> [CA[TCHing,>
17  Joanne:   [it's got RUins -
18                          [and it's got-
19                                                         [.hh
20                                                              [<<f> and it's got
```

21		reSO:RTS;=>
22		you know i- Oh:;
23	**Lenore:**	**<<falsetto+laughing> GOD LISten [to you;>**
24	**Joanne:**	**[<<breathy+len> GO:::D;**
25		[the the [caribBEan is inCR:E:Dible.>
26	**Lenore:**	**[.hh**
27		[<<smiley+h+p> re:SO:RTS;>
28	**Joanne:**	**.hh**
29		<<breathy+len> it's this bl-
30		B^{h}EAU:tiful;
31	**(0.11)**	
32		BEAU:tiful;>
33		<<len> BLUE: WAter,>
34	(1.35)	
35		**<<breathy+p> ↑WHA:T.>**
36	(0.89)	
37		[tsk
38	**Lenore:**	**[I KNOW:;**
39		**i KNOW the cari[bbean is in[crEdible.**
40	**Joanne:**	[beau-
41		[BEAUtiful BEAUtiful blue hehe,
42		blue WAter,
43		and and
44		.hh
45		WARM Water -
46		and like CORal -
47		and TROPical F:ISH - =
48		**and inCREDible <<creaky> r- like;>**
49		reSORT -
50	(1.26)	
51		lIke Uh::m;
52		<<p> hoTEL:S,
53		and REStaurants,>
54	Ken:	.hh
55		Oh when we were there LAST;
56		**we-**
57		**th- it was JUST after an eLECtion;** 🙶

The first instance of change into a different vocal setting occurs in Ken's turn at line 8:

8 Ken: I'd kind of like to <<creaky> go to guateMAla but:^{h};>

Ken's drop into a lower pitch range halfway through the intonation phrase can be seen clearly in Figure 10.3. By delivering the main turn component in creaky voice quality, that is *Guatemala*, which has not been mentioned previously,

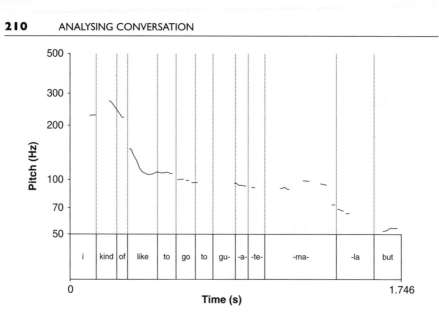

Figure 10.3 *I kind of like to go to Guatemala but,* **line 8 in Extract 10.5**

Ken designs it prosodically as belonging within the transitional space. Having reached the lowest pitch register, the turn is designed as nearing completion even before reaching its main lexical element, which is incorporated into the low pitched turn ending. By designing his turn in this way, Ken presents himself as not contending for the floor beyond this turn, in spite of his introduction of a new item to be talked about. The sequential result is that coparticipant Joanne does not treat Ken's turn as initiating a new sequence – a status which a different prosodic design may easily have brought about – but rather as an aside, not requiring uptake. She continues with her new sequence initiation regarding Mexico (*i think Mexico's like the place to go,* lines 9–10).

Ken changes into creaky voice quality once again at lines 15–16:

```
13  Joanne:  it's got HIStory: -
14           it's [got big CITies -
15  Ken:          [<<creaky+p> YEAH it's got-
16           [it's got disEA[Ses that i keep> <<laughing> [CA[TCHing,>
17  Joanne:  [it's got RUins -
18                      [and it's got-
19                                            [.hh
20                                            [<<f> and it's got
21           reSO:RTS;=>
```

This time, Ken's use of creaky voice is accompanied by reduced loudness. Once again, it co-occurs with a turn design that does not present a serious threat to the floor. Ken's utterance is a collaborative, if sarcastic, continuation of Joanne's ongoing list *it's got history it's got big cities* (lines 13–14). This practice has been described as *borrowing* a co-participant's turn, in order to insert a continuation of one's own without taking full responsibility for the turn as a whole (Szczepek Reed, 2006, pp. 197–201). The prosodic delivery of creaky voice, its resulting low pitch and reduced loudness play an important role in the design of Ken's utterance as taking up borrowed turn space. The use of creaky voice places his talk within the bottom range of his pitch register, and in combination with the reduced loudness this presents his talk as nearing completion from the moment it starts, rather than as a full-fledged turn in its own right.

However, Ken's utterance is not received as entirely non-competitive. Joanne raises her loudness gradually throughout the simultaneous talk, clearly reaching a louder delivery at lines 20–21, *and it's got resorts*. She thus shows firstly that she is not relinquishing the floor and secondly that she is determined to complete the list in the way she has intended, that is without acknowledgement of Ken's sarcastic list item.

The next change in vocal setting occurs in Lenore's turn at line 23:

```
20 Joanne:                                      <<f> and it's got
21        reSO:RTS;=>
22        you know i- Oh:;
23 Lenore:  <<falsetto + laughing> GOD LISten [to you;>
24 Joanne:                                    [<<breathy> GO:::D;
25        [the the [caribBEan is inCR:E:Dible.>
26 Lenore:  [.hh
27               [<<smiley + h + p> re:SO:RTS,>
28 Joanne:  .hh
29        <<breathy> it's this bl-
30        BʰEAU:tiful;
31 (0.11)
32        BEAU:tiful;>
33        BLUE: WAter,
34 (1.35)
35        <<breathy + p> ↑WHA:T.>
36 (0.89)
37        [tsk
38 Lenore:  [I KNOW:;
39        i KNOW the caribbean is incrEdible.
```

Lenore's change into falsetto, and later smiley voice co-occurs with her laughter in response to Joanne's immediately previous turn, which depicts Mexico as famous for its resorts. Prior talk amongst these participants has been about international issues from a broadly political perspective, and later on in this same sequence Ken resumes this approach (*oh when we were there last we th- it was just after an election*, lines 55–57). Joanne's talk about leisure and holiday-related issues is an isolated occurrence within this part of the interaction, and she is the only participant to raise it. With this in mind, Lenore's amused turn *god listen to you resorts* (lines 23 and 27) can be interpreted as light mockery. Her vocal

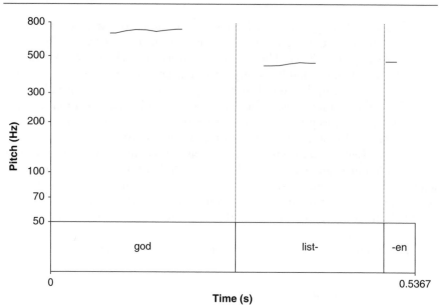

Figure I0.4   *God listen*, line 23 in Extract I0.5

setting of falsetto voice for the first part of this turn takes her to a pitch of
726 Hz (see Figure 10.4; note the extended window of analysis to accommodate
the higher pitch).

Overlapping with Lenore's turn is Joanne's continuing display of appreciation
for Mexico as a holiday destination. On her continuation *god the caribbean is
incredible* (lines 24–25) her speech takes on an extremely breathy voice quality. In combination with the syllable lengthening on *go:::d* and *inc:re:dible*,
this highly marked prosodic delivery contributes greatly to the positive emphasis expressed by the lexical content of this turn. Joanne continues in breathy
voice for her delivery of *it's this bl- bʰeautiful beautiful*, with added initial
aspiration on the first instance of *bʰeautiful*. The lexical repetition of the
word *beautiful* increases the degree of 'adding' to this turn. The breathy vocal
setting, the syllable lengthening, the additional aspiration and the lexical repetition all work together to embellish further the high level of appreciation
expressed.

As Joanne reaches the end of this TCU her voice suddenly loses its breathy
quality as she reverts into a neutral setting (*blue water*, line 33). This phrase
is followed by a lengthy pause (line 34) and a repair initiating *what*, produced
with a rising-falling pitch accent, decreased loudness and a slightly breathy voice
quality. As repair is initiated without immediately prior talk from other participants we must assume that its trouble source is the long silence. Without
a video recording of this interaction we do not know what goes on between
participants in terms of gaze and gestures; however, Lenore's previous mockery and the following absence of recipient uptake show a noticeable lack of
coparticipant involvement in Joanne's turn. Lenore's eventual contribution *i
know i know the caribbean is incredible* (lines 38–39) is delivered in a neutral

setting. While in most interactional environments the neutral setting is used and treated as the default setting, in this instance it is a noticeable prosodic pattern. Typically, when one participant displays such levels of excitement for a conversational item, other participants show affiliation. Szczepek Reed (2006, pp. 127–30) shows that conversational displays of appreciation often involve the type of prosody described above and are routinely followed by prosodically matching turns from other participants. Thus, Lenore's neutral delivery and resulting absence of prosodic matching of Joanne's turn somewhat defies the alignment it expresses in its lexical content (*i know*).

Another change in voice quality occurs in Joanne's turn at line 48:

```
45 Joanne:   WARM Water -
46           and like CORal -
47           and TROPical F:ISH - =
48           and inCREDible <<creaky> r- like;>
49           reSORT -
50 (1.26)
51           lIke Uh::m;
52           <<p> hoTEL:S,
```

Joanne changes into creaky voice for only one word, *r- like*. By employing this vocal setting here the word *like* is dropped to a much lower pitch than surrounding words (see Figure 10.5). Its prosodic delivery thus shows it being literally dropped from an ongoing turn, an interpretation which matches its grammatical

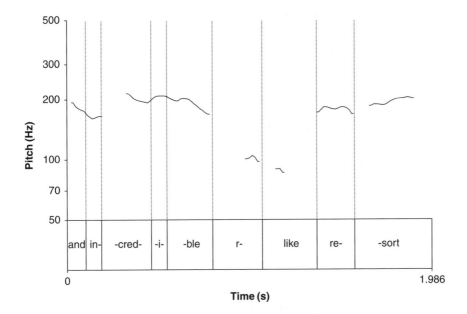

Figure 10.5 *Incredible r- like resort*, lines 48–49 in Extract 10.5

status as an interjection, that is a word without any grammatical connection to other parts of the sentence.

Towards the end of this extract, Ken initiates a new sequence. His voice changes into a creaky voice quality on individual words, such as *we* (line 56) and *election* (line 57).

```
54  Ken:   .hh
55         Oh when we were there LAST;
56         we-
57         th- it was JUST after an eLECtion;
```

This intermittent change into creaky voice is part of the overall setting of Ken's voice, at least for this particular conversation, and can be heard on the entire recording. It is therefore most probably not interactionally relevant, but part of his sociolinguistic identity as a speaker of American English.

10.2.1 Exercises

Identify different voice qualities in the following extracts.

EXERCISE 10.1

Jeff is on the phone to his girlfriend Jill, describing a scene outside his window.

SBC028 Hey Cutie Pie 🎧

```
 1  Jeff:   you knOw what i just REalized?
 2  Jill:   [what -
 3  Jeff:   [she LOOKED at me,
 4          she's wAlking dOwn the STAIRS?
 5  Jill:   uhu -
 6  Jeff:   she LOOKED at mE: - =
 7          and she-
 8  (0.19)
 9          .hh
10          she didn't SEE me;
11  (0.95)
12  Jill:   REally?
13  (0.11)
14  Jeff:   YEAH;
15  (0.1)
16          i WAVED at her and –
17          she jUst KEPT GOing,
```

EXERCISE 10.1

(Continued)

18	(0.2)	
19	Jill:	.hh
20		MAYbe uhm –
21	(0.69)	
22		(if) there's a reFLECtion or something –
23	(0.37)	
24	Jeff:	what a BOdy she has -
25	(0.45)	
26	Jill:	.hh
27		isn't that inCREDible,
28		are our BOdies gonna do thA:t?
29	(0.23)	
30	Jeff:	't's like-
31	(0.67)	
32		It's like –
33	(0.3)	
34		SHE'S eVOLVing.
35	(0.99)	
36		you KNOW like;
37	(0.86)	
38		[(funny)
39	Jill:	[(( ))
40		hh.
41		deGENerating.
42		[huh-
43	Jeff:	[deGENera-
44		YEAH:.
45	Jill:	[hh.
46	Jeff:	[it's KINDa WEIRD.=
47		HUH. 🙸

EXERCISE 10.2

In the following extract, sisters Sherry and Beth and their mother Rosemary are picking their choices for lunch from a restaurant menu.

SBC031 Tastes very special 🎧

🙶 1 Sherry: hOw about if I pick for yOU and < <laughing> yOU pick for mE ->
   2 (0.73)

EXERCISE 10.2

(Continued)

3		[.hh
4	Beth:	[he
5	Sherry:	it's EASier thAt way;
6		ehe
7	(0.71)	
8	Rosemary:	what in the WORLD is a philadElphia-
9	(0.16)	
10	Sherry:	it's r- ROAST BEEF with;
11	(0.4)	
12		mElted CHEESE and;
13		SAUtéed Onions.
14	Rosemary:	m;
15		that [DOES sound GOO:D;
16	Sherry:	[on a HOAgy RO:LL. 🔊

10.3   Research on voice quality in natural conversation

Not a large amount of research has been carried out on voice quality in natural talk. This section summarises two examples. Ogden (2004) shows that creak, breathiness and whisper are employed by Finnish speaking participants in their negotiations over turn-taking. Szczepek Reed (2006, pp. 52–4) investigates how conversationalists repeat other speakers' voice qualities in specific contexts.

10.3.1   Richard Ogden (2004): Non-modal voice quality and turn-taking in Finnish

Ogden shows that in a corpus of ten Finnish radio phone-in programmes non-modal voice quality co-occurs with turn finality in almost 70 per cent of turn transitions. By the term 'non-modal voice quality' Ogden refers to non-default phonatory settings, such as creaky voice, whisper and breathy voice. The most frequent voice quality he finds in relation to turn completion is creaky voice – an observation made previously by non-empirical research such as Laver (1980/2009, p. 126, 1994, p. 196). However, he is able to show that it is not only creak, but also breathiness, whisper and exhalation that contribute to turn finality.

Ogden accounts for those 30 per cent of cases in which there is no non-modal voice quality present at turn completion by showing that those turn endings typically are either highly predictable, as in the case of a first pair part, or are followed by pauses longer than 0.2 seconds, and thus potentially problematic, or involve prosodic stylization, as is frequently the case in routine exchanges, such as openings and closings. Ogden argues that a change to non-modal voice quality is one of a number of practices employed by participants for initiating turn transition. Other practices include syntactic completion, action completion and falling pitch. He then goes on to show that instances in which a change to non-modal voice quality is not followed by speaker transition do not threaten his overall hypothesis that non-modal voice quality is turn-transition relevant. He shows that in those cases, current speakers themselves orient to the potential of a turn transition in other areas of their ongoing turn, for example by completing their utterance syntactically and pragmatically and by noticeable pausing. Other instances of non-modal voice qualities which are not followed by turn transitions involve turns ending in particles which may or may not project more talk to come from the same speaker.

The final part of Ogden's chapter concerns the relation between non-modal voice quality and intonation. He presents a potential argument for considering creaky voice an independent intonational system, as it meets the criteria that have been set out by Ladd (1996, p. 4) for such a classification: its domain stretches over the single syllable, it occurs at sentence, rather than lexical, level and it is categorically structured. However, because of its low pitched quality, it may also be considered a variant of low-falling intonation and therefore a part of the system of intonation. In response to this open question, Ogden shows an example in which creaky voice co-occurs with rising intonation in a turn that contains other instances of rising intonation prior to its ending. Only when speakers design their turns as complete do they add creaky voice quality to their rising pitch. This finding implies that creaky voice is potentially employed by participants separately from intonation and could therefore be considered an independent system.

10.3.2   Beatrice Szczepek Reed (2006, pp. 52–4): Prosodic matching of voice quality

As part of my work on prosodic orientation I found that participants have a tendency to match each others' voice quality in certain interactional settings. By 'prosodic orientation' I mean speakers' display of awareness of each others' prosody in their own prosody, for example by repeating prosodic patterns used by prior speakers in their immediately preceding turns. In terms of voice quality, I found prosodic orientation for harsh, creaky and breathy voice. In the following example, taken from a radio phone-in programme, radio host Leo gradually adopts a breathy voice quality, which is matched by caller Marie in her opening turn, and subsequently continued in Leo's return greeting.

Extract 10.6   Gulf war: Hi Leo 🎧

1 LE: <<all> marie on the line from paCIFica;
2   YOU'RE on the giant sixty eight knbr;
3   <<becoming breathy> thAnks for CALLing marie.>>

4 **MA:**   <<p+breathy> HI lEo.>
5 **LE:**   <<p+breathy> HI.>
6 MA: I just had a cOmment about the: um PROtesters, 99

This extract shows the matching of voice quality during a telephone opening sequence. The vocal setting separates the three-part opening from surrounding talk, as Marie changes into a neutral setting for her next turn (line 6). Like other forms of prosodic matching, continuing a vocal setting for the length of an adjacency pair is often the default case, while prosodic non-alignment is treated by participants as a noticeable absence in such contexts. Matching of voice quality as exemplified above typically occurs with closely connected turns, such as adjacency pairs or next turn agreements; in turn, the prosodic matching itself contributes to the design of a next turn as closely connected to a prior turn.

FURTHER READING

General descriptions of voice quality can be found in Catford (1964), Clark and Yallop (1995, pp. 19–22, 328–32), Honikman (1964), Ladefoged (2001, pp. 122–32) and most importantly Laver (1979, 1980/2009, 1994, pp. 152–5, 184–201, 394–420). In interactional linguistics, contributions have been made by Ogden (2001, 2004) and Grivičić and Nilep (2004).

Several socio-phoneticians have researched the role of voice quality for different accents and social varieties; see for example Coadou (2006), Esling (1978), Henton and Bladon (1988) and Stuart-Smith (1999). Gobl and Chasaide (2003) have studied voice quality and the display of emotions and attitude.

Outlook: Future Issues in Research on Prosody in Conversation

11

I have attempted to give an overview of the current state of interactional linguistic knowledge of conversational prosody, covering the parameters of pitch, time, loudness and voice quality. As the preceding chapters have shown, some of these areas have received more attention from research than others; and there are some, such as loudness and voice quality, in which many basic gaps still need to be filled. In all of the areas of prosody introduced here, interactional linguists are still only scratching the surface of what there is to know about prosody and talk.

Since the first studies investigated the role of prosody for interaction over 30 years ago, research in this field has been predominantly concerned with exploring three areas: the role of prosody for turn-taking, sequence organisation and individual conversational actions.

Turn-taking is accomplished through orientation to a number of linguistic and other interactional cues: potentially complete turns are often characterised by syntactic, pragmatic and prosodic completion (Ford and Thompson, 1996). The main contribution to the definition of the prosodic design of smaller interactional units, in particular TCUs, has been made by Margret Selting (1995, 1996a, 2001, 2005). The prosodic parameters that seem particularly relevant for turn design and turn-taking are changes on the (potentially) final pitch accent in terms of intonation, syllable duration, loudness and voice quality, as well as the rhythmic organization of potentially final stressed syllables. Rhythm has been shown by Couper-Kuhlen (1993) and Auer et al. (1999) to be a highly relevant cue for participants' timing of their next turn onsets (see Chapter 7.3.2). Potentially final pitch accents have been investigated by Schegloff (1998), Wells and Macfarlane's (1998) and Fox (2001) for their role in foreshadowing upcoming transition places. As chapter 3 on intonation has shown, participants orient, at least in part, to the nature of the potentially last accent for their placement of next turns. While Schegloff (1998) and Fox (2001) describe a stepping up or rising-falling pitch accent (a 'peak'), Wells and Macfarlane show that in the variety of English they investigate, West Midlands English, the potentially final pitch accents take the shape of a pitch 'valley'. They come to the conclusion that while participants seem to orient to the presence of a final pitch accent as such as a potential turn-taking cue, the precise prosodic form of this pitch accent is not necessarily predictable.

This finding repeats an earlier, very important aspect of research on prosody and turn-taking, concerning the issue of differences in languages and linguistic varieties. For example, Local et al. (1986) show that the prosodic cues for turn completion in Tyneside English specifically involve a slowing down in speech rate; a sudden increase and subsequent decrease in loudness on the final stressed syllable; lengthening of the final syllable; centralized quality on the final vowels; and either a step-up or a drop in pitch on the last stressed syllable. Local et al. (1985) present similar work on London Jamaican English; and Wells and Peppé (1996) describe prosodic cues for turn-taking in Ulster English. All three pieces emphasise the nature of prosodic turn-taking cues as clusters of prosodic features, rather than individual signals. In fact, Szczepek Reed (2004) demonstrates that, provided a stretch of talk is designed as complete in other, non-prosodic respects, such as syntax and pragmatics, any intonation pattern that exists in English can potentially occur in turn-final position. This reminds us that, although some intonation contours may be regularly used for certain interactional practices, such as 'completing' or 'projecting continuation', those concepts do not necessarily have to refer to turn-taking. Participants may use and interpret a certain prosodic pattern as completing a turn in one instance and a narrative sequence in another. They may also be designing an utterance as 'incomplete' in terms of their own state of knowledge, although it may well be treated as a complete turn, with a speaker transition following it.

When it comes to the role of prosody for sequence organization, research has focused on one of the most fundamental decisions participants have to make on a turn-by-turn basis: is a next turn *continuing* what was done before or is it a *new beginning*? In this decision, prosody seems to play a particularly significant role. For example, John Local (1992) describes participants' interruptions of their own turns-in-progress and the prosodic design of the talk that follows them. In cases in which following talk continues the previously aborted turn, it is delivered with continuing prosody: for example, the pitch register used is exactly the same as that used in the aborted turn and the continuing turn begins at precisely the pitch level at which the aborted turn was left. In contrast, those cases in which participants abandon the previous project and start again are characterised by a higher pitch onset than the one at which the previous turn was abandoned.

Similar evidence for the role of pitch in designing talk as either new or continuing is provided by Couper-Kuhlen (2004), summarised in Chapter 3.3.1. She describes how participants use a sudden increase in pitch and loudness when they begin a new conversational sequence and continue previous pitch and loudness levels when they are continuing a previous sequence.

Szczepek Reed (2009), summarised in Chapter 8.3.2, shows that high pitch and increased loudness does not always design talk as new or noticeably different. From this work it seems that 'newness' is prosodically achieved by doing something prosodically new compared to, for example, a previous speaker. If that previous speaker used high pitch and increased loudness, a next participant's use of those prosodic features does not necessarily design his or her talk as starting something new. Instead, participants' overall orientation to prosody, rather than their employment of specific patterns, appears once again as the main determining factor.

The prosody of specific conversational actions has been a third area of study for interactional linguists, and a very broad one indeed. Numerous studies have been conducted, describing the precise prosodic characteristics of interactional practices, such as repair (Couper-Kuhlen, 1992; Selting, 1996b; Curl, 2004); news delivery and news receipt (Local, 1996; Freese and Maynard, 1998; Ogden et al., 2004); telephone openings and closings (Auer, 1990; Couper-Kuhlen, 2001a); reported speech (Couper-Kuhlen 1996a, 1999; Klewitz and Couper-Kuhlen, 1999); and questions and answers (Couper-Kuhlen and Auer, 1991; Selting, 1992b; Ford et al., 2004; Couper-Kuhlen, forthcoming), to name only a few.

Our understanding of any of these areas – prosody and turn-taking, sequence organisation and single conversational actions – is still far from complete, and it is therefore necessary for research to continue exploring these issues. However, as the majority of discourse-related language study has moved towards a largely undisputed acceptance of the importance of prosody for interaction, the coming years and decades will also enable analysts of conversation to move beyond specifically functional analyses of prosody and towards an exploration of the relationship between prosody and other interactional modes.

As many of the examples in this book have demonstrated, very few conversational actions are accomplished by prosodic means alone. Instead, participants typically use prosody in combination with a variety of other resources, such as grammar, lexis, information structure and, if the interaction is face-to-face, gesture, gaze and body posture, to name only the most obvious. Prosody almost always works alongside other modes when it is employed for the achievement and the structuring of conversational actions. At the same time, achievement of conversational actions is not the only aspect of language and interaction for which prosody is an important resource. Prosody is also a language-specific cue for phonetics (such as in the distinction of long and short vowels); lexis (such as in determining word stress); and syntax (such as in the distribution of focus). Furthermore, prosody is a cue for other aspects of social interaction, such as the display of participants' attitudes and the marking of emotion. Thus, prosody always fulfils a multitude of functions, but rarely are any of those functions fulfilled exclusively by prosody. The challenges for future research lie in an approach that is aware of, and sensitive to, the multilayered combination of those different spheres of prosodic influence.

However, while the role of prosody for interaction will remain a fruitful area of future study for some time, there is further uncharted territory in another direction. Up to now, most interactional linguistic research has been devoted to applying the conversation-analytic approach to the study of language-in-interaction. However, one could also imagine an application of that same approach to the study of the language system itself. Some preliminary work has been done in this area, exploring, for example, the relevance of linguistic categories such as the sentence (Lerner, 1991, 1996) or the intonation phrase (Szczepek Reed, 2010a, 2010c) for conversational participants. In these works, the participant perspective is used to throw light on the nature of linguistic categories previously only studied through linguistic introspection and experimentation. However, the interpretations and perspectives of those who use language in the immediate context of its emergence could be applied to a variety of other areas of linguistic interests. For example, a participant's reference to an extremely high falsetto voice quality in terms of 'volume', rather than pitch (see Extracts 9.2 and 10.3), may tell us something about participants' ways of categorising language events. Alternatively, a participant's packaging of an utterance, which cannot be defined as a syntactically complete unit, as an intonation phrase (as in Extract 3.12), may tell us something about the kinds of utterances participants consider to be possible units. This kind of investigation of language is still in its infancy; however, as the interactional linguistic approach gains ground, research will inevitably turn to some of the theoretical implications to be revealed by a study of language as an interactional achievement.

Finally, there is large scope for future investigations of prosody as a resource for the construction of social meaning, in terms of identity, affect and stance. While research up to now has been primarily interested in the local organisation of talk, many of the areas traditionally studied by sociolinguists are also greatly affected by prosody. As our understanding of the role of prosody for local turn and sequence organisation grows, students of discourse from a variety of disciplines will be better equipped to turn to some of the wider aspects of social interaction.

Answers to Exercises

EXERCISE 3.1

Intonation phrases

Phil: I would like to / talk to you about / these three items / I have here / some ice in a pan / water in this glass / and steam rising from this pot / now / I would like to ask you / how these three things / tell me please / how are they all alike / these three things / this ice here in this pan / this water in this glass / and the steam rising from this pot / just yell it out / we are informal here / yes / correct / they are all forms of water / this ice here of course is water / I told you there was water in this glass / and you have all seen water boil at home / so you are familiar with steam

EXERCISE 3.2

Stressed syllables

Phil: I would like <u>to</u> / <u>talk</u> to you about / <u>these</u> three <u>items</u> / <u>I</u> have <u>here</u> / some <u>ice</u> in a pan / <u>water</u> in this glass / and <u>steam</u> rising from this <u>pot</u> / <u>now</u>/ i would like to <u>ask</u> you / <u>how these three</u> things / <u>tell</u> me <u>please</u> / <u>how</u> are they all <u>alike</u> / <u>these three</u> things / this <u>ice</u> here in this <u>pan</u> / this <u>water</u> in this <u>glass</u> / and the <u>steam</u> rising from this <u>pot</u> / just yell it out / we are <u>informal</u> here / <u>yes</u> / <u>correct</u> / they are <u>all forms</u> of <u>water</u> / this <u>ice</u> here of course is <u>water</u> / I <u>told</u> you there was water in this <u>glass</u> / and you have <u>all</u> seen water boil at <u>home</u> / so you <u>are</u> familiar with <u>steam</u>

EXERCISE 3.3

Pitch accents

Phil: I would like <u>to</u>;
        <u>talk</u> to you about;
        <u>these</u> three <u>items</u>.
        <u>I</u> have <u>here</u>,
        some <u>ice</u> in a pan,
        <u>water</u> in this <u>glass</u>,
        and <u>steam</u> rising from this <u>pot</u>.
        <u>now</u>.

i would like to <u>ask</u> <u>you</u>.
<u>how</u> <u>these</u> <u>three</u> <u>things</u>.
<u>tell</u> me <u>please</u>.
<u>how</u> are they <u>all</u> <u>alike</u>.
<u>these</u> <u>three</u> <u>things</u>.
this <u>ice</u> here in this <u>pan</u>.
this <u>water</u> in this <u>glass</u>;
and the <u>steam</u> rising from this <u>pot</u> -
just <u>yell</u> it out;
we are <u>informal</u> here;
<u>yes</u>.
<u>correct</u>.
they are <u>all</u> <u>forms</u> of <u>water</u>.
this <u>ice</u> here of course is <u>water</u> -
I <u>told</u> you there was water in this <u>glass</u> -
and you have <u>all</u> seen water boil at <u>home</u> -
so you <u>are</u> familiar with <u>steam</u>.

EXERCISE 3.4

SBC047 On the lot

```
 1  Fred:       and on my proDUCtion card;
 2  (0.8)
 3              see;
 4  (0.31)
 5              the dAY before YESterday.
 6  (0.14)
 7              i did ICE cream.
 8  (0.15)
 9              RIGHT.
10              BALian,
11  (0.28)
12  Richard:    uhU,
13  (0.17)
14  Fred:       and you gOtta PACK those;
15              in CAses;
16  (0.24)
17              .hh
18  Richard:    ri[ght;
19  Fred:          [And SO like -
20              I didn't put that down on my proDUCtion car[d.
21  Richard:                                              [hOw many CAses;
22              you PACKED;
23  Fred:       .hh
24              I don't KNOW mAn;
```

25	(0.3)	
26		i PACKED two PALlets.
27	(0.37)	
28		YOU know;
29	(0.43)	
30		I don't know how many (0.12) CAses [that Is but;
31	Richard:	[(uh)
32	Fred:	.hhh
33		YOU know that-
34	(0.3)	
35		THAT shit was HEAVy man.

EXERCISE 4.1

A book about death

1	Darryl:	you have NO idEa;
2		what happens beFORE or AFter.
3	(2.52)	
4		**<<h> you have NO idEa.>**
5	(1.67)	
6		you can read BOOKS about it,
7		you can (0.4) TALK about it –
8	(1.25)	
9		but the most pragmAtic thing to DO is jUst –
10	(0.33)	
11		↑LIVE it.
12	(1.85)	
13	Pamela:	m –
14	(0.86)	
15	Darryl:	LEARN the RULES of the GAME,
16	(0.97)	
17		play the GAME,=
18	**Pamela:**	**<<h>for WHAT – >**
19	(0.83)	
20	**Darryl:**	**<<h> for whatEver you ↑ WANT;>**
21	(2.68)	
22		**for what<<h>Ever you ↑ WANT.>**
23	(2.1)	
24		be a: DOCtor,
25		a SCREEN writer,
26		or an ACtress,
27		or a phiLANthropist,
28		or a:n exPLORer,
29	(3.44)	
30	Pamela:	ts <<p> an exPLORer;>
31	(0.78)	

32 **Darryl:** <<h> **do what you WANT;**
33 **with the time you ↑ HAVE.=>**
34 LEARN,
35 (0.93)
36 GIVE,
37 (2.01)
38 <<h> **whatEVer.>**

EXERCISE 4.2

Hey cutie pie

1 Jeff: you knOw what i'm SAYing,=
2 like could you get-
3 is it POSsible that you could still be POSi- (0.23) POSitive,
4 (0.49)
5 Jill: .hh
6 I thInk (0.19) there'd be a S::L:IGHT CHANCE,
7 (0.33)
8 of it being a FAL:SE NEGative,
9 (0.43)
10 .hh
11 bUt –
12 (0.18)
13 <<h> **I don't THINK so;**
14 **cause i'm PRETty LATE?**
15 **(0.13)**
16 **and i thInk> i'm LATE enOUgh,**
17 .hh
18 where I would HA:VE;
19 (0.45)
20 like (0.19) eNOUGH of;
21 (0.32)
22 **the HORmone <<l> that;**
23 **(0.17)**
24 **the prEgnancy tEst TESTS for?>**
25 (0.22)
26 .hh
27 **i thInk i would have eNOUGH of <<l> that in my Urine;**
28 **thAt – >**
29 (0.19)
30 of ↑ COURSE it would show up;
31 if i had any IN there?
32 (0.37)
33 Jeff: <<p> YEAH;>
34 Jill: you KNOW?=
35 <<h> **sO I-**

```
36  (0.1)
37          I i'm pret-
38          i tOOk that;>
39          as a prEtty GOO:D;
40  (0.36)
41          <<l> SI:GN.>
42  (1.4)
43  Jeff:   <<p> Oh my GO:D;
44          HONey;
45          HOW come you've been;
46  (0.15)
47          KEEPing all this in[SI:DE;>
48  Jill:                 [ts
49          <<h> I:: KN:OW;
50          i didn't MEAN to keep it inside- >
51          i mean i i didn't [mean-
52  Jeff:        .          [<<p> dOn't you LOVE mE ->
```

EXERCISE 5.1

Hey cutie pie

```
 1  Jeff:   so was thAt all the DRAma?
 2  (0.22)
 3  Jill:   tch
 4          <<h> thAt was the ↑DRAma;>
 5          and thAt was the susPENSE,
 6          .hh
 7          and thAt was the reLIEF,
 8          and thAt was the ECStasy.
 9  (0.93)
10  Jeff:   <<h> REALLY?>
11  Jill:   uHU?
12  (0.46)
13  Jeff:   .hh
14          OH::: HONEY:::;
15  Jill:   <<h> ehehO::: - >
16  Jill:   little B:UNNy::;
17          is going thrOUgh: the whOle wIde SPECtrum of eMOTions;
```

EXERCISE 5.2

Zero equals zero

```
 1  Nath:   SO:;
 2  (0.44)
```

3   **let's tAlk about this SLOW:ly:,**
4   **as i WR:ITE this DOWN as you're SAYing it.**
5   all RIGHT,

EXERCISE 5.3

Appease the monster

1 Marci: dOn't forget to buy yourself a COOKie sheet,=
2   before you go to make COOKies,
3 Wend: [YEAH.
4 Kevin: [and DON'T forget to take the TUPperware out of your Oven;
5   before you turn it O[N;
6 Wend: **[SH:::USH up.**
7 (0.46)
8 Marci: ehehe[hehehe
9 Kendr: [ehehe OH YEAH;
10   THAT TOO;

EXERCISE 6.1

New Yorkers Anonymous

1 Sean: well FRAN –
2   I'VE been lOOking –
3 (0.29)
4   REALly;
5   for a year or TWO;=
6   at different PLACes to LIVE.=
7   i went bAck to EUr:ope –
8 (0.7)
9 Fran: mhm,
10 Sean: <<p> to lOndon and PARis –
11 (1.66)
12   i've been in <<p+len> SUN vAlley -
13   TUCsO:n - >
14   <<p> i've been-
15   and mOnTANa;>
16   SEA:Ttle;
17   i LIKED seattle a LOT.
18 Fran: m[hm,
19 Sean: [<<all> but i couldn't LIVE there;>
20 (1.31)
21   and –
22 (0.51)
23   OUTside of new yOrk;
24   and <<all> i COULDn't go back to live in new yOrk again;>=

```
25          it's been-
26  (0.3)
27          i'm Over it;
28  (0.33)
29  Fran:   [mhm,
30  Sean:   [thIs is the best PLACE;
31          i've FOUND;
```

EXERCISE 6.2

Hey Cutie Pie

```
 1  Jill:   well it's NOT –
 2  (0.35)
 3          <<all> aVAILable here in the united stAtes;
 4          it's only> <<len> in F::RA:NCE,>
 5  (0.58)
 6  Jeff:   ENGland,
 7  (0.2)
 8  Jill:   and –
 9  (0.24)
10          <<all> YEAH;=
11          and> <<len> S:WE:de::n ->
```

EXERCISE 7.1

Actual blacksmithing

```
 1  Lynne:  tsk uh Oh and it's rEAlly TIRing though.
 2  (0.61)
 3          .hh and it-
 4  (0.11)
 5          you KNOW like;
 6  (0.47)
 7          YOU get stu-
 8          I:'ve (0.33) only dOne like.
 9          .hh
10  (1.36)
11          <<h> WELL –
12          hh.
13  (0.92)
14          at the END of the yEAr;>=
15          now sEE i tOOk the sEcond hAlf of the COURSE;
16  (0.79)
17          A:nd –
18  (0.91)
```

19		<<len> rIght NOW:;
20		i've PROBably: Only SHO:D abOUt;
21		**FIVE HORSES ->**

EXERCISE 7.2

He knows

1	Lajuan:	**i lIstened to my sIster when my nEphew;**
2	(0.3)	
3		started COLlege how she was sAYing;
4		.hh
5		**SHE filled out All of his applicAtions for where he was gOing: and;**
6		.hh
7		SHE did all of these THINGS;=
8		when he had to apply for a SCHOLarship or whatEver;
9		.hh
10		**SHE filled out Everything and I'm lI:ke;**
11		**hh. I did it bY mySE:LF;**
12	(0.34)	
13		.hh
14		you READ the fOrm;
15	(0.14)	
16		**And you fIll it OUT.**
17	(0.41)	
18	Cam:	[m;
19	**Lajuan:**	**[NO one dId it for ME:;**
20	(0.51)	
21		.hh you knOw and I was vEry (0.47) mUch –
22	(0.39)	
23		whatEver i NEEDed;
24	(0.53)	
25		.hh
26		**i I gOt my mOney from my FA:ther,**
27	(0.12)	
28	·	he paid for SCHOO:L,
29	(0.47)	
30		.hh
31		but –
32	(0.13)	
33		I <<all> did everything on my OWN.>

EXERCISE 8.1

He knows

1	Cam:	thIs is the guy who doesn't know he's GAY.
2	**(0.42)**	

```
 3  Lajua:   [YES.
 4  Cam:     [OR -
 5           Isn't SURE if he's gay.
 6  (0.32)
 7  Lajua:   YES.
 8           who's nOw in the AIR force and lives in in sOUth carolIna.
 9  (0.73)
10           SO.
11  (0.74)
12  Cam:     <<p> WAIT a second.
13  (0.75)
14           I thought this w- guy t- was was MARried.>
15  (0.69)
16  Lajua:   RON.
17  (0.56)
18  Cam:     RON.
19           he's MARried RIGHT,
20  (0.26)
21  Lajua:   thAt's DARren.
```

EXERCISE 8.2

Oh you need a breadbox

```
 1  Cindy:   did uh ↑ (Andy) <<all> mention anything about> the uh CARDS,
 2           that we got for CHRISTmas,
 3  (0.37)
 4  Darle:   UH uh;
 5  Cindy:   <<all> CHRISTmas cards,>
 6           .hh
 7  (0.2)
 8           Oh WHY don't i let (0.08) hIm tell you because - =
 9           it was SOMEthing wE rEAlly got strUck by it because it's uh;
10  (0.1)
11           whAt is the <<p> POet?
12           or SOMEthing?
13           that DID the VERSE,
14  (0.2)
15           .hh
16  (0.14)
17           that your MOM really liked?
18  (0.32)
19           whAt was [ it?>
20  Darle:            [OH:[:: uh:m -
21  Andre:               [<<background> hElen stEIner rIce;>
```

22	**(0.27)**	
23	Cindy:	YEAH.
24	**(0.14)**	
25		what's uh-
26	**(0.15)**	
27		[wait a se-
28	Andre:	[HELen,
29	**(0.12)**	
30	Cindy:	.hh
31		HELen [stEIner RICE or some[thing;
32	Darle:	[(HEL-)
33		[HELen **(0.19)** KELLer RICE.
34	**(0.38)**	
35	Cindy:	or SOMEthing like that.=
36		but ANnyway hE was All excIted so we -
37	**(0.25)**	
38		KINDa made sUre that we -
39		sEnt them all to YOU guys;

EXERCISE 9.1

On the lot

1	Richard:	it's LONEly coming home after pUtting in t- twelve hours on the LOT - =
2		and wOrking All DAY and -
3		yOU know wOrking all EVEning - =
4		and then you don't have anybody to come home and <<p> SHARE it
5		with.>
6	(0.32)	
7	Fred:	YEAH;
8	(0.54)	
9		.hh
10		a- are y-
11		**are yOU <<dim> WORKing twelve hours?>**
12	(0.23)	
13		you're go[nna be-
14	**Richard:**	**[<<p> YEAH,>**
15	(0.13)	
16	Fred:	**you're [<<dim> gonna be DOing that?>**
17	**Richard:**	**[<<p> YEAH,>**
18	(0.23)	
19	Fred:	[NINE to NINE?
20	**Richard:**	**[<<p> DEFinitely;**
21		**NINE to NINE.>**
22		WELL I m-
23		IF I wA:nt.

EXERCISE 9.2

This retirement bit

1	Doris:	is your CIGarette OUt -
2	(0.31)	
3		EverybOdy's -
4	(0.22)	
5	**Angela:**	**<<p+l> yEAh.=**
6		**it's OUT.>**
7	(1.95)	
8	Doris:	you smOked it dOwn into the (0.18) CORK.=
9		DIDn't you.
10	(1.1)	
11	**Angela:**	**<<f+h> PARdon?>**
12	(0.41)	
13	Doris:	.hh
14		**<<f+h> you SMOKED it DOWN Into the CORK.>**
15	(0.54)	
16	Angela:	.hh
17		WELL;
18		YEAH;
19		YOU don't LIKE that;
20		DO you but;
21	(0.38)	
22	Doris:	NO it CHOKES me to DEATH.
23	(0.2)	
24	Angela:	it's-
25	Doris:	ehehe
26	(0.3)	
27	Angela:	It's THE:RE;=
28		might as well SMOKE it;
29	(0.28)	
30	Doris:	OH:;
31	(0.36)	
32	Angela:	hehe
33	(1.4)	
34	Doris:	.hh
35		NO GOOD.
36	(0.33)	
37	**Angela:**	**<<p> NO GOOD.>**

EXERCISE 10.1

Hey Cutie Pie

1	Jeff:	you knOw what i just REalized?
2	Jill:	[what -

```
 3 Jeff:    [she LOOKED at me,
 4          she's wAlking dOwn the STAIRS?
 5 Jill:    <<breathy> uhu - >
 6 Jeff:    she LOOKED at mE: - =
 7          and she-
 8 (0.19)
 9          .hh
10          she didn't SEE me;
11 (0.95)
12 Jill:    REally?
13 (0.11)
14 Jeff:    YEAH;
15 (0.1)
16          i WAVED at her and –
17          she jUst KEPT GOing,
18 (0.2)
19 Jill:    .hh
20          MAYbe uhm –
21 (0.69)
22          (if) there's a reFLECtion or something –
23 (0.37)
24 Jeff:    what a <<breathy> BOdy she has - >
25 (0.45)
26 Jill:    .hh
27          <<breathy> isn't that inCREDible,
28          are our BOdies gonna do thA:t?>
29 (0.23)
30 Jeff:    't's like-
31 (0.67)
32          It's like –
33 (0.3)
34          SHE'S eVOLVing.
35 (0.99)
36          you KNOW like;
37 (0.86)
38          [(funny)
39 Jill:    [(( ))
40          hh.
41          deGENerating.
42          [huh-
43 Jeff:    [deGENera-
44          YEAH:.
45 Jill:    [hh.
46 Jeff:    [it's KINDa <<creaky> WEIRD.=
47          HUH.>
```

EXERCISE 10.2

Tastes very special

```
 1  Sherry:    hOw about if I pick for yOU and <<laughing> yOU pick for mE - >
 2  (0.73)
 3             [.hh
 4  Beth:      [<<falsetto> he>
 5  Sherry:    it's EASier thAt way;
 6             ehe
 7  (0.71)
 8  Rosemary:  what in the WORLD is a philadElphia-
 9  (0.16)
10  Sherry:    it's r- ROAST BEEF with;
11  (0.4)
12             mElted <<creaky> CHEESE and;>
13             SAUtéed <<creaky> Onions.>
14  Rosemary:  m;
15             that [DOES sound GOO:D;
16  Sherry:         [on a HOAgy RO:LL;
```

Appendix: Transcription Conventions

GAT-Transcription Conventions (adapted from Selting et al. 1998)

Turn and sequence structure

[ ]   overlap
[ ]
=   latching

Pauses

(2.85)   measured pause in seconds

Sound and syllable production

:, ::, :::   lengthening, according to duration
asp^{h}iration   aspirated pronunciation of individual sound
break off-   aborted word and/or intonation phrase

Laughter

haha, hehe   syllabic laughter
((laughing))   description of laughter
<<laughing>>   laughter accompanying speech

Stress

ACcent   primary stress
Accent   secondary stress

Phrase-final pitch accents

?   rise-to-high
,   rise-to-mid
-    level pitch

; fall-to-mid
. fall-to-low

Additional pitch accents

↑   pitch step-up
↓   pitch step-down

Change of pitch register

<<l>>   low pitch register
<<h>>   high pitch register

Volume and speech rate changes

<<f>>   forte
<<ff>>   fortissimo
<<p>>   piano
<<pp>>   pianissimo
<<all>>   allegro
<<len>>   lento
<<cresc>>   crescendo
<<dim>>   diminuendo
<<acc>>   accelerando
<<rall>>   rallentando

Voice quality changes

<<breathy>>   breathy voice quality
<<creaky>>   creaky voice quality
<<falsetto>>   falsetto voice quality
<<smiley>>   smiley voice quality

Breathing

.h, .hh, .hhh   breathing in
h., hh., hhh.   breathing out

Other conventions

(( ))   unintelligible passage
(such)   presumed wording
(such/which)   possible alternatives

Notes

2 Pitch: Introduction

1. PRAAT software can be downloaded free at www.fon.hum.uva.nl/praat/
2. Adobe Audition (formerly Cool Edit Pro) is a software typically used for recording and mastering in music production; however, it can also be used for speech analysis. For more information go to www.adobe.com/products/audition/

3 Pitch: Intonation

1. However, some syllables take more time to articulate than others, for example because they contain clusters of consonants. Therefore overall syllable length is not always a reliable descriptor of how stress is perceived. At times it can be more accurate to measure vowel length rather than overall syllable length. On the other hand, this assumes that participants only lengthen vowels in stressed syllables, which is not the case. Chapter 5 on lengthening and shortening of syllables provides more information on this topic.
2. The final pitch movement on *will* is delivered in creaky voice quality and is therefore not picked up by the speech analysis software. The final fall-to-low does therefore not appear in Figure 3.11.

10 Voice Quality

1. Other languages, however, do make use of voice quality changes as linguistic contrasts. See, for example, Gordon (2001); Kirk et al. (1993).

Glossary

Adjacency pair – The smallest type of conversational sequence, consisting of two consecutive turns, of which the second is made expectable by the first. Examples are question/answer, greeting/return greeting.

Approximant – A manner of articulation for consonants in which one articulator approaches another without producing audible friction. English approximants are /w r j l/.

Articulation – The production of speech sounds through the use of the speech organs.

Articulator – An organ used for the production of speech, such as the tongue, the palate or the teeth.

Aspiration – A puff of air following the release of a stop consonant, such as [pʰ].

Assimilation – The change of one sound into another under the influence of a neighbouring sound, as in 'ten pence', pronounced /tempens/, rather than /tenpens/.

Auxiliary verb – A verb, such as *to be* or *to have*, used with a main verb to indicate grammatical information, such as tense (*I have found it*) or aspect (*I am running*).

Breathy voice – A vocal setting involving excessive air escaping through the vocal folds, which remain slightly open during speech production.

Citation form – The dictionary pronunciation of a word in isolation.

Coarticulation – Overlapping articulation in adjacent sounds.

Consonant – A type of sound produced by partially or completely obstructing the airflow, creating an audible change, such as friction or closure, in the airflow.

Contour – An intonation movement across more than one syllable.

Creaky voice – A vocal setting in which the vocal folds vibrate with low frequency.

Declination – The overall falling intonation contour across an intonation phrase.

Diphthong – A vowel during the production of which the tongue and potentially the lips change shape.

Falsetto – A vocal setting for which the vocal folds are stretched very thin, especially at the edges, typically resulting in extremely high pitch.

Frequency – Number of (vocal fold) vibrations per second.

Fricative – Consonant produced by partially obstructing the airflow, causing audible friction. Examples are /s f ð/.

Glottis – The narrow space between the vocal folds in the larynx.

Intensity – The degree of energy in a sound wave; perceived as loudness.

Intonation – The emerging pitch movement during voiced talk.

Intonation phrase – A chunk of talk produced under one intonation contour.

Larynx – The part of the windpipe in which the vocal folds are located. Also referred to as 'Adam's apple'.

Loudness – Perceived intensity of a sound as loud or soft.

Marked – Linguistically non-default.

Nasal – A sound whose production involves lowering the velum and allowing air to pass through the nasal cavity. Examples are /m n/.

Noun phrase – A grammatical phrase whose head is a noun or a pronoun. Examples are 'table', 'the table', 'the wooden table', 'the table that belongs to Mary', 'all the tables in this room'.

Nucleus – The primary pitch accent in an intonation phrase.

Onset – Onset of a syllable: the consonants preceding the vowel; onset of an intonation phrase: the first pitch accent.

Pharynx – The part of the throat above the larynx.

Phonetics – The study of speech sounds, their articulation and their perception.

Phonology – The study of speech sounds in a given language, their categories, system and patterns.

Pitch – The perceived frequency of (vocal fold) vibration as high or low.

Pitch accent – Pitch movement on a stressed syllable and potential subsequent unstressed syllables.

Pitch range – A speaker's overall speaking range between the highest and lowest pitch value during a given conversation.

Pitch register – A speaker's local pitch span during a given interactional sequence, turn or intonation phrase.

Pragmatics – The study of language in use and in context.

Received Pronunciation (RP) – The variety of English traditionally considered the most prestigious.

Repair – A sequence in conversation involving the identification of a prior utterance as requiring modification, clarification or correction.

Segment – Speech sound.

Semantics – The study of the meaning of words and sentences.

Sequence – A group of turns by more than one participant which are designed as coherent by those participants.

Sequence organization – The design of groups of turns as coherent and of individual turns as continuing or breaking with the coherence of such a group.

Speech rate – The tempo of an utterance.

Speech rhythm – The structuring of spoken language in terms of regular patterns through time.

Stop – A consonant produced by obstructing the airflow through complete closure of the vocal tract. Examples are /p t k/.

Stress – Prominence of one syllable over another, minimally through additional air force, maximally through additional loudness, duration and pitch movement.

Suprasegmental features – Aspects of speech that are relevant beyond the domain of the individual segment.

Syllable – A phonological unit typically consisting of at least a vowel sound, and potential preceding and/or subsequent consonants.

Syntax – The (study of the) structure of sentences.

Turn-taking – Participants' negotiation over speaker change in conversation.

Universal – A linguistic feature or pattern to be found in all languages of the world.

Variety – An accent or dialect of a language.

Voice quality – A suprasegmental articulatory setting.

Voicing – Voicing in phonetics: vibration of the vocal folds, caused by an egressive air-stream, resulting in voiced articulation. Voicing in pragmatics: adopting the voice of another, as, for example, in reported speech.

Vowel – A type of sound produced with relatively little blockage of the airflow and no audible friction.

Whisper – A setting in which air passes freely through the glottis, resulting in an absence of voicing.

Bibliography

Abercrombie, D. (1967) *Elements of General Phonetics* (Edinburgh: Edinburgh University Press).

Altenberg, B. (1987) *Prosodic Patterns in Spoken English: Studies in the Correlation Between Prosody and Grammar* (Lund: Lund University Press).

Ashmore, M. and Reed, D. (2000) 'Innocence and nostalgia in conversation analysis: the dynamic relations of tape and transcript', *Forum Qualitative Sozialforschung/Forum: Qualitative Social Research*, 1/3. http://www.qualitative-research.net/index.php/fqs/article/view/1020/2200

Atkinson, J.M. and Heritage, J. (eds) (1984) *Structures of Social Action: Studies in Conversation Analysis* (Cambridge: Cambridge University Press).

Auer, P. (1990) 'Rhythm in telephone closings', *Human Studies*, 13, 361–92.

Auer, P. (1999) *Sprachliche Interaktion. Eine Einführung anhand von 22 Klassikern* (Tübingen: Niemeyer).

Auer, P. and Couper-Kuhlen, E. (1994) 'Rhythmus und Tempo in konversationeller Alltagssprache' in B. Schlieben-Lange (ed.) *Rhythmus. Zeitschrift für Literaturwissenschaft und Linguistik*, 24/96, 78–106.

Auer, P. and di Luzio, A. (eds) (1992) *The Contextualization of Language* (Amsterdam: Benjamins).

Auer, P. and Rönfeldt, B. (2004) 'Prolixity as adaptation: prosody and turn-taking in German conversation with a fluent aphasic' in E. Couper-Kuhlen and C.E. Ford (eds) *Sound Patterns in Interaction* (Amsterdam: Benjamins), 171–200.

Auer, P., Couper-Kuhlen, E. and Müller, F. (1999) *Language in Time: The Rhythm and Tempo of Spoken Interaction* (New York: Oxford University Press).

Barden, B. (1991) 'Sprechgeschwindigkeit und thematische Struktur', *Kontextualisierung durch Rhythmus und Intonation*, 15, University of Konstanz.

Barry, W.J., Andreeva, B., Russo, M., Dimitrova, S. and Kostadinova, T. (2003) 'Do rhythm measures tell us anything about language type?' in *Proceedings of the 15th International Congress of Phonetic Sciences*, Barcelona, pp. 2693–2696. http://pascal.kgw.tu-berlin.de/gnom/Lehre/hs-rhythm/literatur/Barry-Barcelona.pdf.

Barth-Weingarten, D. (2007) 'Prosody, Construction Grammar and language change' in S. Volk-Birke and J. Lippert (eds) *Anglistentag 2006 Halle. Proceedings* (Trier: Wissenschaftlicher Verlag), pp. 421–433.

Barth-Weingarten, D., Reber, E. and Selting, M. (eds) (2010) *Prosody in Interaction* (Amsterdam: Benjamins).

Barth-Weingarten, D., Wichman, A. and Nehe, N. (eds) (2009) *Where Prosody Meets Pragmatics* (Bingley: Emerald).

Bell-Berti, F., Gelfer, C.E. and Boyle, M. (1995) 'Utterance-final lengthening: the effect of speaking rate' in *Proceedings of 13th International Congress of Phonetic Sciences*, Stockholm, 1, 162–165.

Benton, M., Dockendorf, L., Jin, W., Liu, Y., and Edmondson, J.A. (2007) 'The continuum of speech rhythm: Computational testing of speech rhythm of large corpora from natural Chinese and English speech' in *Proceedings of the 16th International Congress of Phonetic Sciences*, pp. 1269–1272. http://www.icphs2007.de/conference/Papers/1591/1591.pdf

Berger, P.L. and Luckmann, T. (1966/1991) *The Social Construction of Reality: A Treatise in the Sociology of Knowledge* (London: Penguin).

Bergmann, J.R. (1994) 'Ethnomethodologische Konversationsanalyse' in G. Fritz and F. Hundsnurscher (eds) *Handbuch der Dialoganalyse* (Tübingen: Niemeyer), pp. 3–16.

Berkovits, R. (1984) 'Duration and fundamental frequency in sentence- final intonation', *Journal of Phonetics,* 12, 255–265.

Billig, M. (1999a) 'Whose terms? Whose ordinariness? Rhetoric and ideology in conversation analysis', *Discourse and Society*, 10, 543–558.

Billig, M. (1999b) 'Conversation analysis and the claims of naivety', *Discourse and Society*, 10, 572–576.

Boden, D. (1990) 'The world as it happens: Ethnomethodology and conversation analysis' in G. Ritzer (ed.) *Frontiers of Social theory: The New Synthesis* (New York: Columbia University Press), pp. 185–213.

Boden, D. and Zimmerman, D.H. (eds) (1991) *Talk and Social Structure: Studies in Ethnomethodology and Conversation Analysis* (Cambridge: Polity Press).

Bolinger, D.L. (1963) 'Length, vowel, juncture', *Linguistics,* 1, 5–29.

Brazil, D., Coulthard, M. and Johns, C. (eds) (1980) *Discourse intonation and language teaching.* (London: Longman).

Button, G. (ed.) (1991) *Ethnomethodology and the Human Sciences* (Cambridge: Cambridge University Press).

Cambier-Langeveld, T. (1999) 'The interaction between final lengthening and accentual lengthening: Dutch versus English' in *Proceedings of 14th International Congress of Phonetic Sciences,* San Francisco, pp. 467–470.

Carr, P. (1999) *English Phonetics and Phonology: An Introduction* (Cambridge: Cambridge University Press).

Catford, J.C. (1964) 'Phonation types' in: D. Abercrombie, D.B. Fry, P.A.D. MacCarthy, N.C. Scott and J.L.M. Trim (eds) *In Honour of Daniel Jones* (London: Longmans), pp. 26–37.

Catford, J.C. (2002) *A Practical Introduction to Phonetics*, 2nd edn (Oxford: Oxford University Press).

Cauldwell, R. (1996) 'Stress-timing: observations, beliefs and evidence', *Eger Journal of English Studies,* 1, 33–48.

Clark, J. and Yallop, C. (1995) *An Introduction to Phonetics and Phonology*, 2nd edn (Oxford: Blackwell).

Clayman, S and Gill, V.T. (2004) 'Conversation Analysis' in A. Bryman and M. Hardy (eds) *Handbook of Data Analysis* (London: Sage), pp. 589–606.

Coadou, M. (2006) 'Voice quality and variation: a pilot study of the Liverpool accent' in *Proceedings of the 3rd International Conference on Speech Prosody*, Dresden. http://aune.lpl.univ-aix.fr/~sprosig/sp2006/contents/papers/PS7–06_0123.pdf

Collins, B. and Mees, I.M. (2008) *Practical Phonetics and Phonology* (Oxon: Routledge).

Cook-Gumperz, J. and Gumperz, J.J. (1976) 'Context in children's speech' in J. Cook-Gumperz and J. Gumperz (eds) *Papers on Language and Context*. Working Paper No. 46 (Berkeley: University of California, Dept. of Anthropology).

Cooper, W.E. and Danly, M. (1981) 'Segmental and Temporal Aspects of Utterance-Final Lengthening', *Phonetica*, 38, 106–115.

Couper-Kuhlen, E. (1983) 'Intonatorische Kohäsion. Eine makroprosodische Untersuchung', *Zeitschrift für Linguistik und Literaturwissenschaft*, 49, 74–100.

Couper-Kuhlen, E. (1986) *An Introduction to English Prosody* (Tübingen: Max Niemeyer; London: Edward Arnold).

Couper-Kuhlen, E. (1991) 'A rhythm-based metric for turn-taking' in *Proceedings of the 12th International Congress of Phonetic Sciences*, 1, 275–278.

Couper-Kuhlen, E. (1992) 'Contextualizing discourse: The prosody of interactive repair' in P. Auer and A. di Luzio (eds) *The Contextualization of Language* (Amsterdam: Benjamins), pp. 337–364.

Couper-Kuhlen, E. (1993) *English Speech Rhythm: Form and Function in Everyday Verbal Interaction* (Amsterdam: Benjamins).

Couper-Kuhlen, E. (1996a) 'The prosody of repetition: On quoting and mimicry' in E. Couper-Kuhlen and M. Selting (eds) *Prosody in Conversation* (Cambridge: Cambridge University Press), pp. 366–405.

Couper-Kuhlen, E. (1996b) 'Intonation and clause combining in discourse: The case of because', *Pragmatics*, 6/3, 389–426.

Couper-Kuhlen, E. (1999) 'Coherent voicing: On prosody in conversational reported speech' in W. Bublitz and U. Lenk (eds) *Coherence in Spoken and Written Discourse: How to Create it and How to Describe it* (Amsterdam: Benjamins), pp. 11–32.

Couper-Kuhlen, E. (2001a) 'Interactional prosody: High onsets in reason-for-the-call turns', *Language in Society*, 30, 29–53.

Couper-Kuhlen, E. (2001b) 'Intonation and discourse: Current views from within' in D. Schiffrin, D. Tannen and H. Hamilton (eds) *Handbook of Discourse Analysis* (Oxford: Blackwell).

Couper-Kuhlen, E. (2002) 'Prosody' in J. Verschueren, J. Östman, J. Blommaert and C. Bulcaen (eds) *Handbook of Pragmatics* (Amsterdam: Benjamins), pp. 1–19.

Couper-Kuhlen, E. (2003) 'On initial boundary tones in English conversation' in M.J. Solé, D. Recasens and J. Romero (eds) *Proceedings of the 15th International Congress of Phonetic Sciences*, Barcelona, pp. 119–122.

Couper-Kuhlen, E. (2004) 'Prosody and sequence organization in English: The case of new beginnings' in E. Couper-Kuhlen and C.E. Ford (eds) *Sound Patterns in Interaction* (Amsterdam: Benjamins), pp. 335–376.

Couper-Kuhlen, E. (2007a) 'Situated phonologies: patterns of phonology in discourse contexts' in M. Pennington (ed.) *Phonology in Context* (Basingstoke and New York: Palgrave Macmillan).

Couper-Kuhlen, E. (2007b) 'Prosodische Prospektion und Retrospektion im Gespräch' in H. Hausendorf (ed.) *Gespräch als Prozess. Linguistischen Aspekte der Zeitlichkeit verbaler Interaktion* (Tübingen: Narr), pp. 69–94.

Couper-Kuhlen, E. (forthcoming) 'Some truths and untruths about prosody in English question and answer sequences' in J.P. de Ruiter (ed.) *Questions: Formal, Functional and Interactional Perspectives* (Cambridge: Cambridge University Press).

Couper-Kuhlen, E. and Auer, P. (1991) 'On the contextualizing function of speech rhythm in conversation: Question-answer sequences' in J. Verschueren (ed.) *Levels of Linguistic Adaptation. Selected papers of the International Pragmatics Conference, Antwerp 1987.* (Amsterdam: Benjamins), pp. 1–18.

Couper-Kuhlen, E. and Ford, C.E. (eds) (2004) *Sound Patterns in Interaction* (Amsterdam: Benjamins).

Couper-Kuhlen, E. and M. Selting (eds) (1996a) *Prosody in Conversation* (Cambridge: Cambridge University Press).

Couper-Kuhlen, E. and Selting, M. (1996b) 'Towards an interactional perspective on prosody and a prosodic perspective on interaction' in E. Couper-Kuhlen and M. Selting (eds) *Prosody in Conversation* (Cambridge: Cambridge University Press), pp. 11–56.

Cowley, S. (1994) 'Conversational functions of rhythmical patterning', *Language and Communication*, 14/4, 353–376.

Cruttenden, A. (1997) *Intonation*, 2nd edn (Cambridge University Press. Cambridge).

Crystal, D. (1969) *Prosodic Systems and Intonation in English* (Cambridge: Cambridge University Press).

Cummings, F. and Port, R. (1998) 'Rhythmic constraints on stress timing in English', *Journal of Phonetics*, 26, 145–171.

Curl, T. (2004) ' "Repetition" repairs: The relationship of phonetic structure and sequence organization' in E. Couper-Kuhlen and C.E. Ford (eds) *Sound Patterns in Interaction* (Amsterdam: Benjamins), pp. 273–298.

Cutler, A. (1980) 'Syllable omission: errors and isochrony' in *Temporal Variables in Speech: Studies in Honour of Frieda Goldman-Eisler* (The Hague: Mouton), pp. 183–190.

Cutler, A. and Pearson, M. (1986) 'On the analysis of prosodic turn-taking cues' in C. Johns-Lewis (ed.) *Intonation and Discourse* (London: Croom Helm), pp. 139–156.

Dauer, R.M. (1983) 'Stress-timing and syllable-timing reanalyzed', *Journal of Phonetics*, 11, 51–62.

Darwin, C.J. and Donovan, A. (1980) 'Perceptual studies of speech rhythm: isochrony and intonation' in J.C. Simon (ed.) *Spoken Language Generation and Understanding* (Dordrecht: D. Reidel Publishing), pp. 77–85.

Dellwo, V., Fourcin, A. and Abberton, E. (2007) 'Rhythmical classification of languages based on voice parameters' in *Proceedings of 16th International Congress of Phonetic Sciences*, Saarbrücken, 1129–1132. http://www.icphs2007.de/conference/Papers/1169/1169.pdf

Drew, P. (2003) 'Conversation Analysis' in J. Smith (ed.) *Qualitative Psychology: A Practical Guide to Research Methods* (London: Sage), pp. 132–158.

Drew, P. (2005) 'Conversation Analysis' in K.L. Fitch and R.E. Sanders (eds) *Handbook of Language and Social Interaction* (Mahwah, NJ: Lawrence Erlbaum), pp. 71–102.

Du Bois, J.W. (1991) 'Transcription design principles for spoken discourse research', *Pragmatics*, 1(1), 71–106.

Du Bois, J.W. and Englebretson, R. (2004) *Santa Barbara Corpus of Spoken American English, Part 3* (Philadelphia: Linguistic Data Consortium).

Du Bois, J.W. and Englebretson, R. (2005) *Santa Barbara Corpus of Spoken American English, Part 4* (Philadelphia: Linguistic Data Consortium).

Du Bois, J.W., Chafe, W.L., Meyer, C., and Thompson, S.A. (2000) *Santa Barbara Corpus of Spoken American English, Part 1* (Philadelphia: Linguistic Data Consortium).

Du Bois, J.W., Chafe, W.L., Meyer, C., Thompson, S.A. and Martey, N. (2003) *Santa Barbara Corpus of Spoken American English, Part 2* (Philadelphia: Linguistic Data Consortium).

Du Bois, J.W., Schuetze-Coburn, S., Cumming, S. and Paolino, D. (1993) 'Outline of discourse transcription' in J.A. Edwards and M.D. Lampert (eds) *Talking Data. Transcription and Coding in Discourse Research* (Hillsdale: Lawrence Erlbaum), pp. 45–89.

Duranti, A. and Goodwin, C. (eds) (1992) *Rethinking Context: Language as an Interactive Phenomenon* (Cambridge: Cambridge University Press).

Edwards, J.A. and Lampert, M.D. (eds) (1993) *Talking Data: Transcription and Coding in Discourse Research* (Hillsdale: Lawrence Erlbaum).

Erickson, F. (1992) 'They know all the lines: Rhythmic organization and contextualization in a conversational listing routine' in P. Auer and A. di Luzio (eds) *The Contextualization of Language* (Amsterdam: Benjamins), pp. 365–397.

Erickson, F. and Shultz, J. (1982) *The Counsellor as Gatekeeper. Social Interaction in Interviews* (New York: Academic Press).

Esling, J. (1978) 'The identification of features of voice quality in social groups', *Journal of the International Phonetic Association*, 7, 18–23.

Faure, G., Hirst, D.J., and Chafcouloff (1980) 'Rhythm in English: Isochronism, pitch, and perceived stress' in L.R. Waugh, and C.H. Van Schooneveld (eds) *The Melody of Language* (Baltimore: University Park Press), pp. 71–79.

Flowe, W.C. (2002) 'The Form and Function of Prosodic Stylization in Spoken Discourse', PhD thesis Universität Konstanz. http://kops.ub.uni-konstanz.de/volltexte/2002/748/pdf/doktorarbeit.pdf

Ford, C.E. and Couper-Kuhlen, E. (2004) 'Conversation and phonetics: Essential connections' in E. Couper-Kuhlen and C.E. Ford (eds) *Sound Patterns in Interaction* (Amsterdam: Benjamins), pp. 3–25.

Ford, C.E., Fox, B.A. and Hellerman, J. (2004) ' "Getting past *no*" ' in E. Couper-Kuhlen and C.E. Ford (eds) *Sound Patterns in Interaction* (Amsterdam: Benjamins), pp. 233–269.

Ford, C.E., Fox, B.A. and Thompson, S.A. (eds) (2002) *The Language of Turn and Sequence* (Oxford: Oxford University Press).

Ford, C.E. and Thompson, S.A. (1996) 'Interactional units in conversation: Syntactic, intonational, and pragmatic resources for the management of turns' in E. Ochs, E.A. Schegloff and S.A. Thompson (eds) *Interaction and Grammar* (Cambridge: Cambridge University Press), pp. 134–84.

Fox, B.A. (2001) 'An exploration of prosody and turn projection in English conversation' in M. Selting and E. Couper-Kuhlen (eds) *Studies in Interactional Linguistics* (Amsterdam: Benjamins), pp. 287–315.

Freese, J. and Maynard, D.W. (1998) 'Prosodic features of bad news and good news in conversation', *Language in Society*, 17, 195–219.

French, P. and Local, J. (1983) 'Turn-competitive incomings', *Journal of Pragmatics*, 7, 701–715.

French, P. and Local, J. (1986) 'Prosodic features and the management of interruptions' in C. Johns-Lewis (ed.) *Intonation and Discourse* (London: Croom Helm), pp. 157–180.

Fry, D.B. (1979) *The Physics of Speech* (Cambridge: Cambridge University Press).

Garfinkel, H. (1967) *Studies in Ethnomethodology* (Englewood Cliffs, NJ: Prentice-Hall).

Garfinkel, H. (1996) 'An overview of ethnomethodology's program', *Social Psychology Quarterly*, 59, 5–21.

Giegerich, H.J. (1992) *English Phonology. An Introduction* (Cambridge: Cambridge University Press).

Gobl, C. and Chasaide, A.N. (2003) 'The role of voice quality in communicating emotion, mood and attitude', *Speech Communication*, 40(1–2), 189–212.

Goldberg, J.A. (1978) 'Amplitude shift' in J. Schenkein (ed.) *Studies in the Organization of Conversational Interaction* (New York: Academic Press), pp. 199–218.

Goodwin, C. (1980) 'Restarts, pauses, and the achievement of a state of mutual gaze at turn-beginning', *Sociological Inquiry*, 50(3–4), 272–302.

Goodwin, C. (1981) *Conversational Organization: Interaction Between Speakers and Hearers* (New York: Academic Press).

Goodwin, C. and Heritage, J. (1990) 'Conversation Analysis', *Annual Review of Anthropology*, 19, 283–307.

Gordon, M. (2001) 'Linguistic aspects of voice quality with special reference to Athabaskan' in S. Tuttle and G. Holton (eds) *Proceedings of the 2001 Athabaskan Languages Conference* (Fairbanks: Alaska Native Language Center), pp. 163–178. http://www.linguistics.ucsb.edu/faculty/gordon/athabphonation.pdf

Grabe, E. and Low, E.L. (2002) 'Durational variability in speech and the Rhythm Class Hypothesis' in C. Gussenhoven and N. Warner (eds) *Papers in Laboratory Phonology 7* (Cambridge: Cambridge University Press), pp. 515–546.

Grivičić, T. and Nilep, C. (2004) 'When phonation matters: The use and function of yeah and creaky voice', *Colorado Research in Linguistics*, 17, 1–11.

Gumperz, J. (1982) *Discourse Strategies* (Cambridge: Cambridge University Press).

Gumperz, J. (1992) 'Contextualization revisited' in P. Auer and A. di Luzio (eds) *The Contextualization of Language* (Amsterdam: Benjamins), pp. 39–53.

Gumperz, J. (1993) 'Transcribing conversational exchanges' in J.A. Edwards and M.D. Lampert (eds) *Talking Data. Transcription and Coding in Discourse Research* (Hillsdale: Lawrence Erlbaum), pp. 91–121.

Günthner, S. (1996) 'The prosodic contextualization of moral work. An analysis of reproaches in why-formats' in E. Couper-Kuhlen and M. Selting (eds) *Prosody in Conversation* (Cambridge: Cambridge University Press), pp. 271–302.

Günthner, S. (1999) 'Polyphony and the "layering of voices" in reported dialogues: An analysis of the use of prosodic devices in everyday reported speech', *Journal of Pragmatics*, 31, 685–708.

Halliday, M.A.K. (1967) *Intonation and Grammar in British English* (The Hague: Mouton de Gruyter).

Halliday, M.A.K. (1970) *A Course in Spoken English: Intonation* (London: Oxford University Press).

Have, P. ten (2002) 'Reflections on transcription', *Cahiers de Praxématique*, 39, 21–43.

Have, P. ten (2004a) *Understanding Qualitative Research and Ethnomethodology* (London: Sage).

Have, P. ten (2004b) 'Ethnomethodology' in C. Seale, D. Silverman, J. Gubrium and G. Gobo (eds) *Qualitative Research Practice* (London: Sage), pp. 151–64.

Have, P. ten (2007) *Doing Conversation Analysis. A Practical Guide*, 2nd edn (London: Sage).

Have, P. ten and Psathas, G. (eds) (1995) *Situated Order: Studies in the Social Organization of Talk and Embodied Activities* (Washington, DC: University Press of America).

Henton, C.G. and Bladon, R.A.W. (1988) 'Creak as a sociophonetic marker' in L. Hyman and C.N. Li (eds) *Language, Speech and Mind: Studies in Honor of Victoria A Fromkin* (Beckenham: Croom Helm), pp. 3–29.

Heritage, J. (1984a) *Garfinkel and Ethnomethodology* (Cambridge: Polity Press).

Heritage, J. (1984b) 'A change-of-state token and aspects of its sequential placement' in J.M. Atkinson and J. Heritage (eds) *Structures of Social Action: Studies in Conversation Analysis* (Cambridge: Cambridge University Press), pp. 299–345.

Heritage, J. (1995) 'Conversation analysis: Methodological aspects' in U.M. Quasthoff (ed.) *Aspects of Oral Communication* (Berlin/New York: Walter de Gruyter), pp. 391–418.

Hirst, D. and Di Cristo, A. (eds) (1998) *Intonation Systems. A Survey of Twenty Languages* (Cambridge: Cambridge University Press).

Hoequist, C.J. (1983) 'The Perceptual Center and Rhythm Categories', *Language and speech*, 26(4), 367–376.

Honikman, B. (1964) 'Articulatory settings' in D. Abercrombie, D.B. Fry, P.A.D. MacCarthy, N.C. Scott and J.L.M. Trim (eds) *In Honour of Daniel Jones* (London: Longman), pp. 73–84.

Hutchby, I. and Wooffitt, R. (2008) *Conversation Analysis*, 2nd edn (Cambridge: Polity Press).

International Phonetic Association (1999) *Handbook of the International Phonetic Association. A Guide to the Use of the International Phonetic Alphabet* (Cambridge: Cambridge University Press).

Jasperson, R. (2002) 'Some linguistic aspects of closure cut offs' in C.E. Ford, B.A. Fox and S.A. Thompson (eds) *The Language of Turn and Sequence* (Oxford: Oxford University Press), pp. 257–286.

Jassem, W., Hill, D.R. and Witten, I.H. (1994) 'Isochrony in English Speech: Its statistical validity and linguistic relevance' in D. Gibbon and H. Richter (eds) *Intonation, Accent and Rhythm. Studies in Discourse Phonology* (Berlin: de Gruyter), pp. 203–225.

Jefferson, G. (1973): 'A case of precision timing in ordinary conversation: Overlapped tag-positioned address terms in closing sequences', *Semiotica*, 9(1), 47–96.

Jefferson, G. (1983) 'Another Failed Hypothesis: Pitch/Loudness as Relevant to Overlap Resolution', *Tilburg Papers in Language and Literature*, 38, 1–24. Tilburg University.

Jefferson, G. (1986) 'Notes on 'latency' in overlap onset', *Human Studies*, 9, 153–183.

Jefferson, G. (1989) 'Notes on a possible metric which provides for a "standard maximum silence" of one second in conversation' in D. Roger and P. Bull (eds) *Conversation* (Clevedon: Multilingual Matters), pp. 166–96.

Johns-Lewis, C. (1986) *Intonation and Discourse* (London: Croom Helm).

Johnson, K. (2003) *Acoustic and Auditory Phonetics* (Oxford: Blackwell).

Kallmeyer, W. and Schütze, F. (1976) 'Konversationsanalyse', *Studium Linguistik*, 1, 1–28.

Kelly, J. and Local, J. (1989) *Doing Phonology: Observing, Recording, Interpreting* (Manchester: Manchester University Press).

Kingdon, R. (1958) *The Groundwork of English Intonation* (London: Longmans).

Kirk, P.L., Ladefoged, J., and Ladefoged, P. (1993) 'Quantifying acoustic properties of modal, breathy and creaky vowels in Jalapa Mazatec' in A. Mattina and T. Montler (eds) *American Indian Linguistics and Ethnography in Honor of Laurence C. Thompson* (Ann Arbor: University of Michigan), pp. 435–450.

Klewitz, G. and Couper-Kuhlen, E. (1999) 'Quote–unquote. The role of prosody in the contextualization of reported speech sequences', *Pragmatics*, 9(4), 459–485.

Kohler, K. (1991) 'Isochrony, units of rhythmic organization and speech rate' in *proceedings of 12th International Congress of Phonetic Sciences*, Aix-en-Provence. vol. 1, pp. 257–261.

Ladd, D.R. (1996) *Intonational Phonology* (Cambridge: Cambridge University Press).

Ladefoged, P. (1962/1996) *Elements of Acoustic Phonetics*, 2nd edn (London: University of Chicago Press).

Ladefoged, P. (2001) *A Course in Phonetics*, 4th edn (Fort Worth: Harcourt College Publishers).

Ladefoged, P. (2005) *Vowels and Consonants. An Introduction to the Sounds of Language.* Second Edition (Oxford: Blackwell).

van Lancker, D., Kreiman, J., and Bolinger, D. (1988) 'Anticipatory lengthening', *Journal of Phonetics*, 61, 339–347.

Lass, R. (1984) *Phonology. An Introduction to Basic Concepts* (Cambridge: Cambridge University Press).

Lass, R. (2009) *English Phonology and Phonological Theory. Synchronic and Diachronic Studies* (Cambridge: Cambridge University Press).

Laver, J. (1979) *Voice quality: a classified bibliography* (Amsterdam: Benjamins.)

Laver, J. (1980/2009) *The Phonetic Description of Voice Quality* (Cambridge: Cambridge University Press).

Laver, J. (1994) *Principles of Phonetics* (Cambridge: Cambridge University Press).

Lehiste, I. (1977) 'Isochrony reconsidered', *Journal of Phonetics*, 5, 253–263.

Leiter, K. (1980) *A Primer on Ethnomethodology* (Oxford: Oxford University Press).

Lerner, G.H. (1991) 'On the syntax of sentences in progress', *Language in Society* 20, 441–458.

Lerner, G.H. (1996) 'On the "semi-permeable" character of grammatical units in conversation: Conditional entry into the turn space of another speaker' in E. Ochs, E.A. Schegloff and S.A. Thompson (eds) *Interaction and Grammar* (Cambridge: Cambridge University Press), pp. 238–276.

Lerner, G.H. (Ed.) (2004) *Conversation Analysis: Studies from the First Generation* (Amsterdam: Benjamins).

Levinson, S.C. (1983) *Pragmatics* (Cambridge: Cambridge University Press).

Liddicoat, A.J. (2007) *An Introduction to Conversation Analysis* (London: Continuum).

Lieberman, P. and Blumstein, S. (1988) *Speech Physiology, Speech Perception and Acoustic Phonetics* (Cambridge: Cambridge University Press).

Local, J. (1992) 'Continuing and restarting' in P. Auer and A. di Luzio (eds) *The Contextualization of Language* (Amsterdam: Benjamins), pp. 273–296.

Local, J. (1996) 'Conversational phonetics: Some aspects of news receipts in everyday talk' in E. Couper-Kuhlen and M. Selting (eds) *Prosody in Conversation* (Cambridge: Cambridge University Press), pp. 175–230.

Local, J. (2003) 'Phonetics and talk-in-interaction' in *Proceedings of the 15th International Congress of Phonetic Sciences*, Barcelona, pp. 115–118.

Local, J. and Kelly, J. (1986) 'Projection and 'silences': notes on phonetic and conversational structure', *Human Studies*, 9, 185–204.

Local, J. and Walker, G. (2004) 'Abrupt-joins as a resource for the production of multi-unit, multi-action turns', *Journal of Pragmatics*, 36(8), 1375–1404.

Local, J.K., Wells, B.H.G. and Sebba, M. (1985) 'Phonology for conversation. Phonetic aspects of turn delimitation in London Jamaican', *Journal of Pragmatics*, 9, 309–30.

Local, J., Kelly, J. and Wells, B. (1986) 'Towards a phonology of conversation: turn-taking in Tyneside English', *Journal of Linguistics*, 22(2), 411–437.

Local, J., Ogden, R. and Temple, R. (eds) (2003) *Phonetic Interpretation. Papers in Laboratory Phonology VI* (Cambridge: Cambridge University Press).

Local, J., Wells, B. and Sebba, M. (1985) 'Phonology for conversation: phonetic aspects of turn delimitation in London Jamaican', *Journal of Pragmatics*, 9, 309–330.

Low, E.L. (2006) 'A review of recent research on speech rhythm: Some insights for language acquisition, language disorders and language teaching' in R. Hughes (ed.) *Spoken English, TESOL and Applied Linguistics. Challenges for Theory and Practice* (Basingstoke: Palgrave Macmillan), pp. 99–125.

Low, E.L., Grabe, E. and Nolan, F. (2000) 'Quantitative characterizations of speech rhythm: syllable-timing in Singapore English', *Language and Speech*, 43(4), 377–402.

Lynch, M. (2000) 'The ethnomethodological foundations of conversation analysis', *Text*, 24, 517–532.

MacWhinney, B. (2007) 'The TalkBank project' in J.C. Beal, K.P. Corrigan and H.L. Moisl (eds) *Creating and Digitizing Language Corpora: Synchronic Databases, Vol. 1.* (Basingstoke: Palgrave Macmillan), pp. 163–180.

Marks, J (1999) 'Is stress-timing real?', *ELT Journal*, 53(3), 191–199.

Miller, J., Grosjean, F. and Lomanto, C. (1984) 'Articulation rate and its variability in spontaneous speech: A reanalysis and some implications', *Phonetica*, 41, 215–225.

Miller, M. (1984) 'On the perception of rhythm', *Journal of Phonetics*, 12, 75–83.

Miura, I. (1993) 'Switching pauses in adult-adult and child-child turn takings: An initial study', *Journal of Psycholinguistic Research*, 22(3), 383–395.

Mulder, J. and Thompson, S.A. (2008) 'The grammaticization of *but* as a final article in English conversation' in R. Laury (ed.) *Crosslinguistic Studies of Clause Combining* (Amsterdam: Benjamins), pp. 179–204.

Nofsinger, R.E. (1991) *Everyday Conversation* (Newbury Park: Sage).

Ochs, E. (1979) 'Transcription as theory' in E. Ochs and B. Schiefflin (eds) *Developmental Pragmatics* (New York: Academic Press), pp. 43–72.

Ochs, E., Schegloff, E.A. and Thompson, S.A. (1996) *Interaction and Grammar* (Cambridge: Cambridge University Press).

O'Connel, D.C. and Kowal, S. (1994) 'Some current transcription systems for spoken discourse: A critical analysis', *Pragmatics*, 4, 81–107.

O'Connor, J.D. and Arnold, G.F. (1973) *Intonation of Colloquial English: A Practical Handbook* (London: Longman).

Ogden, R. (2001) 'Turn-holding, turn-yielding and laryngeal activity in Finnish talk-in-interaction', *Journal of the International Phonetics Association*, 31, 139–152.

Ogden, R. (2004) 'Non-modal voice quality and turn-taking in Finnish' in E. Couper-Kuhlen and C.E. Ford (eds) *Sound Patterns in Interaction* (Amsterdam: Benjamins), pp. 29–62.

Ogden, R. (2009) *An Introduction to English Phonetics* (Edinburgh: Edinburgh University Press).

Ogden, R., Hakulinen, A. and Tainio, L. (2004) 'Indexing "no news" with stylization in Finnish' in E. Couper-Kuhlen and C.E. Ford (eds) *Sound Patterns in Interaction* (Amsterdam: Benjamins), pp. 299–334.

Patzelt, W.J. (1987) *Grundlagen der Ethnomethodologie* (München: Fink).

Pennington, M. (ed.) (2007) *Phonology in Context* (Basingstoke: Palgrave Macmillan).

Peräkylä, A. (2004) 'Conversation analysis' in C. Seale, D. Silverman, J. Gubrium and G. Gobo (eds) *Qualitative Research Practice* (London: Sage), pp. 165–179.

Pfitzinger, H.R. (1999) 'Local speech rate perception in German speech' in *Proceedings of 14th International Congress of Phonetic Sciences,* San Francisco, 893–896.

Pierrehumbert, J. (1980) 'The Phonology and Phonetics of English Intonation', Ph.D. thesis, MIT.

Pike, K.L. (1947) *Phonemics* (Ann Arbor: University of Michigan Press).

Pomerantz, A. and Fehr, B.J. (1997) 'Conversation analysis: An approach to the study of social action as sense making practices' in T.A. van Dijk (ed.) *Discourse Studies: A Multidisciplinary Introduction* (London: Sage), pp. 64–91.

Psathas, G. (Ed.) (1979) *Everyday Language: Studies in Ethnomethodology* (New York: Irvington).

Psathas, G. (1995) *Conversation Analysis* (Thousand Oaks, CA: Sage).

Psathas, G. and Anderson, T. (1990) 'The "practices" of transcription in conversation analysis', *Semiotica*, 78, 75–99.

Ramus, F., Nespor, M. and Mehler, J. (1999) 'Correlates of linguistic rhythm in the speech signal', *Cognition*, 73(3), 265–292.

Roach, P. (1982) 'On the distinction between 'stress-timed' and 'syllable-timed' languages' in D. Crystal (ed.) *Linguistic Controversies* (London: Edward Arnold), pp. 73–79.

Roach, P. (1998) 'Some languages are spoken more quickly than others' in L. Bauer and P. Trudgill (eds) *Language Myths* (London: Penguin), pp. 150–58.

Roach, P. (2001) *Phonetics* (Oxford: Oxford University Press).

Roach, P. (2003) *English Phonetics and Phonology: A Practical Course,* 3rd edn (Cambridge: Cambridge University Press).

Rogers, H. (2000) *The Sounds of Language: An Introduction to Phonetics* (Zug: Pearson).

Sacks, H. (1992) *Lectures on Conversation* (Oxford: Blackwell).

Sacks, H., Schegloff, E.A. and Jefferson, G. (1974) 'A simplest systematics for the organization of turn-taking for conversation', *Language*, 50, 696–735.

Schegloff, E.A. (1980) 'Preliminaries to preliminaries: "Can I ask you a question"', *Sociological Inquiry*, 50(3–4), 104–152.

Schegloff, E.A. (1986) 'The routine as achievement', *Human Studies*, 9, 111–52.

Schegloff, E.A. (1987) 'Between macro and micro: contexts and other connections' in J. Alexander, B. Giesen, R. Munch and N. Smelser (eds) *The Micro–Macro Link* (Berkeley and Los Angeles: University of California Press), pp. 207–234.

Schegloff, E.A. (1998) 'Reflections on studying prosody in talk-in-interaction', *Language and Speech*, 41(3–4), 235–263.

Schegloff, E.A. (2007) *Sequence Organization in Interaction: A primer in Conversation Analysis* (Cambridge: Cambridge University Press).

Schegloff, E.A. and Sacks, H. (1973) 'Opening up closings', *Semiotica*, 8(4), 290–327.

Schegloff, E.A., Jefferson, G. and Sacks, H. (1977) 'The preference for self-correction in the organization of repair in conversation', *Language*, 53(2), 361–382.

Schenkein, J.N. (1978) *Studies in the Organization of Conversational Interaction* (New York: Academic Press).

Schubiger, M. (1958) *English Intonation. Its Form and Function* (Tübingen: Niemeyer).

Scollon, R. (1981) *Tempo, Density, and Silence: Rhythms in Ordinary Talk* (Fairbanks: University of Alaska, Center for Cross-Cultural Studies).

Selkirk, E.O. (1984) *Phonology and Syntax. The Relation Between Sound and Structure* (Cambridge, MA: MIT Press).

Selting, M. (1992a) 'Intonation as a contextualization device: Case studies on the role of prosody, especially intonation, in contextualizing story telling in conversation' in:

P. Auer and A. di Luzio (eds) *The Contextualization of Language* (Amsterdam: Benjamins), pp. 233–257.

Selting, M. (1992b) 'Prosody in conversational questions', *Journal of Pragmatics*, 17, 315–345.

Selting, M. (1994) 'Emphatic speech style – with special focus on the prosodic signaling of heightened emotive involvement in conversation' in C. Caffi and R.W. Janney (eds) *Involvement in Language, Journal of Pragmatics* 22, 375–408.

Selting, M. (1995) *Prosodie im Gespräch. Aspekte einer interaktionalen Phonologie der Konversation* (Tübingen: Niemeyer).

Selting, M. (1996a) 'On the interplay of syntax and prosody in the constitution of turn-constructional units and turns in conversation', *Pragmatics*, 6(3), 371–388.

Selting, M. (1996b) 'Prosody as an activity-type distinctive cue in conversation: The case of so-called "astonished" questions in repair initiation' in E. Couper-Kuhlen and M. Selting (eds) *Prosody in Conversation* (Cambridge: Cambridge University Press), pp. 231–270.

Selting, M. (2000) 'The construction of units in conversational talk', *Language in Society*, 29, 477–517.

Selting, M. (2001) 'Fragments of units as deviant cases of unit-production in conversational talk' in M. Selting and E. Couper-Kuhlen (eds) *Studies in Interactional Linguistics* (Amsterdam: Benjamins), pp. 229–258.

Selting, M. (2004) 'The "upward staircase" intonation contour in the Berlin vernacular: An example of the analysis of regionalized intonation as an interactional resource' in E. Couper-Kuhlen and C.E. Ford (eds) *Sound Patterns in Interaction* (Amsterdam: Benjamins), pp. 201–231.

Selting, M. (2005) 'Syntax and prosody as methods for the construction and identification of turn-constructional units in conversation' in A. Hakulinen and M. Selting (eds) *Syntax and Lexis in Conversation* (Amsterdam: Benjamins), pp. 17–44.

Selting, M. and Couper-Kuhlen, E. (eds) (2001) *Studies in Interactional Linguistics* (Amsterdam: Benjamins).

Selting, M., Auer, P., Barden, B., Bergmann, J.R., Couper-Kuhlen, E., Günthner, S., Meier, C., Quasthoff, U., Schoblinski, P. and Uhmann, S. (1998) 'Gesprächsanalytisches Transkriptionssystem (GAT)', *Linguistische Berichte*, 173, 91–122. http://www.mediensprache.net/de/medienanalyse/transcription/gat/gat.pdf

Sharrock, W.W. and Anderson, Robert J. (1980) *The Ethnomethodologists* (Chichester: Ellis Horwood).

Silverman, D. (2006) *Interpreting Qualitative Data: Methods for Analyzing Talk, Text and Interaction,* 3rd edn (London: Sage).

Silverman, D. (1998) *Harvey Sacks and Conversation Analysis. Key Contemporary Thinkers* (Cambridge: Polity Press).

Stevens, K.N. (2000) *Acoustic Phonetics* (Cambridge, MA: MIT Press).

Streeck, J. (1983) 'Konversationsanalyse. Ein Reparaturversuch', *Zeitschrift für Sprachwissenschaft*, 2(1), 72–104.

Stuart-Smith, J. (1999) 'Glasgow: Accent and voice quality' in P. Foulkes and G. Doherty (eds) *Urban Voices: Accent Studies in the British Isles* (London: Edward Arnold), pp. 201–220.

Szczepek Reed, B. (2004) 'Turn-final intonation in English' in E. Couper-Kuhlen and C.E. Ford (eds) *Sound Patterns in Interaction* (Amsterdam: Benjamins), pp. 97–117.

Szczepek Reed, B. (2006) *Prosodic Orientation in English Conversation* (Basingstoke: Palgrave Macmillan).

Szczepek Reed, B. (2009) 'Prosodic orientation: A practice for sequence organization in broadcast telephone openings', *Journal of Pragmatics*, 41(6), 1223–1247.

Szczepek Reed, B. (2010a) 'Units of interaction: Tone units or Turn Constructional Phrases?' in E. Delais-Roussarie (ed.) *Conference Proceedings: Interface Discourse and Prosody.* University of Chicago. Paris, 9–11 September 2009.

Szczepek Reed, B. (2010b) 'Speech rhythm across turn transitions in cross-cultural talk-in-interaction', *Journal of Pragmatics*, 42(4), 1037–1059.

Szczepek Reed, B. (2010c) 'Intonation phrases in natural conversation: A participants' category?' in D. Barth-Weingarten, E. Reber, and M. Selting (eds) *Prosody in Interaction* (Amsterdam: Benjamins).

Tanaka, H. (1999) *Turn-taking in Japanese Conversation: A Study in Grammar and Interaction* (Amsterdam: Benjamins).

Tanaka, H. (2000) 'Turn-projection in Japanese talk-in-interaction', *Research in Language and Social Interaction*, 33(1), 1–38.

Tanaka, H. (2004) 'Prosody for marking transition-relevance places in Japanese conversation: The case of turns unmarked by utterance-final objects' in E. Couper-Kuhlen and C.E. Ford (eds) *Sound Patterns in Interaction* (Amsterdam: Benjamins), pp. 63–96.

Tannen, D. (ed.) (1982) *Analyzing Discourse: Text and Talk* (Georgetown: Georgetown University Press).

Tannen, D. and Saville-Troike, M. (eds) (1985) *Perspectives on Silence* (Norwood, NJ: Ablex).

Tauroza, S. and Allison, D. (1990) 'Speech rates in British English', *Applied Linguistics,* 11, 90–105.

Taylor, T.J. and Cameron, D. (1987) *Analysing Conversation. Rules and Units in the Structure of Talk* (Oxford: Pergamon Press).

Trouvain, J. and Grice, M. (1999) 'The effect of tempo on prosodic structure' in *Proceedings of 14th International Congress of Phonetic Sciences,* San Francisco, vol. 2, 1067–1070.

Uhmann, S. (1989) 'On some forms and functions of speech rate changes in everyday conversation', *Kontextualisierung durch Rhythmus und Intonation 7*, University of Konstanz.

Uhmann, S. (1992) 'Contextualizing relevance: On some forms and functions of speech rate changes in everyday conversation' in P. Auer and A. di Luzio (eds) *The Contextualization of Language* (Amsterdam: Benjamins), pp. 297–336.

Uhmann, S. (1996) 'On rhythm in everyday German conversation: Beat clashes in assessment utterances' in E. Couper-Kuhlen and M. Selting (eds) *Prosody in Conversation* (Cambridge: Cambridge University Press), pp. 303–365.

Walker, G. (2007) 'On the design and use of pivots in everyday English conversation', *Journal of Pragmatics*, 39(12), 2217–2243.

Wells, B. and Macfarlane, S. (1998) 'Prosody as an interactional resource: Turn-projection and overlap', *Language and Speech*, 41(3–4), 265–294.

Wells, B. and Sue Peppé (1996) 'Ending up in Ulster: prosody and turn-taking in English dialects' in E. Couper-Kuhlen and M. Selting (eds) *Prosody and Conversation* (Cambridge: Cambridge University Press), pp. 101–130.

Wells, J.C. (2006) *English Intonation. An Introduction* (Cambridge: Cambridge University Press).

Wennerstrom, A. (2001) *The Music of Everyday Speech* (Oxford: Oxford University Press).

Wennerstrom, A. and Siegel, A.F. (2003) 'Keeping the floor in multiparty conversations: Intonation, syntax, and pause', *Discourse Processes*, 36(2), 77–107.

Wichmann, A. (2000) *Intonation in Text and Discourse: Beginnings, Middles and Ends* (Harlow: Longman).

Wooffitt, R. (2005) *Conversation Analysis and Discourse Analysis. A Comparative and Critical Introduction* (London: Sage).

Zimmerman, D.H. (1988) 'On conversation: The conversation analytic perspective' in J. Anderson (ed.) *Communication Yearbook 11* (Beverly Hills, CA: Sage), pp. 406–432.

Index